Navigating The River of Time

Stuart Perrin

BLUE KITE PRESS

Cover design: Ana Cissa Pinto
acpcreativelab.com

Layout & Design: Robert Sink
webworksnyc.com

Library of Congress Control Number: 2016912165
CreateSpace Independent Publishing Platform, North Charleston, SC

Perrin, Stuart, 1942 -
Navigating The River of Time / by Stuart Perrin
ISBN: 978-1534919365
1. Perrin, Stuart — Meditation, Yoga, Spirituality, Self-Help
2. Author, American

Author's Note

A combination of wisdom teachings and memoir, *Navigating The River of Time* shares incidents from the life of a confused but gifted young man's journey halfway around the world and return to his hometown where he meets his spiritual teacher. It's a tapestry that brings together years of meditation practice with day-to-day practical living.

If its readers recognize their own struggle in the author's struggle, if they understand that they can connect their consciousness with Higher Energy in the universe and build a strong inner life, the book is a success. All they have to do is master the tools of meditation: mind, breath, need, will, gratitude, and the chakra system. They're born with them and live with them until the day they leave the world. What's missing is knowledge of how to use them to build an inner life.

If no social class, intelligence quotient, racial or religious upbringing, economic status or country of birth makes us happy, if chakras exist in every human being and are a direct link to God or Higher Energy in the Universe, what determines spiritual growth is the daily work one does to develop their inner life and become a more conscious person. If we prioritize that work, the universe will take care of the rest.

My spiritual teacher Rudi once told me: "A guru is like a cow. If you don't milk a cow, it will scream into the night." A teacher has to give away his teachings to fulfill his destiny; a teacher will always be available to anyone who wants to listen. He's like a "gadfly" that reminds us to live a life based on truth, a mirror guiding us on a path to enlightenment.

Stuart Perrin – June 10, 2016

Acknowledgments

Alice Stipak, Anne Kolhstaedt, and Bob Sink for an incredible job of editing the book. Alice Stipak for transcribing many of the lectures that made this book possible. Bob Sink for the book's interior design and Ana Cissa Pinto for the cover.

I would also like to thank the people who attended meditation intensives held in different parts of the United States. They drew out of me many of the teachings that are in this book.

Dedication

To my daughter Ania Devi who I love dearly.

CHAPTER 1

Meditation has little or no value unless there's a practical application for it in daily life. It's one thing to dilly-dally on the astral plane and wig oneself out with Bardo creatures and other cosmic entities, and another to use meditation to build an inner life that is strong enough to transform the mind's chaos and confusion into a well-balanced state of being. Activated kundalini can be a turn-on. A practitioner will experience light, auras, cosmic entities, gods, demigods, and many other higher forms. All of this is secondary to the real purpose of meditation. An instructor of kundalini yoga must teach a technique that helps his students to develop balance, harmony, and inner strength. He must teach them to keep the mind focused on the chakra below the navel, or the strength of kundalini could result in both spiritual and physical burnout.

Plants and trees have roots that draw nourishment from the earth. When storms hit, they uproot trees that have weak roots. Healthy trees survive and continue to flourish after the storm is over. What amazes me is how detached nature can be. After a hurricane, clouds part, the sun peeks through, and life moves on as if the hundred-mile-an-hour wind had never happened. There's no guilt, remorse, or unhappiness, just the sun's warmth reminding us that the storm has passed, calm has returned; we can step out of our houses and observe trees with healthy roots stand upright and embrace the sky.

If people took time to learn what nature has to teach, there would be less conflict, greater detachment, and the ability to stay calm when the going gets tough. We try to convince ourselves that the going won't get tough again. At the same time we're eaten alive by inner conflicts. In a strange sense, we need disruption. It reminds us that we have to do something about ourselves. If a tree can be rooted, why can't a human being follow suit? Certainly we have more intelligence than a tree. But most people don't know where to find their internal center of balance. They are lost in a mental and emotional fog that diminishes their capacity to function.

The human mind consumes people's energies. It's a nonstop voice that analyzes, confuses, creates excessive tension, and never shuts up; it's a voice that exhausts us by the end of the day. It forces us to drink alcohol, take pills, and do whatever we can to stop the chatter. The mind plays a surreal game of ping pong with us. It bounces back and forth from the past to the future, and never roots itself in the present.

The past is like a shadow that follows us around, and the future is simply today becoming tomorrow. We look at them through a prismatic lens that never reveals the truth. The present eludes an active mind that swings like a pendulum from one illusion to another. We conveniently forget that the *now* exists. So much time is wasted worrying about the future that the present is buried beneath a mound of fear, insecurity, and a neurotic need to fabricate plans that never seem to work out. The best way to deal with the future is to focus on the present. Make life work today and the future will take care of itself.

My teacher Rudi spoke about spiritually malnourished people, a pandemic situation that touches just about everyone on earth. With all the books written on the human condition, with all the research and testing that's been done, real solutions still hide in places no one dares enter. Chaos and confusion run rampant in the human mind, and pill-popping, drug-induced solutions turn creative people into zombies. Because we rely on external answers to problems deeply rooted inside us, the mind never shuts up, and human beings continue on their half-crazed journey till they are put in a grave. Prescribe a pill and the problem goes away; fit a person into society like a cog in a machine. No internal foundation is developed, no inner life that's strong enough to transform suffering into spiritual energy. Creativity is deadened and we produce a society of spiritually starved misfits that haven't enough inner strength to function in a healthy way.

Human beings are masters at procrastination. Unless money

is involved or we're confronted by tragic circumstances, people's tendency is to put off opportunities to develop strong inner lives. Day and night creep into the next day and night until old age takes over, and it's difficult to conjure up enough energy to overcome inner problems. When life becomes unbearable people take time to do something about it. Otherwise, they live in a black hole. They think age and death only affects other people, not themselves, and they can put off until tomorrow what is so needed today.

❖❖❖❖

A meditation master is like a plumber who unclogs pipes to keep water from gushing out the kitchen sink. The power of *shakti*—spiritual Drano—when transmitted from teacher to student, opens the chakra system and enables energy to flow in a healthy way. If one's mind is focused in the *hara*, if we build the foundation, balance, and inner strength that elude most people and take it with us into everyday activities, we discover that the chakra below the navel is a vertex in a triangle that connects the inner life of a human being with the external world and higher energy. By conditioning ourselves to focus there, we develop enough *chi* to keep our hearts open and minds quiet. Connected to spirit, we no longer have to cannibalize other people's energy to fuel our depleted selves.

It takes time to master one's inner life, time and hard work to transform the things that are killing us into life-giving energies. As long as the mind dictates action, as long as ego and tension run rampant inside us, chaos will reign, and conflict will hinder our interactions with other people. Love, forgiveness, openness and compassion get lost in layers of tension. The heart stays closed, and we see the world through a prism that distorts reality.

❖❖❖❖

The outer world is a reminder of who I am and exactly how far I've come in my spiritual development. Family, friends, jobs, and social interactions mirror the evolution of my inner life. Am I judgmental? Do I attract situations that create overwhelming tension? Can I deal with the tension? There's so much wrong with life that one doesn't have to be a genius to complain about it. There are no perfect people, but imperfection is still the best teacher. As long as people irritate me it means I haven't fully developed my own humanity. It's better to listen to them, to grow inside, and be grateful to them for reminding me that I have to work on myself. They reflect imperfections that exist inside me or I wouldn't get annoyed. No argument, lecture or verbal abuse will change other people. But I can change myself. I can elevate my own humanity and live a life full of love and compassion.

It's the responsibility of a meditation teacher to help students develop strong chakra systems and make it possible for wisdom to find its way into their consciousness. Trumpets sound in the cosmos and angels sing a rowdy version of Handel's "Hallelujah Chorus" when the universe finds a human being with a developed chakra system. "Let the wisdom flow," it cries out. "Let spiritual practice continue on earth."

The Buddhist sutras have taught wisdom and compassion for thousands of years. So have the Old and New Testaments . . . and all the other great religious texts. This doesn't mean that we have to become religious. An agnostic can do it, so can an atheist if they learn to develop their chakra systems. Religion often interferes with a spiritual life. There's too much dogma, too much ritual, too many rules and regulations that restrict people. There's too much "You gotta do it this way or you're gonna roast in hell." The sad thing is that most people are already roasting in hell. Can hell get ghastlier than the chaos, tension, and insecurity that exist in the human mind? Can hell be any worse than people starving, than war and persecution, slavery, and "man's inhumanity to man" on earth? We don't need religion to paint a grim picture of suffering in an afterlife.

No matter how high one's IQ, no matter how extensive their studies, no matter how much people cram into memory, the human mind is limited to what it can grasp. It's like trying to fit an ocean into a teacup. The alternative is much more mysterious. Instead of analysis and logic, instead of thoughts that imprison infinite energy in a limited sphere, a spiritual life aligns us with the flow of energy in the universe. We become nothing. This is a scary proposition to people who rely on ego and self-importance to drive their lives, but nonetheless, a way of living that allows us to tap spirit and be nourished by a force much higher than ourselves.

The human mind resembles a birdcage filled with thousands of parakeets that chirp from morning to night—an inner life cannibalized by nonstop thinking that eats one alive. The intellect interprets wisdom through a prismatic lens that restricts it to what an individual's mind can comprehend. The universe waits patiently for us to make room for wisdom to find a home. We have to learn the most basic lesson: how to free ourselves from ourselves and allow higher energy to be part of our lives. Mastery of mind comes with time and a good deal of patience. If we don't invest that time and work on ourselves, the mind will dry up emotion and keep the heart from opening. It robs us of our humanity.

We can analyze "love" to the nth degree, but to live it is another matter. We can feign compassion and go through its motions, but how is it possible to love another person if one's incapable of loving oneself? The human mind is like a minor-league dictator with its own set of rules that must be followed. If no one complies, tension and conflict stare us in the face. If the mind's energy is used to develop the *hara*, rules change, and we let the world be. We don't have to know better than anyone else. When focused in the *hara*, the mind helps develop foundation, inner balance, and a root system that can handle life's difficulties. It transforms our thoughts into *chi* and gives us enough inner strength to keep the heart open. Tension falls away and we make room inside ourselves to receive the wisdom of the universe.

❖❖❖❖

There must be a bit of rebel in a person who's determined to change his own perceptions and not accept the mundane as a prototype for living. We satisfy ourselves with familiar, unthreatening environments that insulate us from problems. No matter how bored we become, no matter how conditioned we get by daily routine, no matter how terrible that reality, we cling to it and are afraid to make changes.

A stagnant environment doesn't mean our inner lives lack problems. The inevitable always lingers in the distance. Even the most conservative of people succumb to age and death and can't hide in a haze of mediocrity. Inside every human being there's a force of energy that does battle with the world—a mind that's in a perpetual state of conflict and a mirror image of pain and suffering experienced by every other person, a mind that exhausts our creative energy. Any attempt to fix the external world becomes a manipulation of shadows. It never works. We must return to a place where it's possible to make real change: the self. Once we learn how to do it, the process will free us from poisonous habits gleaned at an early age. They say, "If you save one life in your lifetime, the gates of heaven open and you're welcome." That life should be one's own. Suffering doesn't come to an end. What does end is our inability to transform suffering into love and joy. We share happiness with people who are ready to receive it. The alternative is simple: to reincarnate again and again, to go through a wind tunnel of pain and suffering until we free ourselves from life's invisible prison, and learn that happiness is the only real success on earth.

Meditation brings clarity, self-love and forgiveness; it also brings joy and compassion, and enables us to live here like human beings. We emerge from a shadow world that's full of illusion and embrace the sun. It's similar to the martial arts, but the battle isn't with an opponent in a ring. The battle is with life's nonstop succession of problems dumped in our laps. Without highly developed *chi*, we're like dust in the wind. We live in a daily meat grinder of unmanageable tension that consumes us whole. There's no rootedness, no foundation, and like Oscar Wilde's *Dorian Gray*, the external image of self becomes hideous with age when we look at it in life's cracked mirror.

In the movie *Young at Heart*, a documentary about a group of elderly people who come together to sing jazz, rock and roll, and popular songs, one member of this group (a ninety-year-old man) was sprawled out on an armchair. With a smile on his face, he spoke to the camera, "Nobody gets out of life alive," he said. The wisdom in this simple sentence made me laugh. It reminded me of my spiritual teacher's insistence that I should never take time for granted. "We can escape most things in life," Rudi said, "but death is a certainty. Its very presence reminds us of how important it is to live with open hearts and embrace the miracle of each day."

Life and death are woven together like threads in a sacred

tapestry. One gives birth to the other. Without death there is no rebirth, and life teaches us how to detach ourselves from illusion. They are both the children of time. One cannot exist without the other, and both create draconian fear in people who rely on mind and emotion to get through the day. We also discover that there's nothing to fear if we're connected to spirit. Life, death, and time become teachers that help us on the path to enlightenment. A conscious use of meditation enables us to transcend the precincts of time, embrace both life and death, be happy, and work out our karma on earth.

CHAPTER 2

Two thirty a.m.—I woke up with a splitting headache. I massaged my neck and head and the area of the third eye. The pain was so intense that I couldn't fall back to sleep again. I got out of bed, drank a glass of water, took a pee, and walked about, but nothing rid me of the pain in my forehead. Like an uncontrollable fire that clears underbrush, dead and dying trees, and anything else in its path, the heat changed the contour of my forehead and expanded an already-open third eye. Bones shifted, ridges and valleys formed, and the wings of a phoenix spread from my third eye to the crown chakra. I had undergone a major death and rebirth. Cosmic physicians had come and performed a psychic operation. This wasn't the first time I had this experience. I had also seen Rudi in the throes of this type of inner transition.

In 1972, on a trip I made to New York from Texas, Rudi met me at the airport. In many letters and phone conversations he spoke about the changes that had taken place inside him. "You won't believe what's happened to my head," he said in one of our conversations. When we met at the airport I realized Rudi was a changed person. There was an aura of golden light that surrounded him. From a large indentation at the center of his forehead, I saw the wings of a phoenix bird touch the crown of his head— a symbol of rebirth, of deep inner change, of a person whose consciousness has broken through to realms that were outside of time and space. "Stop staring at my head," he laughed. "I can't see anything else," I responded. He wasn't the same person I had spent time with three months before. "Cosmic physicians came," he laughed, "and performed surgery on my head. It was so painful, I was laid up for three days." "I've never seen anything like it," I said. "Nor have I," he responded. I couldn't take my eyes off his head. It had expanded, grown, changed in such a dramatic way that the markings in his forehead were like a chart that revealed profound spiritual growth and inner awakening. He asked me to put my hand on his forehead. I experienced a heat so intense that I thought it would burn my hand, the same kind of heat I felt when I touched my own forehead many years later.

Rudi and I went for dinner at a restaurant on the Upper West Side of Manhattan. "How am I different than anyone else?" he asked me. "I like to dine out, watch TV, go to the movies, have friends, and live a good life." I started to laugh. My hand was still burning. His head had expanded, and the love in his heart was beyond anything I had experienced before. "I don't know," I smiled. "It's a mystery to me how you're like anyone else."

When I experienced a similar opening in my head there wasn't much I could do but absorb the changes that took place inside me. A major operation had transformed the shape of my forehead, and I didn't want to waste a drop of the energy. I wrote a little bit, watched some television, taught meditation class, rested, and tried to be reclusive. Activity would come after the energy of change was absorbed. "I'm off to Oregon in a few days to hold a meditation retreat. Stay quiet," I thought. "A new level of spiritual teaching will rise to the surface. A retreat is the perfect place for this to take place."

❖❖❖❖

Headaches are often a by-product of congested chakra systems. When the heart chakra isn't open, energy will back up and create so much tension that the result can be a splitting headache. It's like faulty plumbing. If the pipes are clogged, everything comes out the kitchen sink.

A friend of mine once complained to me about a migraine. The pain in her head was so intense she could barely move. I asked her to sit in a chair opposite me. I went into a deep meditative state. I could see that the problem wasn't her head. It was her heart. "Close your eyes," I said to her. I stood up, walked over to her, put my finger on her forehead and drew tension out of the chakra. After about a minute of this, I put my finger on her heart center. When I finished the healing, I asked the woman to open her eyes. They were aglow, full of life, and she looked ten years younger. "The headache's gone," she said to me with a big smile. "What did you do? I've never felt better." "It's not your head," I responded. "It's your heart. It was closed. Energy ceased to flow, and excess tension backed up and created the migraine."

I've healed hundreds of people with serious headaches. Often in jest I've told them that I've discovered a new kind of aspirin. "Most people refuse to take the time to learn how to do this for themselves," I said to one of my students. "They need a pill, a doctor, or a healer, someone or something external to themselves to resolve the problem."

Headaches should be renamed heartaches. When gratitude dries up and the heart chakra closes, pressure builds that affects the head. The intensity of this pressure can create migraines. Gratitude and *shakti* are like Liquid Plum'r. They will unclog the heart, get energy to flow, release tension in the brain and help to rid us of serious headaches.

My two thirty a.m. headache was different. My heart wasn't closed. When cosmic physicians operated on my third eye, when they separated bone and muscle and made room inside me for higher energy, I felt nothing but gratitude. And today there's newfound inner awareness, more wisdom, and a deeper connection with my spiritual teacher, Rudi. I'll never forget that the day I met him transformed my life.

❖❖❖❖

In the mid-1970s, I went to Memorial Sloan Kettering Hospital to visit a cousin of mine who had cancer. The doctors had given her a few weeks to live. "You do meditation and all that kind of stuff," her mother said to me. "Do you think you can help Sandy?" "I don't know," I replied, "but I'll go to the hospital tomorrow."

I hadn't seen my cousin Sandy in years. She was barely recognizable. Pale, sickly, tired, and with a huge belly, she had accepted the fact that death was a few weeks away. A bit of a shock for me to see her like that, my first question was, "Do you want to live?"

I had to know that from the start. If she wanted to die there was nothing I could do for her. She whispered in a desperate voice, "Yes."

I sat down by her bedside and asked her to close her eyes and listen to her breathing. In a deep meditative state, I put my finger on her forehead and performed the healing meditation practice I'd learned from Rudi. Over the next few days I returned to the hospital to continue the treatment. When the cancer went into remission she told everyone she met at Memorial Sloan Kettering Hospital about the miracle her cousin had performed. "You've got to get him to meditate with you," she said. The hospital released her four days later. The doctors had no explanation except, "Things like this sometimes happen."

"Come to Texas and learn what I teach," I said to her just before she left the hospital. "Six months of study will get you strong enough to keep the tumors from ever coming back." "I've got a husband," she replied, "children. My life is here in New Jersey." I pleaded with her. She refused to come. A year later, she died. She might have died anyway, I'll never know. Nor will her husband and children. But somehow, deep in myself, I always feared for her. I told myself, "It's her decision. I can't interfere with the choice she's made with the organic process of life and death."

CHAPTER 3

I'm often asked, "Do ambition and will have relevance in meditation practice?" This isn't an easy question to answer, especially in a world where ambition and will (the by-products of strong egos) are almost always used to attain money, position and power. We objectify our ambition and focus it on external goals without a thought about our internal life. It's the next score that's going to make us happy. We accumulate vast wealth, bask in it, and create insulated, gilded palaces that force the rest of the world to look at us through sunglasses. The need for a spiritual life is almost non-existent. There are countless obstacles in the way, many psychological, emotional and physical blocks that hinder an attempt to open and develop chakras. Most people don't want to be bothered with change. They cling to the familiar. Change forces one to step into the unknown—a kind of death and rebirth that threatens comfort zones and demands re-examination of a benign micro-world, and exit from a safety net to embrace the new.

The meditation class I teach is like a gym. Practitioners come there to develop psychic muscle systems, or chakras. If the chakras aren't worked every day they atrophy the same way physical muscles turn to flab when we don't exercise. The real test of meditation isn't the class. It's when one leaves the class and has to confront the rest of life. Do we leave our psychic muscle system in the classroom, or do we take what we've learned with us? There's a bridge that connects meditation with the rest of the world. To cross that bridge we must maintain inner balance. There's always a barrage of things to test us. It could be a clerk in a grocery store, a taxi driver or someone on the subway; it could be a member of our family or a co-worker; it could be just about anyone or anything. A loss of inner balance reminds us to work harder in the next meditation class. It's not easy to keep one's mind focused in the *hara*. If we blow it once or twice or a hundred times the inner work shouldn't stop. It take time and patience and results come when we least expect it. A loss of inner balance should remind us to work harder in the next meditation class.

Meditation is a craft, and the tools of this craft are mind, breath, need, will and gratitude. If there isn't a deep need to grow spiritually, then nothing we do is going to strengthen the chakra system. There are too many obstacles to hinder the effort. The first and foremost is the mind: an overactive place that twists and turns, drifts and pounds until it exhausts us, a creature that must be tamed. When the need for a spiritual life becomes strong, obstacles are no longer a hindrance. The mind becomes a surgical instrument that cuts through tension, strengthens the *hara* and develops equilibrium and foundation. We've taken the first step on a path that leads to enlightenment.

The world is spiritually famished, but instead of junk-food energy diets, instead of cigarettes, alcohol, pills and dope, we can put an end to spiritual hunger by learning to develop chakras; we can put an end to hunger that gnaws at our gut and reminds us that material gain won't fill the void. The other remedies are short-lived fixes for deep-rooted problems, for a chakra system that's atrophied, for spiritual growth that's been blocked. Our chakra system isn't strong enough to receive energy of a higher nature, and mind, emotion, and sexuality take us only so far. They will never satisfy the discomfort we feel inside. It's like living on a diet of bread and potatoes. We become full, even bloated, but slowly starve to death.

❖❖❖❖

My gallery in New York City had clients that pursued art objects with ravenous zeal. Obsessed with the next treasure . . . and the next . . . and the next, they'd run to my gallery when I called them. When I visited their homes, statues were hidden in showcases filled to the brim with other statues. The owners had become so familiar with them that their rarity had vanished. One of my clients had a large collection of ancient Tibetan *phurbas* (ritual knives) and spent tens of thousands of dollars to acquire them. On a visit to his apartment he asked me what the *phurbas* were used for. He hadn't the faintest idea. He liked their shape and knew they were rare, and had a passion for them. "*Phurbas* are used in Tibetan ritual ceremonies to transform inner blocks and tensions into spiritual energy," I said to him. He didn't respond and looked at me as if I were crazy. "Do you have any more in stock?" he asked me. "Not now," I replied, "but as soon as I get one I'll call you."

Facebook, Twitter, Google, and Microsoft are corporations founded by strong-willed and very smart entrepreneurs. They refuse to let anything interfere with success. Their ambition is so strong it overcomes any obstacle. The need for power, the need to accumulate ludicrous sums of money, to be king of the heap, to bask in success and lord it over others—that need stems from uncompromising will and an unwavering desire to succeed. A spiritual life requires an even stronger will. It's the single most difficult thing to attain on earth. Intangible and beyond the limited comprehension of mind, it is always out of reach. We can't touch it or taste it or smell it. Any movement towards enlightenment requires a gradual reduction of ego and image of self. We can't be attached to anything that we possess. As Rudi once said: "It's not, not to have, but to not let what we have own us." We can't possess the infinite, but we can receive its wisdom and let it guide our daily lives.

The same energy that goes into building an economic empire can be used to attain enlightenment. It depends on need and how one wants to invests their time and energy. It also depends on karma: what one is ready to do in their lifetime. Material success and spiritual development are not mutually exclusive. They say, "It's easier for a camel to go through the eye of a needle than a rich man to go to heaven," but a rich man also has a chakra system, a mind and breath, all the instruments that can be used to build an inner life. If he takes time from his busy schedule to develop them an inner life is possible. If he loses himself in the glitter of money, if he feeds his ego with greed and power, his chakra system will atrophy, mind and emotions will cannibalize his energy, and unconditional joy, love, and compassion will disappear in a mirror of self-delusion.

The political and business worlds are replete with men and women who are caricatures of their former selves—less human and more possessed by power and the trappings of power, driven by greed and blinded by money, they don't give a damn who gets trampled in a struggle for material things. The tensions are so severe that they weaken the body's immune system. Organs and cells deteriorate and once-healthy people fall prey to disease. Medical advances can't compete with the rapid deterioration of human bodies. Excessive tension keeps the body from remaining fit. When people equate inner work with flakiness and ignore organic means by which they can transform their tension into positive energy, when the tension leads to burnout and early aging, one wonders if they ever take a good look in the mirror. Charisma doesn't hide deep unhappiness. The eyes of a human being reveal whether or not their heart is open.

The human mind is a conflicted creature that enslaves us every day. But spirit can outfox the mind and turn the master into a servant. It takes a remarkable effort to focus the mind in the *hara*. A lifetime of habit must be revamped and the mind transformed into a surgical instrument that cuts through tension and opens the navel chakra. It takes time and patience to do this and the only person we're up against is one's self.

There's a silent, but steadily growing epidemic on earth today of spiritually destitute people. It crosses every border. It touches folks that live in cities, towns, and villages around the globe; it touches people because they replace spiritual need with material things. Their inner lives dry up and they lose touch with the source of creative energy. The chakra system is like a musical instrument. If we don't fine-tune it every day, it atrophies, and our psychic muscle system won't support a connection with higher energy.

Five essential tools are used when we meditate: mind, breath, will, gratitude, and need. The most basic of these tools is need. Without it, the rest are useless. One can chant day and night, one can perform hundreds of rituals, meditate, memorize sacred texts, and prostrate one's self before statues, one can follow strict rules and regulations set forth by gurus, but if real hunger for enlightenment isn't there, all this activity becomes form without substance…and spirit moves past like river water over a rock.

If the need to grow is strong enough, mind and breath become instruments that develop the chakra system. They work together to open and strengthen the heart and navel chakra. When focused in the *hara*, the mind, like a surgical instrument, will cut through tension and help to create strong inner foundation. Gratitude opens the heart and breath will expand both the heart and the *hara* and make it possible to absorb *shakti*. Our emotions will diffuse themselves, the mind will get quiet, and there will be room inside us to receive wisdom and compassion. Our internal life, external life, and higher energy become one, and the navel chakra the vertex of a triangle that connects the three.

When we're full of ourselves there's no room for the wisdom that the universe wants to share with us. Daily activity is fueled by thought, emotion, sex, and the drive to make money. As the chakra system refines itself we not only experience profound inner silence, we no longer rely on the mind's limited intelligence to guide our lives. We connect to a higher intelligence that's attached to the infinite. For us to embrace this intelligence we must arrive at a place in ourselves where "less is more," where we are detached from the past and future, and live our lives in the moment. We discover that Genesis isn't a magical event that took place in ancient history. It's a living experience that takes place every moment of our lives. We discover that the universe is constantly recreating itself and that we live at its vertex. We also discover that most people are asleep, unconscious, too wrapped up in their own problems to recognize this simple reality; most people bumble about in a world that lacks consciousness. It's like the old Zen saying, "Before enlightenment, chop wood, carry water. After enlightenment, chop wood, carry water."

The only thing that changes with enlightenment is our inner life. Our senses sharpen: food tastes better, what we see and hear has more resonance, and the words that we utter take on deeper meanings. We listen to people and discover that the art of listening enables us to engage in good conversation. When we listen to other people we learn about them and speak without condescension or fear, with trust, and with the ability to communicate. Thought and emotion don't interfere; our tensions are at bay, we defer to life as our teacher, and let the world be.

The path to enlightenment often appears to be a half-crazed

attempt to dehumanize one's self—a costume ball attended by saints, *nagababas, sadhus*, and other strange characters. The very notion that Milarepa built four different houses at the whim of the *mahasiddha* Marpa; the idea that Ramakrishna dressed in drag and danced before a statue of Kali; that Ramana Maharshi spent sixteen years meditating in a cave in order to get his enlightenment; the very notion that great saints had to divest themselves of normalcy appeals to many people. It's something to be analyzed, thought about, gloated over, but never experienced.

Altars are set up in urban and suburban households. On these altars are pictures of half-naked saints. Books by and about these saints are read by millions of people. It's like T. S. Eliot in his poem about J. Alfred Prufrock:

And indeed there will be time
To wonder, 'Do I dare?' and 'Do I dare?'
Time to turn back and descend the stair,
With a bald spot in the middle of my hair.

"There's time to procrastinate—there's always another excuse, and another, until both time and excuses run dry and we're left with "a bald spot in the middle of [our] hair." The ordinary never becomes extraordinary, because we're afraid to step into the unknown. We stand on the outside and look in at a world that fascinates us, titillates us, even excites us, but there's always the presence of a strange door that we're afraid to enter, a door that leads to a playground where "normal" people have transformed themselves into the children of God, a place that looks wacko to the outsider, but a place that's full of joy, unconditional love, and compassion, a place where everyone is invited but few dare enter. The question is, "Where is that place?" The answer: It's not very far away from any of us. In fact, all we have to do is look inside ourselves and we'll see God's children living there; all we have to do is go beyond the chaos and confusion in our minds and emotions and enter a doorway to this playground; all we have to do is learn how to use need, will, mind and breath to develop our chakra systems . . . and we'll find a path that leads to spiritual enlightenment.

I stepped into that world when I met Rudi. For six years I sat at his feet, learned from him, and discovered that the real "battlefield of truth" took place every day inside myself. I marveled at Rudi's ability to create harmony out of chaos, to love people who lived in his ashram that were of such diverse natures that under any other circumstance there would have been war instead of peace. It was the first time I'd seen unconditional love at work in the world.

One evening Rudi and I went to dinner at a friend's apartment. The conversation evolved around Rudi's spiritual practice and his ashram on Tenth Street. "How can people live that way?" the friend asked. On any given day, ten to twenty people slept on the second floor of his ashram. The morning wait to use the bathroom was impossible. Rudi smiled and said, "People are there for only one reason, to get their spiritual training. Isn't that true, Stuart?" I smiled and answered, "There can be no other reason." "I saw Swami Nityananda asleep on a potato sack," Rudi said, "and wished that my life could get that simple." Rudi was the most loving, beautiful, irascible, sacrilegiously spiritual person I'd ever been around. He taught me to overcome discomfort, to not sit in judgment of others, and to use the difficult circumstances karma dishes out to strengthen my inner life and get closer to God.

If there's an insatiable need inside you to get to God, you do whatever it takes to make that journey. Friends and relatives might think you're crazy, but so what? It doesn't matter what people think. The only thing that matters is that you get free of yourself and live in the light of God. The truth is that I've never met a sane person in my life. Being a little wacko is all right. It allows me to fit in with everyone else on this planet. Most people are half-dead before they are put in the grave. They are spiritually undernourished, and can't find enough creative energy in themselves to make life enjoyable. As Christ said, "Let the dead bury the dead." Follow your inner life on a path that leads to enlightenment.

There has to be love for one's self, one's family, one's friends and fellow workers, because each human being lives on God's playground. Some are conscious that they live there . . . most are not. It doesn't matter. We're in no position to judge other people. Once we sit in judgment of them, we open ourselves to be judged, and there's no one dead or alive who hasn't committed some stupid infraction that's hurt another person. As we refine our inner lives, need, will, mind and breath dissolve into nothingness. The path to enlightenment also disappears. We *are* . . . that's it, and we live our lives in the moment. We're conscious, free, open and happy, and we've attained the highest level of what it means to be human.

In a world that's replete with cynicism, vengeance, and anger, not many people live this way. The word *love* is just another word that's bandied about in popular songs, plays, movies, etc. Unless we develop an inner life that's strong enough to keep our hearts open, the word love is without meaning. No matter how good it sounds, it still amounts to nothing when the human heart is closed.

I've given up trying to understand spirit. I also realized that I know nothing about life—a profound realization because it opened up the world to me. I don't have to know more than other people, I don't have to be right. I can listen and learn and allow life to be my teacher. It takes a good deal of courage to look in the mirror at a reflection of myself and accept that the universe is much bigger than I am. I had never known that kind of humility; I had never known that every person I met was my teacher. When my heart opened fear diminished, and for the first time in my life, both inner and outer realities took on a magical sheen.

CHAPTER 4

"I'm a lesbian. How can I study with you; how can I have a spiritual life?" A student once said to me. She had tears in her eyes. It was the early 1970s in Denton, Texas, a conservative township in which gays and lesbians were tightly locked in closets. They didn't dare come out. "I don't care if you sleep with sheep," I responded. "Do you want to be with God?" "More than anything," she said. "I've wanted that since I was a little girl." "That's the only thing that matters. You can study with me. I don't give a damn who or what you sleep with. We're all children of God. What I do care about is that you have a deep need for a spiritual life."

There's too much righteousness in the world, I thought after she left. It creates prisons from fundamentalist ideas that punish people whose belief systems, race, and sexuality differ from one's own, a dogmatic set of principles that say there's only one possible path to God: the righteous path— often a boring, almost deadly approach to life that limits experience and denies other people their beliefs. It turns innocent and loving children into half-crazed fanatics that haven't enough intelligence or wisdom to allow people that differ with their beliefs to live peacefully in this world.

Diversity of belief creates a rich environment. There's no one uniform that will fit all—a uniform that limits creative expression and keeps people out of touch with their true selves. In the minds of righteous people, the *I am* has become a logical, well-worked-out formula that attempts to fit a gallon of water in a shot glass. It creates boundaries that can never be crossed. It limits compassion to an insulated world of members who walk the same path and who cannot tolerate diversity—a small-minded, fascistic approach to life that reduces everything to a caricature of itself. The *I am* is no longer an expression of infinite energy.

What works for myself doesn't necessarily have to work for other people. To set up a soapbox in Times Square and preach the benefits of kundalini yoga would not only denigrate the meditation practice I learned from Rudi, it would transform sacred spiritual work into something ridiculous. Meditation's wellspring of silence creates dialogue with spirit and a love of God that can't be explained. Nor can it be stuffed down the throats of other people. The dialogue teaches gratitude, tolerance, patience, and whatever one has to learn to work out their karma. In meditation sessions I've had Christian, Buddhist, Jewish, Muslim and Hindu experiences, and each of them has helped me get closer to enlightenment. It's foolish to limit myself when the universe provides countless paths that come from and return to the exact same place.

❖❖❖❖

In my late teens and early twenties I'd visit holy men of every religious persuasion. I'd hear poetic words about happiness, joy, and compassion being the key to a spiritual life. I was urged to become celibate and vegetarian, to study the Old and New Testaments, the Bhagavad Gita, the Koran, the Vedas, and many other sacred texts. I was urged to chant, pray, meditate, and participate in ritual practices. I'd read the texts over again and studied many profound subjects. I chanted and prayed, visited temples and churches, wise and holy men, but no one could tell me how to quiet my mind and emotions; no one was prepared to teach a technique that was strong enough to overcome my inner chaos. The words they spoke were often profound, even inspiring, and there were times that I'd leave on a high note, but then discovered that little or nothing took root. I still had to deal with myself— an unhappy, lonely, often depressed person, at times half-crazy and incapable of quieting my unruly, demonic mind.

❖❖❖❖

The day after I met him, I returned to Rudi's Asian art gallery on Seventh Avenue South to learn the breathing technique and to attend his meditation class. The exercise was simple: focus my attention on the chakra below the navel and ask deeply to open, to surrender and to grow spiritually. The next step was to open the heart. "Keep your attention below the navel and feel gratitude," he said. "You don't need your mind to open the heart. It will just get in the way. Gratitude is the quickest way to open the heart center. Take a deep breath into the center of your chest and hold it for about ten seconds. Let joy and love spread through the chakra, and while you are holding your breath, swallow a little saliva to relax the throat muscles. After holding your breath for about ten seconds, exhale a little of the air, stop, wait a few seconds, and continue to exhale until you are comfortable. Then take another deep breath. This time bring all the air down to the chakra below the navel. Your mind and breath are there, and ask deeply for help to open, to surrender and to grow spiritually. Hold the breath for about ten seconds then exhale a little of the air, stop, wait a few seconds and continue to exhale until you're comfortable.

"After the second breath," Rudi continued, "just breathe naturally, but try to keep your mind focused below the navel. Once the mind loses this focus the whole system of a human being goes off balance. If you feel energy move through the sexual area, bring about five per cent of your attention to the base of the spine. Try to draw the energy up the spine to the top of the head where it will accumulate and ripen. When the crown chakra (the thousand-petaled lotus) opens, a connection will be made between the soul of a human being and the soul of the universe.

"Use the double-breathing exercise only when necessary," he said. "If your mind is quiet and heart open, if you're centered, it isn't necessary to do the double breathing. If you begin to think, daydream, and want to look around the room, then you have to re-center yourself. You have to focus your attention in the navel chakra, and do the double-breathing exercise again. It's a very simple technique that will open and develop the chakra system. Like any other craft, it takes time to learn. You have to discipline the mind and master the flow of breath. They are the tools of meditation and they must be used properly."

Rudi taught an open-eye meditation. Most meditation practices require closed eyes. At first I didn't understand the reason for open eyes. Later on it became clear to me. There are three things going on in the meditation practice. The first is the internal use of mind and breath to develop the chakra system—an inner life that connects us to spirit. When our eyes are open, we're not only focused on the navel chakra, we're also connected to the world. A triangle forms, and its vertex is in the *tan t'ien* or *hara*. We're focused on the inner, the outer and a higher plane of consciousness at the same time. We discover that there's no separation between the three. We can live in the world and be free of the world at exactly the same time. In meditation class, *shakti* transmitted by the teacher will enter the practitioner through the eyes and act as a catalyst to help build their inner lives.

The conscious use of breath will expand the chakra system. With every inhalation we open to the entire universe; and with every exhalation we let go of a part of ourselves. The Hindus have a mantra called *So-Hum*. When you inhale, you say to yourself *So*, and when you exhale you say *Hum*, "I am that" or "I am one with God." There's a simple exercise I teach that can be done during meditation. It helps to master breathing. When one inhales, say "I." As one brings the air into the heart chakra, say "am." After one holds the breath for about ten seconds, say "that," while exhaling. The words should be said internally and each breath should be slow and extended. You may feel a bubbly sensation— a lightness of being that comes when one connects with higher energy. This same breathing exercise can also be used to strengthen the chakra below the navel.

The inner lives of people are like a cauldron full of tension that goes so deep it begins to erode the mind and body. The older we get the deeper that tension embeds itself inside us. It eats away our energy and keeps us from being productive. It transforms a lifetime of accumulation into a sickly person that has difficulty getting through the day. People invest their time and energy in external things like money, family, power, and success. Over the years, age and illness suck them dry. There wasn't time to master tension and inner chaos. They were too busy chasing external turn-ons that never made them happy; turn-ons creating momentary surges of pleasure that disappeared as quickly as they manifested.

People have told me: "I'm getting sick, my wife is getting sick. There's so much tension, my only relief is a pill." When I ask them why they didn't practice some form of meditation, they often look at me with a dull stare: "Meditation? It sounds good, but I never had time." We have enough time to kill ourselves in the pursuit of money, but no time to invest in something that brings life. Tension is an untreatable illness from which masseuses, chiropractors, acupuncturists, and other body workers give us temporary relief. It accumulates in every joint, organ and bone of our bodies. It takes remarkable inner strength to transform tension into life-giving energy. A student of Rudi's once asked him why he wore orange t-shirts all the time. "It's a symbol of fire," he replied, "of surrender." "What are you surrendering?" the student asked. Rudi thought for a moment and replied with a smile on his face: "Tension."

The first step is to bring the tension to the area below the navel, transform it into *chi*, and draw the *chi* through the sexual area to the base of the spine and activate kundalini. Positive and negative energies merge. They rise up the spine and connect the human soul with the soul of the universe. Once we learn how to do this, our tension will reduce itself. We'll no longer have need for addictive prescription drugs, for triple shots of scotch to relax us, for marijuana, cocaine, or any other kind of drug that does damage to our systems. Kundalini burns our tension and transforms it into energy that rises up the spine and connects us to the universal soul. If the double-breathing meditation technique is practiced every day, gradually over a period of time one will learn to master inner chaos.

❖❖❖❖

The seven basic chakras are all connected to the spine—the only area in a human being where energy rises. It's important to sit straight when one meditates so the force of kundalini can move from the base of the spine to the crown chakra without obstruction. Once there's heat at the base of the spine and energy rises to the crown, we can draw *shakti* through the heart center to the spine and it will also rise to the top of our head. The same holds true with each of the other chakras. When energy rises from the base of the spine to the crown chakra, it forms a bump that's no different than the bump one sees on the head of a statue of Buddha. The energy accumulates there, and over time the chakra will ripen. When it opens the soul is released, and there's union with higher energy in the universe. The bump on the top of a meditation practitioner's head is a sign that kundalini has awakened. Often pictured as a lotus flower with a thousand petals or as a radiance that connects one's consciousness to higher energy, an awakened crown chakra touches on divine mysticism and makes it possible for a human being to attain enlightenment.

Each chakra plays its role in the awakening of kundalini. There has to be rootedness in the *hara* that makes it possible for us to do two things: work out our karma, and have enough inner strength to support a spiritual life. The heart needs to be open. Happiness and a compassionate lifestyle are the highest attainments on earth. An open heart means we've fulfilled our humanity. The sexual area can't be clogged up or energy will cease to flow; kundalini won't be activated. Tantra (sexual energy) is essential if we want to develop higher consciousness. When internalized, it's a healing energy that stokes kundalini at the base of the spine and makes it possible for our soul to embrace the soul of the universe through the crown chakra. The throat chakra connects us to the source of sound, and each spoken word reveals whether or not we've elevated our consciousness. Finally, there's the third eye, or the chakra in the forehead. When open it becomes a repository of wisdom and knowledge, and it enables us to distinguish what's real from what's an illusion. Each chakra is like a finely tuned instrument. It must be played in tandem with the other chakras, or life's symphony will be out of tune. If our chakras malfunction, there'll be little joy or love in the human heart; pain and suffering won't be transformed into *chi*. We were born with the tools to refine and develop chakras. We just have to master the use of mind and breath to turn chaos into balance and harmony.

People often confuse *chi* with a spiritual life. When they experience a sense of balance, power, and calm, they equate it with elevated consciousness. But *chi* is a powerful force that can be used to succeed in the world. It brings money, relationships, success, and a circle of friends that respect, fear, and adore us.

If a person's *chi* embraces ego and is used to cut a path through the material world, there's no limit to the amount of damage that can be done if their heart is closed. *Chi* becomes a sinister tool in political and business realms where most people rely on logical, well-worked theorems to deal with problems, theorems that often go awry as soon as they are applied to moment-to-moment change. A person with highly developed *chi* focuses on the present and makes decisions according to what life brings. They don't try to fit the universe into a little box. Like a dancer who responds to each musical note, improvises when necessary, and is totally alive in the moment; if a businessman, lawyer, or a politician has powerful *chi* they can tune into the moment and outwit other people.

Highly developed *chi* doesn't mean that a person is spiritual. Hitler, Stalin, and Mussolini probably had highly developed *chi*. Putin definitely has highly developed *chi*— a powerful energy that emanates from his person, strength of purpose, and a no-nonsense decisiveness. What's missing in him is heart. There's little or no compassion for others. A wellspring of protective energy gushes from his mind and gut— a force of energy that could easily torture or kill people who cross him. There must be checks and balances. What are they? The answer is simple: humility, love, compassion— a heartfelt empathy for the suffering of others; an ear that listens to their cries; a need to conquer one's own demons and bring kindness to the world.

Without a well-developed chakra system, *chi* creates power-crazed men and women who use their gifts to subjugate other people and control lives. A fine line separates sainthood from madness—a line that is easily crossed when one lives with a closed heart and loses touch with their humanity.

CHAPTER 5

People construct internal walls of self-defense: mental walls, emotional walls, economic walls, societal walls, and racial walls to name a few. Years of conditioned behavior determine response when a person interacts with other human beings. They have to protect themselves from an onslaught of intentional or unintentional bad vibes. The lack of parental love for their children diminishes trust, closes the heart, and stunts emotional growth at a very early age. A forty-year-old adult could have the inner life of a seven-year-old child, an unrecognizable condition when we first meet them. When friendships or relationships grow, as pressure builds to truly love and confide in another human being, emotional insecurity becomes apparent.

It's all very understandable. An infant reaches out to parents who are crippled inside. When the love isn't provided for the child, its heart closes, insulated walls are built, and it protects itself from being hurt . . . protection that's carried into teenage years and adulthood. Emotionally and mentally crippled people peek out from behind fortresses. They try to connect with other men and women who are in the same condition, and it's almost impossible for them to do so. They're like short-circuited wires in an old house. If these people have children of their own the legacy of unhappiness and emotional immaturity is passed on from generation to generation. They suffer from a case of spiritual malnutrition, a disease not genetic in its makeup or listed in medical handbooks, but a condition that affects the entire human race.

Well-insulated internal walls keep people from being vulnerable: an unconscious defense mechanism that's developed over years of being hurt. Most of us are not even aware that it exists. Our minds and bodies are conditioned to believe that these walls are beneficial. Life can't touch us if we're secure in our insulated cell. But we can't escape being touched by life. In fact there's no way around it unless we want to live like turtles. An internal voice cries out for attention—a deafening cry produced from loneliness and despair, a desperate voice that somehow must commune with the world from a well-insulated fortress that transforms human beings into the living dead. Nothing can enter its precincts; no one can live within its walls. Not wanting to be hurt, we're skeptical when approached with love and we try to keep the demon-kindness away from us. Our teachers, friends and partners must have patience for an emotionally crippled person's heart center to open and for them to trust.

What does it mean to be vulnerable? If every act is one in which we give and receive, we discover that neither is possible without some degree of vulnerability. We can't interact with other people unless we make room inside ourselves for them to be around us. Can we deal with their tension? Can we relate to them in a compassionate way? They are no longer the enemy, but a friend or a teacher, someone who doesn't intimidate us, because we can deal with their problems and use what we like or dislike about them as a reason to deepen our own inner lives.

There's a seed of life in the most despicable person, a voice that cries out for love. Hidden behind a thick veneer of self-hatred and anger, their inner child wants to come out. It hungers for love and acceptance, but doesn't know how to get them. The question is: Are we intimidated by another person's anger? Do we have enough spiritual development to connect with their inner child? Are we vulnerable enough to love them anyway, forgive them their past indiscretions, and help them find a place in the world?

In order to live a compassionate life, strong foundation and balance are essential. Without them, life runs right over us. Weak people can't sustain open hearts, and we can't be vulnerable if we live insulated lives and hide from the world. We forget that age, illness and death will crack the walls of our fortress; we forget that pain and suffering have no borders; we forget that people dish out anger, depression, hatefulness, chicanery and a host of other negative vibes that test us every day. Can we deal with these people without getting into trouble? Can we open ourselves to human interaction? Do we pick and choose what's comfortable for us? If so, life, in all its complexity, will teach us that fear and insecurity dictate the kind of world we live in. We forget that God hides behind thousands of masks, and each of these masks is a reminder that we're born on earth to evolve, grow, and learn to embrace humanity.

There's no way to avoid getting hurt by life. No matter how we try to protect ourselves, life will find a way to bite us in the ass. It's never what we expect, always unreasonable, and it creates more conflict than our systems can handle. No one looks forward to war, massive fires, turbulent weather, extreme poverty, loved ones and friends dying—tragic events that manifest in the lives of people every day. No one looks forward to illness or death, but they pay us all a visit, a great equalizer that couldn't care less if we live in a crystal palace or a hovel. No philosopher or theologian can successfully debate this matter with the universe. Shit happens to each of us in its own unique way. It's impossible to avoid the smell, even if we delude ourselves with thoughts of invincibility. If we work on ourselves to build inner lives that are strong enough to deal with tragic circumstances, when shit happens (and it always does), at least we'll be able to maintain balance. We won't close up like clams, but we'll take whatever lesson life teaches us and build a stronger base. If we're not vulnerable, wisdom eludes us, and we're left with trauma that rips apart our fragile natures.

Between now and the time of death, human beings will get hurt again . . . and again . . . and again. We can't avoid it until we learn to use our hurt in a positive way. If we bring the pain to the chakra below the navel and transform it into harmony and balance, the problem becomes another opportunity to grow. We cease to live in our own personalized Jericho, and walls of insulation tumble down. The best protection in life is to be open and full of spiritual energy. We need to let life in, we need to learn what it has to teach. If we allow that to happen, vulnerability stops being a problem.

CHAPTER 6

"I want you to go to the Denton, Texas, ashram for three weeks," Rudi said to me. "They need a teacher there." It was a town of about forty thousand people thirty-five miles north of both Dallas and Fort Worth. I had lived in New York City most of my life and spent a good deal of time in Paris, Rome, Marrakech, Athens and many other cities in Europe and North Africa. I had studied art history and literature, and spent hours in museums like The Louvre, The Prado, The Uffizi, and Denton wasn't my idea of a place I wanted to hang out in for a very long time. When I arrived in Denton I had a couple of dollars in my pocket, and a desire to teach Rudi's meditation practice. He had saved my life, and I believed that his meditation could help many people who wanted to grow spiritually.

A group of young men and women ran a vegetarian restaurant in Denton called the Cosmic Kitchen. They lived commune-style in a rented house on North Locust Street. They had met Rudi and wanted to study his meditation. On my first day in Denton I discovered their house was rife with drugs—marijuana, cocaine, LSD, some heroin, and I told them that I would leave if they didn't get rid of the drugs. There was only one rule in Rudi's meditation practice: no drugs. Most of the young people stormed out of the house. They were pissed that Stuart, a guy from New York, had the gall to ask them to flush their hallucinogens down a toilet. I didn't blame them. It was their choice. If they wanted to get stoned it was all right with me, but there was no way that drugs and deep spiritual practice could work together. It was my first test in Denton. After the "revolution," I was left with four or five students—young people who committed themselves to Rudi's spiritual practice because it meant more to them than getting stoned.

About six months later Rudi came to visit me in Denton. "It's been a helluva three weeks," I said to him. "You're on your fourth day," he replied with a big smile on his face.

What scared me was that I would become like the locals in Denton. I kept hearing, "It's a nice town, a quiet town, a religious town full of good people that don't cause much trouble. Ya'll come back now." The refrain from Simon and Garfunkel's song "My Little Town" played itself over again in my head: *Nothing but the dead and dying in my little town.* There's only one way I can avoid becoming a sleepwalker in Denton, I thought. I have to build something extraordinary.

Over the next nine years I developed teachers, helped to start ashrams in Dallas, Austin, Nacogdoches, and Tucson, taught for five years in a prison, taught at universities, hospitals, and started many businesses. I bought the rental house we lived in, then a property adjacent to it, and a small strip mall where we built and ran a restaurant, antique store, delicatessen, and contracting shop. All of this was run under the auspices of the Kundalini Yoga Ashram—a 501(c)(3) not-for-profit organization that I founded in Denton. They were wonderful times. On Friday and Saturday nights we had belly dancing in our restaurant. Over a hundred people lined up outside to get in: doctors, lawyers, politicians, judges, and other town folk who came to the Rudra Restaurant to have a good time. Armie Armstrong, a good friend who'd visit me in my antique store said to me, "You've really goosed this town. You gave it exactly what it needed." He had lived in Denton for over forty years and had never seen anything like it. With all the businesses and projects we had going on, there was one constant: we had meditation classes every day. They were open to the public and free of charge.

Many creative people lived in the commune. Given the opportunity they could produce wonderful things. At times I felt like an overworked midwife who helped people give birth to projects. It wasn't easy. I had to overcome my own resistance as well as theirs. To challenge them, I had to challenge myself. I'd think: Could I continue to support all of this? Could I make my visions practical? Could I finally escape the town of Denton? "You could just leave,"

I thought. But I knew that my three weeks hadn't come to an end. There had to be one final project. What could that project be? The answer was right in front of my nose. We needed to expand our living quarters. Three to six people were crammed into each bedroom of the ashram. Another house had to be bought or built, but why just an ordinary house? Why not build something that was architecturally beautiful—a Tibetan temple-like structure on North Locust Street? I thought about this for a few weeks.

I had a very talented student named Bob Baker. Though untrained, he had genius design capabilities. He had designed and built our restaurant and had done projects in Denton and other places. I called him into my gallery one day, asked him to sit down, and told him what I wanted to do. "A Tibetan temple," he said in a somewhat astonished voice, "cantilevered and made into an apartment complex to house members of the ashram?" "If you design the project," I said to him, "I will get the money." "But I've never designed a building," he replied. "I don't care," I responded. "I know you can do it. You have the talent." Three months later, he walked into my gallery with finished plans for an apartment building. At times Bob resented me because I pushed him too hard. I never lost confidence in him. I saw the genius and it had to be tapped. It never mattered to me when we got into serious arguments about the project. I never doubted that he could do it.

I met with the president of the First State Bank and showed him the plans. He examined them, gave me a strange look, then asked, "Here, in Denton, Texas?" "Why not?" I replied. "We could do it for $150,000." "I'll show it to the board," he said. "Can we meet again in about a week?"

At the next meeting he offered me a mortgage of $75,000 with a hint of greed in his eyes. I'm sure he was thinking, "If this guy takes my offer, in six months the bank will own valuable property on North Locust Street. How could he build this apartment complex for $75,000? If he doesn't take my offer, screw him. He's Mr. K. Y. Ashram and I don't like these New York types in my little town." Word had spread around Denton that I was New York mafia come to take over their precious municipality. When a friend told me about this rumor I laughed and said to her, "I'm a goon teaching free classes in meditation to whoever wants to attend." "Okay, it's a deal," I said to the banker. This money will get most of the project done, I thought. If I needed more, I would get it from somewhere.

It took eight months to build the apartment complex. Four members of the ashram worked on it. At least one of them had no previous carpentry experience. When we ran out of money I scraped the remaining costs from wherever I could find a nickel. Restaurant and antique store profits all went into finishing a place for members of the ashram to live. The final touch was an iron stupa finial that a crane lifted to the top of the apartment building. Bob Baker rode on the stupa and anchored it in place. At that moment I knew my time in Denton had come to an end. The next few years were a coda. We put in a Japanese garden with pavilions and a koi fish pond, we started a wholesale bakery and a candy factory. But I knew that all of this work had one purpose, to keep me busy before I left. I didn't want to just leave, I wanted to leave something extraordinary behind.

"A diamond is the product of fifty thousand years of earth's pressure," Rudi said, and "the body needs roughage to digest food." I wanted to take impossible projects on myself and make them possible. The rewards didn't matter. Deep inner work helped me envision and create these projects, a strange adventure in no man's land. It was a little crazy perhaps, but a tightrope walk that required balance and clarity, sometimes dangerous, but never boring; never for a moment did I permit myself to succumb to Denton's small-town, etherized mentality. When the new apartment building was finished I realized that I had exhausted my creative potential. There was nothing else for me to do in Denton.

On a trip to India in the 1970s I asked His Holiness Kalu Rinpoche whether or not I should move back to New York City. "You must," he replied. "If you live in New York, your teachings will help people around the world."

I had a beautiful place to live in Denton, businesses with great potential for success, real estate, and wonderful students I meditated with every day. But in my heart of hearts I knew that my work there was done. It took nine years for me to complete Rudi's three-week plan. I had to move on and use what I'd learned in Texas to explore new areas of creativity. New York City will be a difficult test, I thought. I'll have to start over, but that is okay. It will be an adventure, something new.

In December of 1980 I left Denton and started a meditation center on Thirteenth Street and Broadway in Manhattan's Greenwich Village. To support myself I opened an Asian art gallery. I lived and taught meditation on the second floor of a loft building that Rudi had purchased a year before he died.

❖❖❖❖

New York City provided opportunities to grow that were impossible to find in Denton. Within four to five years over a hundred people came to study meditation at the ashram. My Asian art business thrived, and opportunities arose to set up centers in Chicago, Portland, Seattle, Philadelphia, Miami and other cities throughout the United States. I held retreats in upstate New York, in Italy, Brazil, and Greece, and helped to set up meditation centers in Paris, Berlin, Zurich, Jerusalem, Athens, São Paulo, Kathmandu, and other cities. The work stretched me thin. I needed to go very deep inside myself to tap sources of energy to support situations that developed around the world. Kalu Rinpoche's words came true. Rudi's meditation practice gave me the strength to undertake these projects. At the same time, I wrote a number of books that were published.

Most people that live in ashram situations hide out in insulated environments that protect them from difficulties in the so-called "real" world. "Life is a temple," I'd say to myself, "and unless we get strong enough to recognize that it's our teacher, enlightenment is a word, not a reality." In New York City I asked people to return to their homes after meditation class, and find God in whatever they did.

❖❖❖❖

In my early twenties, broke and living in Europe, I wanted to return to New York, but couldn't afford a plane ticket. For sixty dollars I was able to book passage to the States on a US Army troop ship. I scraped the money together, hitchhiked to Bremerhaven, Germany, boarded the ship and sailed to New York. One morning before breakfast I had the following conversation with a soldier: "I'll be getting out of the army in a few weeks," he said to me, "but I'm going to re-up." "Why," I asked him." "You think I'm gonna deal with the crap out there? No way, man. I can eat here, have a place to sleep, and everything's taken care of for me."

When I taught meditation in a Fort Worth prison, I had a similar experience. An inmate I had befriended was released about five months after I started the program. Three months later I saw him in the prison yard. "What the hell are you doing here?" I asked him. "Couldn't take it, man," he responded. "Couldn't take the pressure on the streets." He was busted again by the cops for selling marijuana and had to return to prison. "It's easy here," he went on. "I don't have to worry about nothing. If I stay clean, they leave me alone. I get food, a place to sleep, and none of the hassles of the streets."

Meditation classes were held six days a week in New York City, free of charge, and open to anyone who wanted to attend. "People have to build a bridge that connects the meditation class with everyday life," I said to my students, "a bridge they can cross into a world that will give them every opportunity to grow."

I've always been a quiet person, internal, and shy about my gifts. I've never been able to convince people that they should practice kundalini yoga. If they came and asked, I would tell them what I've learned. Some people took my quiet demeanor for weakness. It never bothered me. I embraced students who lived with open hearts. The ones who made the most noise usually produced the least. I enjoyed the company of my students and invited at least twenty of them to dinners at my loft three times a week. There were also parties and concerts, dance performances, weddings, and meditation classes.

Many of my students were made meditation teachers. I supported prison programs at Sing Sing and Riker's Island, and co-founded an anti-human-trafficking safe house at our ashram in Kathmandu. It was wonderful, life-giving work, and it inspired me to get up every morning. I never thought about it. I didn't want to run for the hills.

I had to contend with major egos, with jealousy, with strong personalities of people who proclaimed to know better than me and were full of advice on how I should run my life, with students I mistakenly made meditation teachers who became so important in their own minds that they wrote me out of history and proclaimed themselves to be kundalini yoga masters, people with supercharged egos that created gods out of money, success, and self-importance. A few of them tried to teach a version of Rudi's meditation practice to unwary students without consulting me.

Every person who studied with me had mental and emotional baggage. Their personal problems consumed them and they'd consult with me about marriage difficulties and jobs, people so self-involved they never for a moment would stop and think, Stuart has a marriage to take care of, a child, and a business to run. He has to come up with fifteen to twenty thousand dollars a month for them to study meditation in his loft. He teaches all over the world and has hundreds of people who study with him. It was like Mad magazine—always funny, a little bizarre, but one thing was certain—I knew that the present would recede into the past.

Life provided plenty of day-to-day roughage, both positive and negative varieties that I could use to build a strong inner life. I am grateful for the kind and gentle people that were in my life who supported the work I did in New York City. I am also grateful for those people who attacked me with black magic, huge egos, greed, jealousy, pettiness, rage, small-mindedness, and a hundred other strange and negative vibes that I had to transform into fodder for my inner growth.

None of them took into account how busy I was and what I was supporting. So involved in their own mental, emotional and economic bullshit, they could barely see an inch in front of their noses. They expected me to solve their problems. "There is a solution," I would tell them. "You have to work inside yourself and transform your problems into a spiritual life. That's how I can help you." Very few of them listened. They wanted an immediate fix, and were probably disappointed when I told them there was none.

It's more than sixteen years since I discontinued the ashram on Fourth Avenue and Tenth Street. I've met old students of mine in restaurants or on the streets. When I look into their eyes there's often the same unhappiness, the same insecurity, the same twisted ego problems they brought to me years ago. "Time has passed," I'd say to myself, "and people have done little or nothing about their inner lives." They often ask me, "Do you still teach that meditation practice? It was fantastic. It really helped me."

"Yes," I reply. "Great. I've got to do that again." I almost never see them. It's like the great yawn of life has swallowed them up and digested them whole.

I ran a meditation center in New York City for over twenty years and it freed me of images I had of myself. Busy building a strong chakra system, I never worried about what the future would bring. My time was used to develop a spiritual life. Those years were a miracle and I'm grateful for them. They gave me the strength to maintain a connection with Rudi, Nityananda, and with God.

CHAPTER 7

Dreams provide insight into transcendent-type realities—a step out of our linear perception of the world. They break down preconceived notions and open a doorway to ordinary objects placed in a scene that's totally out of joint. What we envision in a dreamscape makes perfect sense if we don't cling to preconceived ideas.

As a young man, I had convinced myself that art, music, and writing were direct links to enlightenment—a painting by Albrecht Altdorfer like *The Battle of Alexander at Issus*, Turner's incredible use of light and color, Michelangelo, Van Gogh, and other artists whose work touched on beauty so sublime it inspired me to walk a spiritual path. "Imagination opens a door that leads to the divine," I said to myself. When the mundane breaks down into form and color, when words and music guide us to transcendent planes of consciousness, truth and beauty provide insight into the ways of God on earth. They resurrect spirit in a half-dead world.

Dreams and imagination inspired an internal search that opened a doorway to the unknown. Though scholars and therapists interpret dreams and infuse them with logical meanings, in my early twenties, dreams had a singular purpose: to break down existing form and create a new way to see the world. Well-worked-out and logical definitions of things shortchanged reality; and artists, poets and composers needed to transcend the ordinary and lift the soul of a human being into realms of consciousness that touched on higher truths.

As a path to spiritual enlightenment the creative act inspired me to devote time and energy to the study of paintings, music, and the written word. I'd smoke a joint and spend hours listening to Bach's *Mass in B-minor*, to English madrigals and early Renaissance motets, to Mozart, Beethoven, and medieval masses, to music that celebrated divine and earthly beauty—all a product of the imagination of great composers. Hard rock and minimalist-type music were of no interest to me. My hunger for a spiritual life was so deep that I'd seek out artistic and musical forms that celebrated God. I couldn't get enough of them. Not being an artist or musician myself never kept me from exploring worlds that provided a vision of life that transcended the ordinary, and gave entrance to realms of consciousness that touched on the divine. Art and music became spiritual nourishment, a constant reminder that there was something in the universe much higher than myself, something that gives insight into a reality that transcends daily routine. When I listened to Bach's *Mass in B-minor*, it revealed possibility I couldn't find in my ordinary life. It inspired me to write poetry that celebrated God. It's a beginning, I thought. There has to be more to life than nine-to-five jobs, a beer with the boys, and one love affair after the other—routines that nearly drove me to distraction.

A spiritual life was important to me but I had no idea how to get it. The thought of spending my life in a monastery didn't sit well. I was restless, sexually active, and full of chaotic, confused and far-out thoughts of a visionary nature, a person who had no place in a world that reeked of normalcy.

Dreams and imagination became a substitute for daily living. I'd hole up in my apartment, smoke a joint, and spend hours in reveries of a spiritual nature. I'd project slides of paintings by Blake, Pissarro, Modigliani, Soutine and other artists onto my apartment wall and study them for hours. How I didn't wind up in a sanitarium is a mystery to me, that I survived myself is an even greater mystery. Painting and music were my first step out of linear reality, a hazardous step no doubt, but at least an attempt to escape mediocrity imposed by the demands of "Caesar", a new way for me to see the world. Symbols manifested of assorted kinds: images of animals with human heads, of amphitheaters where gods and mortals partied together, visions of the mad and the not so mad in a dance of death . . . a drunken festival that went on forever. I'd sit cross-legged in the heart of the Buddha and experience light and love and a limitless flow of eternal energy. None of it made sense to me, but I knew that my drugged-out reveries had to be transformed into a living reality. Poetry was a beginning, but not enough. There had to be more. There had to be a way to infuse spirit into the mundane, there had to be a way to utilize dream reality on a material plane. All of these different areas of consciousness are connected, I thought. I just have to learn how to unify them inside myself.

I always came up empty when I interpreted dreams. Their surreal imagery wouldn't integrate itself into the dry logic of mind. No interpretation could reveal the true nature of a dream, and my brain wasn't vast enough to wrap itself around the entire landscape. "It takes the juice out of poetry and life," I said to my friend Allan. What difference does it make if I understand my dreams or not? It's better to just experience them, to use them as steps on a ladder into the unknown, a living experience instead of dry and logical explanations that conform with intellect and preconceived ideas. It's all very simple. The body and mind relax and consciousness moves onto another plane. One encounters strange shapes and forms there, like a Van Gogh painting of a room, a starry sky, a pair of shoes or a vase filled with sunflowers, like a Bosch image of the underworld, or a Turner seascape. There's no correlation between dreams and the reality I see around me. I don't understand the images that manifest, I don't want to sterilize imagination.

Dreams are a living expression of my creative effort to explore the unknown. Art, music and writing are means to that end. They provide much that is awesome, and awe has become a healthy thing in my life. Why do we quash our inner child who doesn't interpret anything? When logic takes over the dream world we lock imagination in a prison. Universal knowledge is so extensive that the mind can comprehend about five percent of what exists. Dreams help us step beyond that meager five percent and into the unknown. Why inhibit one's self? Why are we forced to obey the restrictions of the mind? If dreams and imagination touch on truth and beauty, we shouldn't put them on a leash. The question always comes up, will the dream world drive us mad? The answer is yes. But a little madness tips the scales and can give us an inspired vision of life. With inner balance, madness disappears, and dream energy can be used to explore the unknown."

Moby Dick is an adventure story to most kids. When they read it later in life the novel becomes a multilayered tale that touches on profound truths. Dreams are no different. Their imagery is complex and layered, and we comprehend only what we're ready to understand. As strange as they can be, and uplifting, dreams always fall short of ultimate truth. A step above the material plane they have limited scope when the inner life of a person connects to spirit. No matter how bizarre their shapes and forms, the human mind can still interpret them. Spirit is another matter. It transcends human comprehension. It has logic of its own and it takes us outside of time and space. Dreams excited me as a kid. I used them in poems and short stories. When I learned Rudi's deep techniques of inner work, dream reality became just another step on a ladder that led to consciousness outside of time and space.

❖❖❖❖

Teenagers live in a void-like space that's located somewhere between childhood and being an adult, a space that's replete with false self-knowledge, insecurity, ego, and an inherent need to find a place for themselves in the world. One can't lecture them for one simple reason: they won't listen. A telltale sign of immaturity is found in people that know better than everyone else, a sign that exists in most teenagers. A vibrant mix of chaotic hormones, insecurity, fear, tension, dysfunctional families, and playful curiosity, they never give a moment's thought to old age and growing up. The future to them is Wednesday on a Tuesday—the next party, the importance of friends, social networks, video games, and a pimple that just appeared on their face. There's no respect for experience that comes with age, a boring, if not useless, stage of life they are convinced will never take place for them. A teenager's conversation with an adult is like a visit to a wind factory. Words rarely, if ever, find a home because they don't listen. It's a waste of time to lecture them. They know more than their parents, teachers, and friends, more than anyone. We have to love them and have patience. We've all been "wiser" than our parents, we've all made extensive visits to the wind factory.

After decades of battling with life, our minds, emotions, and physical bodies become battered, crippled, and incapable of continuing the fight. We are forced to listen. We discover that other people have important things to teach us, and that self-righteousness is the quickest path to the grave. We discover that it's impossible to love or be loved if we're full of ourselves. No one has been able to touch us, and we're incapable of reaching out. We've inhabited an unchartered island in a sea that's so remote it can only be found in the human mind. One can hear the voice of that child stranded on a island crying for help, for recognition, for someone to reach out and take its hand, for someone who has enough compassion to forgive a thousand wrongs committed in a short lifetime. It's the child in all of us that has grown old and fearful, the child who wants to come out of the shadows and embrace life—a child who never listened, learned, and respected what life has to teach, a battered child who has suffered and felt pain.

Can a parent or teacher embrace this child? The answer is "Yes," but cautiously and with unconditional love, wisdom, and caring. There are no pat answers to this quandary, just love, and more love. No lecture is going to ring true to someone who has lived a protected life on an unchartered island. It will force them deeper into their shell. No voice of reason will change that. Then what works? A little patience, trust, a smile, the ability to listen to them without judgment, a heart that's full of compassion, and someone who cares enough and makes room for them to find their own way. Righteous answers to questions will do nothing but drive people further away. They hear only what they're ready to hear. Everything else is an imposition. If the path to the human heart is jammed up with absurdities, if logic has no place there, if nothing that makes sense will open the door, we have to let go of the right way to do it and let an inner voice guide us. We have to find other ways to navigate the sea that surrounds our own, and other people's islands.

No two people will respond to the same question in the same way. What I teach isn't for everybody, but those who listen and learn from it will expand their consciousness and open deep areas inside themselves. Most people are not ready to hear about dreams and ladders that extend into realms that transcend time and space; and no one wants to be lectured on the right way to live. Who can blame them? When you think about it, is there a right way to live? Rightness is in the mind of each and every one of us. What works for me might not work for anyone else in the world. To try and convert someone to kundalini meditation is foolish; to proclaim that there's only one path to God is even more foolish. No one is an apostate because they happen to differ from me. The very thought is ludicrous and can create monsters out of well-meaning people.

An apple ripens on the tree, a bottle of wine must age to develop bouquet. And like my teacher Rudi said, "It takes nine months to have a baby and one second to die."

When people are ready to listen, nothing gets in their way. Between now and then, there are millions of excuses, procrastinations, and reasons to postpone the inevitable. We've all been through it. We've all had to find a way out of a swamp. There's an insane belief in people that they have to be perfect at whatever they do, and that belief keeps them from ever being happy, an infantile belief drilled into the human psyche at an early age. The very thought "I have to be perfect" does nothing but bring failure. If we can't accept our limitations, if we have to be perfect at everything we do, there's no foothold on which to build an inner life. It's imperfections that make us work on ourselves. We need them as much as we need the strong and creative parts of self. Without them, a human being flounders in the bright lights of ego and never takes interest in anything else. Perfection is either a disease of the psyche or a playground for gods and fools. The former creates a bloated and fragile persona that dangles from tenterhooks, and the latter is outside of human understanding. Somewhere in-between we struggle with our limitations and are reminded that we have to grow every day. We're willing to step into the unknown; we're willing to fail a thousand times if that's what it takes to succeed.

I have never met an easy person, whether they happen to be members of my family, friends, work associates, students or an acquaintance I bump into on the street. Every human being locks himself or herself in a prison of their own making. Some call it reality and walk its terrain with ease. But most of us struggle each day to make sense out of a life that's out of focus . . . and tread carefully when we enter another person's take on reality. We bumble about life with benign absurdity in the outer circle of a three-ringed circus. When miscues turn to anger, when a thought is blown out of proportion and turns to righteousness, when we trespass on another person's space and try to convince them that we know better, connections between people are severed and what often ensues is a fight for one's life. Whether it's two people at odds with each other or countries at war, the struggle is the same. My belief is better than yours. If I beat you up, trample on you, kill you, the path will become clear and my world will be a better place. It's stupid beyond belief, because the world never becomes a better place. It continues on its merry way. Egos still combat each other and the outcome is always death and destruction.

Minor indiscretions often play havoc with a person's nerves: chalk on a blackboard, someone chewing a wad of gum, someone looking at us in a strange way, traffic, a song sung off-key, a guttural voice or a high-pitched sound, anything can set us off if we have no inner balance. People can do it intentionally or unintentionally. It doesn't matter. What does matter is anger, hate, revenge, and assorted other emotions that not only drain us of our own creative energies, but also hurt others. One nasty word tossed in our direction and we find ourselves in a minor war. How many times have we heard: "It's none of your business . . . mind your own business." We don't have to be right all the time. What matters in a fickle society is freedom to express oneself even if that expression does damage to other people. The word freedom is on the tip of everyone's tongue. But we rarely hear talk about responsibility—a key word in a society that values freedom. If we step on people's toes, if we infringe on their space and believe it's okay, there will be nothing but trouble.

Does freedom mean we can do whatever we want? Can no one tell us any different? Can I light up a cigarette in a crowd and blow smoke in people's faces; can I drink myself into a semi-coma, get rowdy, throw up, fight, and become a burden to friends and loved ones; can I sleep with another person if I have AIDS? If I'm free to express myself in any way I want, is there no responsibility? This thought never occurs to people who trespass on another person's space, an important thought that keeps us from fighting wars that make us lose touch with our humanity. Rightness isn't the answer. It only creates more conflict. Then what is the answer? If we listen to other people, if we open our hearts and share kindness and compassion, and let them breathe around us, there are simple answers that come when our hearts are open, when our minds become quiet, and we live with a semblance of balance.

❖❖❖❖

The world we see around us is a mirror image of one's self. There is no better teacher. When life ceases to be our enemy, it will teach us how to repair chaos and confusion in our minds and hearts. Unbearable inner pain almost always forces us to seek help . . . and karma provides it in the form of therapies, religion, meditation, and other practices. But life can't fix the problem. We must learn to do that for ourselves; we must take a good look in the mirror and accept what's wrong. The problem is that we comprehend only what we're ready to hear. The rest of life flows past us like water moves over a river rock. Nothing is absorbed, and spiritual teachings make no sense to people who aren't ready to hear them. They're nonsensical platitudes to be disregarded. If you try to preach religious dogma or a "right way of living" to the general public, you will most likely make an enemy. No one wants to be told that things will change when they take full responsibility for themselves, no one wants to hear that the chaos and confusion we see in the world reflects what exists inside every person. For people to change they have to master their own internal chaos, they have to create harmony and balance out of suffering and despair.

I never talk about my spiritual practice with family, friends or acquaintances. Most of them aren't ready to hear about kundalini yoga, chakras, *shakti*, tantra, inner work and higher energy in the universe. Why intimidate them? Why burden them with knowledge they aren't ready to learn? It's better to talk about sports, the weather, vacations, food —mundane things that won't intimidate people who don't give a damn about meditation and yoga. They'll relegate one's words of wisdom to a flaky world filled with weirdos. It becomes problematic when we deal with family. For us to love them they don't have to fit into our spiritual box. Each family member has his or her own distinct reality. One has to respect it, and not put them down because they have no interest in esoteric things. There's always common ground for conversation if we respect unique qualities we find in every human being. Can we love them if they don't agree with our way of living, even if they try to get us to change? That tests unconditional love and a compassionate heart. A spiritual life is twenty-four hours a day, seven days a week, and every human being is a child of God on earth no matter what his or her beliefs (or non-beliefs) are. A spiritually evolved person recognizes this and respects the thoughts and feelings of other human beings. He doesn't try to change anyone else and forgives people who try to change him.

❖❖❖❖

My daughter has grown up to become her own person, not as I wanted her to be, but as she needs to be if her life is to evolve and change. I've always tried to give her room to find herself. At times her dramas were so intense that I wondered if I was doing the right thing. I watched her battle inner demons. I watched with trepidation until she found her own way and a connection with spirit that will mature, grow, and become, over the course of her lifetime, a unique way for her to use creative energy. A number of years ago I took her to see a movie called *Super Size Me*, an exposé of McDonald's exploitive methods to sell food to the public that contributes to obesity, heart conditions, diabetes, and any number of other diseases that plague mankind. For months after we saw the movie, every time my eight-year-old daughter and I walked past a McDonald's "restaurant," she'd say, "Yuck, yuck, and more yuck." She couldn't understand why people would eat that kind of food. "They'll get sick, Daddy. They'll get very sick." A seed was planted in her, not by lectures on health food, raw food, gluten-free, chemicals, the dangers of dairy products and inorganic produce, not by anything I said to her, but by a visual experience, a movie that made a deep impression on an eight-year-old child and changed her view of things. We both learned important lessons—she about food, and I about patience, how life's rhythms will teach us what we need to know.

❖❖❖❖

People communicate with us in many ways, through silence,

their activity, the clothing they wear, the food they eat, and makeup they put on, their hairstyles, the way they walk and sit, and hundreds of other diminutive actions that reveal inner lives. In my early twenties I studied acting in New York. I quickly learned the secret of a good performance wasn't in the dialogue. Actors had to learn to listen to each other and respond accordingly. Interpretation of the author's words came later and it changed as the play developed and one actor responded to his fellow actor's performance. Our day-to-day interaction with people is no different. Often the words we speak cover up deeper emotions and hide what's really in our thoughts. There's so much static in our heads brought on by nonstop mental chitchat—a virtual chicken coop of ideas that never leave the roost. When we try to communicate, when we try to be clear about what we want to say, thought runs interference, and we never relate exactly what's on our minds. We never listen to what other people want to tell us. Their words bounce off a thick wall created from tension, an invisible wall that scrambles communication and doesn't allow for clarity of ideas. Occasionally there's a crack in the fortress, a slight fissure that permits vulnerability, and we listen to another person's words. Our hearts open, there's a twinkle in our eyes, and we connect the spoken word with its multiple levels of meaning. We hear what another person is saying to us . . . and respond accordingly.

❖❖❖❖

Many of the things Rudi spoke about years ago make more sense to me today than when I first heard them. His prodigious resource of wisdom made it impossible for me to take it all in. I stopped listening . . . at least with my ears. The energy was too strong . . . too overwhelming. So I went deep inside myself, opened my chakra system, and received his words as *shakti*, and they ring clearer to me today than when I first heard them. My inner life is now strong enough to understand what he spoke about.

Though memory gets dim and our minds can't recall most things we've learned, the past takes up residence inside us. Every forgotten word and experience, both positive and negative, will surface when we least expect it. Like a lending library, the chakra system is full of wisdom that's passed down through the ages, sacred pages replete with knowledge that can free us from lifetimes of pain and suffering. The Old and New Testament, the Bhagavad Gita, the Vedas, and the Koran, and every other holy book has been written from a place that's deep inside all of us. If we internalize our search and stop looking for answers in the outer world, we'll find wisdom at the center of our hearts. The uninitiated find it difficult to understand this. They've been told to investigate the external world for answers and to study books written by wise men. They haven't been shown a meditation technique that will help them excavate hidden treasure buried deep inside one's self.

❖❖❖❖

Family and friends teach us compassion, patience, forgiveness, and how to love other people—important lessons that help us to open our hearts. Are they the final goal? I don't think so. Age and illness decimate families. It's difficult (but not impossible) to sustain a joyful and heartfelt love for thirty or forty years and embrace a loved one with the same passion that existed early on. The past is dead, the future doesn't exist, and this moment is all we have. To be fully alive in the present is not only the quintessential goal of a spiritual life, it's indispensable if we want our relationships to work.

❖❖❖❖

A few years ago, I read an interview with Bill Gates, the founder of Microsoft. "I can't sleep at night," he said to the interviewer. "I'm afraid that tomorrow my empire will be gone." The man is worth eighty billion dollars I thought when I finished the article. He lives in a house that's at least thirty thousand square feet and nestled in a forest near a lake. The richest man on earth can't get a good night's sleep. How much money does it take for a person to get eight hours of sleep? It was like reading a Buddhist scripture about the veil of illusion and how it causes pain and suffering.

The material world demands that we invest energy in finite and illusory rewards that disappear as we age and die. If we don't "give unto Caesar what is Caesar's due," life's repercussions are frightening—homelessness, hunger, societal outcast, loneliness, penury—a way of life that defeats us every day. There's no written law that says a successful person can't have a spiritual life. The two aren't mutually exclusive. It depends on whether or not the successful person has done enough inner work to connect with spirit. If they spend their time wallowing in financial success and deluding themselves with false security and grandeur, a spiritual life is almost impossible.

Money transforms ambition into greed, basic responsibility into a power-crazed obsession with numbers that approach the realm of the surreal. To what end? As William Shakespeare said: *To die, to sleep—No more . . . For in that sleep of death . . .* in that "sleep of death" greed, ambition, billions of dollars, kingdoms, and political power are reduced to a seven-foot parcel of land or an urn full of ashes, an absurd result for a lifetime's effort. War, barbaric acts by religious fanatics, and time's erosive nature have desecrated civilizations, multi-billion dollar industries, and works of art. At best, fine painting, sculpture, music and architecture should remind us that every human being is a work of art; every human being is connected to infinite energy in the universe. The greatest treasures on earth are hidden in the human heart: love, happiness, joy and a compassionate way of living.

❖❖❖❖

The uniqueness of each human being creates healthy chaos and makes life more interesting. Robotic or clone-like people, the spitting image of one another, dressed in the same uniform and taught to march to the same tune, smile the same smile, and laugh together at the same jokes, the normalcy of it is enough to turn life into a bad dream. It's like a thin coat of varnish that covers a Pandora's box of nightmarish creatures. Rudi told me many years ago that I could be a "second-rate Rudi or a first-rate Stuart." I realized that imitation wouldn't take me anywhere, even if I imitated the greatest living spiritual master I'd ever met. I also realized what I teach isn't for everyone.

In Denton I ran an Asian art gallery. There were Hindu and Buddhist statues in my gallery from India, Tibet, Nepal, China, Thailand. On a bright, early spring morning, four twenty-something-year-old people entered my gallery (two men and two women), walked gingerly past the statues, and threw (what they called) holy water at them. They sang songs that came from a Christian hymnal. One of these young people turned to me and shouted: "We're gonna exorcise the demons from these statues." My first response was anger, but quickly the anger turned to laughter. "If there are demons in those statues," I told those young people, "I don't want them hangin' out in my store either." I also told them that if they didn't get out of my gallery that minute, I would call the police. They left without another word. I never saw them again.

From an early age I've loved antique Hindu and Buddhist art from India, Nepal and Tibet. Many of the statues channel strong spiritual energy and help me when I sit in meditation. To be told that the devil lives in statues of the Buddha was not only laughable, but a real education in how twisted the human mind can get. No two realities are alike; no two people see exactly the same thing when they look at the world. I couldn't feel angry with young Christian fanatics that threw holy water on what they were taught was evil. A person once walked out of my meditation class because he thought *shakti* was the transmission of the devil's energy. He muttered, as he left the room, that Christ is the only way, and meditators worship Lucifer. There are Christians, Jews, agnostics, Muslims, atheists, Zoroastrians, and hundreds of other belief systems in this world. Each of them acts like a support for sects of people. Uniqueness of belief makes the world a more interesting place. I have no problem with it. I do have a problem with religious or non-religious fanatics who try to convert people to their way of thinking. George Bernard Shaw once said that he'd rather spend an eternity in hell with the Buddha, Socrates, Plato, and a host of other brilliant, but non-Christian souls, than ten minutes in heaven with Holy Rollers that stuff righteousness down one's throat.

❖❖❖❖

Money is a reflection of positive and negative fluctuations of the human mind. No matter how much of it we have, there's always a need for more; no matter how much of it we have, we always live on some kind of financial edge. I can't remember a day in my life when I haven't had financial pressure. No amount of money has ever been enough to cover my expenses. Not that I lived a frivolous life. I know how to budget money. But the more of it I had, the more I spent: bigger apartments, much more expensive art, expensive houses, restaurants, clothing. The pressure reminded me that I had to build a strong inner life. "A diamond is a product of tens of thousands of years of the earth's pressure," Rudi said in one of his classes. At times the pressures were so intense that I thought they'd turn me into a fifty-carat stone. They forced me to build a system inside myself that could handle stress . . . and problems stopped being problems. They turned into opportunities for me to grow. I had no need to become a mega-billionaire and no need for power or fame. My only need was an internal one. Could I master the chaos I found inside? Could I find my path to God? Could I continue to teach the meditation practice I learned from Rudi? Those were my considerations. As my economic pressures grew, my inner work deepened. I discovered that the only way to survive financial crises was to open inside myself and connect with higher energy and keep myself from going crazy.

Years of financial pressure produced an interesting revelation: if I continue to work inside myself, the universe not only listens, it will provide. Money never turned me into a glutton, but it made sure basic stuff like food, shelter, clothing was taken care of. Trust in myself developed, and I became conscious of how things worked out. I never lazed away my day or sat in meditation for twenty hours. I worked and played and lived like other people, and used financial pressure as a reminder that I had to build a strong inner life. I've run my life this way for many years. The only time it ceased to work is when I lost touch with spiritual energy. There were serious setbacks: a failed marriage, sleazy business partners, and students that turned on me. But that was okay. I discovered setbacks were just opportunities for me to build a stronger inner life . . . and to learn how to handle them. I don't presume anything today. I just work at my life and try to use everything that happens as a means of getting closer to spiritual enlightenment.

Projections are delusional because nothing ever works out exactly the way it's planned. Goals have to be real. To succeed at them, I must focus my attention in the present. I can't drape them in fantastical head-trips and spend each day in a future that doesn't exist. A thousand doors may slam in one's face, but another door always opens. If someone doesn't see it open, they'll sit and wait . . . and wait . . . and wait, like the character in a Kafka short story that never dares enter the door because he knows behind it there's some version of truth.

Money is energy, sometimes powerful, always necessary, often problematic, and never easy to deal with. It consumes people, frightens them, fills them with anxiety, makes them both happy and sad, imprisons them or turns them into slaves. The thirst for money can transform innocent and loving human beings into gluttons for severe punishment. It transforms them into thieves, murderers, slave owners, and more often, sly sons-a-bitches who will step over anyone to make a buck. Money can lead to a taste for power and a godlike sense that we're beyond human and divine laws. When we finally realize that time doesn't stop, the fear of age and death becomes ever present, and we're reminded how fragile it is to be human. The kingdom we've built can't be taken to the grave, and we've forgotten the reason why we had to make money in the first place. Like Rosebud in the movie *Citizen Kane*, innocence is buried beneath a lifetime accumulation of stuff we've left behind, and the child in us has disappeared.

Failure is like a vise that grips the minds and hearts of people. When there's no internal balance, tension mounts, and situations look like they're hopeless. We don't trust that a door will open and an answer will come to help resolve the crisis. The real problem is a lack of training. We rely on the external world to provide answers, and never trust an inner voice. If the chakra system is highly developed, if our minds and hearts are quiet, an answer will come, often different than what we expected, but an answer, nonetheless, that will help us move on with our lives. We'll recognize that a crisis isn't really a crisis, but an opportunity to change and grow. If we continue to whip a dead horse nothing will change. The impasse we've arrived at screams that stalemate isn't the answer. Where do we go? That's another quandary, but one that easily resolves itself if we step away from the dead horse and see what else life has to offer.

Financial pressure reminds me that I have deep work to do

on myself. It reminds me that I'm fallible, human, and subjected to conflict that manifests on earth. Real nobility of soul is to have gratitude for my financial problems. The reason is simple: they don't allow me to take my life for granted, they help me get stronger. Most importantly, they never go away. The struggle isn't against financial problems, it's against myself—a complex self that's sometimes insecure, sometimes frightened, a self that could hide behind money, glamour and position, and forget about a deep inner life. Financial problems force me to confront that self and think how foolish it is to get upset about something that won't go away. There are other solutions, but first I have to be clear about something: the external world can't be manipulated. If I try to beat it into submission, it will eventually destroy me. Life and its partner, death, will outmaneuver me, outreach me, and continue to plague me until I learn to make friends with both of them. We delude ourselves into thinking that financial problems vanish. One day, I promise, they will, but that day will come when I'm dead and buried. Meanwhile the task in hand is to juggle those problems, resolve them, know when to move on, and stop the complaints. They're a daily test of whether I can stay centered, open my heart, and maintain a connection with spiritual energy.

❖❖❖❖

"There's one thing no one can ever take away from me," Rudi said. We were sitting in his store late in the afternoon. "It's the joy I feel in my heart, the gratitude I feel for my life."

Chaos and confusion have made me wonder why karma brings us to a place like earth. Years of inner work have helped me to recognize that the answer is in the human heart. Can we transform our suffering into joy, our problems into love; can we learn to be happy? Can we say to ourselves, "I've been born on earth to have a wonderful life"?

In the first place, we have to make friends with one's self—the only person on earth we spend twenty-four hours a day with. If we don't love ourselves, how can we love other people? How can we, if the day is spent in a web of tension and self-loathing, if undercurrents of rage keep us from believing we're good enough to be happy, if we're told by an inner voice that something has to change, and it's not the outside world. The problem is a closed heart, an overactive mind, and no sense of internal balance. I've said it many times: "The only successful people on earth are happy people." We don't need vacations in exotic places to resolve the problem. They provide momentary relief from extreme tension, but wherever we go, the one person we can't leave behind is our self.

The real test of happiness is in everyday life. Can we enjoy a glass of water, our breakfast, the ride to the office, the gum-chewing secretary who complains all the time about her boyfriend, the reckless taxi driver, a nagging friend, the crowded city streets, the stock market's highs and lows? Can we open our hearts and stop complaining about injustice? Can we remember: it's our life, our moment, our day and night? If we don't find joy in other people, in the smell and taste of food, in the warmth of a spring day, in simple things that fill our lives, then money, fame, self-importance, exotic beaches and high-tone cocktail parties are band-aids on a serious wound. Botox and makeup can't hide the sadness in a person's eyes.

I'd be depressed for months at a time in my late teens and early twenties, often driven close to despair, but always conscious that I had to change inside myself. As strange and difficult as the external world was, I never blamed it for my unhappiness. There was as much war, greed, pain, and spiritual famine in me as there was anywhere else on earth. I told myself: you can't fix the planet, but you can fix yourself. It took me time, deep inner work, Rudi's meditation technique and a need for a spiritual life, and I finally kept depression at bay. The dark and dismal months of miserable and paralyzed Stuart vanished. Today, when early states of depression make their appearance, it takes me less than thirty seconds to master the onslaught. I've learned to focus my mind's energy in the navel chakra and draw the depression down. Instead of three months of mental and emotional paralysis, the energy of depression now builds *chi*, in a word—harmony and balance. What could have killed me when I was younger now gives life.

❖❖❖❖

I saw a PBS telecast of documentaries on religion. One of the films was about Buddhism. The narrator pointed to a chair. "If I sit in this chair for an hour I will be comfortable," he said. "If I sit there for six hours I'll get restless. For six days I'll become stiff. For six years I'll most likely become paralyzed."

Things change whether we want them to or not, but much of change isn't apparent: we slowly get older . . . our bodies become different. We're taller, more responsible, less innocent, fearful adults who have lost that childlike ability to improvise with life. Stagnation has become so much a part of our daily routine that we barely notice change. The fear of age drives people to cosmetic surgeons who promise eternal youth. Wrinkles and flab can be removed from one's face, but a worn-out, sad, and stagnant look can't be surgically removed from a patient's eyes. The innocence of childhood has been exorcised by the difficulties of life.

Fifteen years ago, in Woodstock, NY, I received a telephone call. "This is M.," the lady's voice said. "The last time I heard the name M.," I replied, "it was more than thirty years ago in Big Indian, NY." "That's me," the lady responded. "I was three years old at the time." Though her name was familiar to me, if I walked past this woman on the street I would have had no idea who she was. Over thirty years have passed, I thought. So much has happened in my life. It was a shock for me to speak to a thirty-three-year-old woman with three children whom I hadn't seen since she was a child. One thing I can guarantee: we all get older. The days will pass into months and years. The real question is what have we done with the time? Have we used it intelligently or have we just grown old?

Does a reflection of us in the mirror reveal eyes that sparkle with youthful vitality or a tired, weary face that has grown old, frightened and worn, a face that's given up on the wonderment of life, that's a deathlike mask resigned to age, disease and the nearness of the grave?

The world we live in is a quasi-dreamlike place that reflects countless images projected by the human mind. We try to fix a dwelling we shouldn't have messed up in the first place. We never ask ourselves, does this world belong to us? Aren't we tourists issued temporary visas to visit planet Earth? Haven't we come here to enjoy ourselves, to love and be loved, aren't we here to live happy lives? Why make the earth into a polarized reflection of mind? If we're guests in God's house, we must treat it with respect, with dignity, with love and humility. A guest doesn't rearrange the host's furniture. Given sixty or seventy years to be on earth, sometimes more, sometimes less, in that time period, why mess up the decoration? People forget we are children that live in God's playground. We've got to laugh, sing, feel unconditional love and joy, and bring to that playground the highest levels of our humanity.

CHAPTER 8

Before I met Rudi, my internal life was inundated with gods, demons, and Mahasiddhas that one sees painted in Tibetan *thangkas*. I thought that I was crazy until, one day in my late teens, I walked into the Riverside Museum on the Upper West Side of Manhattan. There was an exhibition of Tibetan *thangkas* that belonged to Brandeis University. I had never seen a *thangka* before, but was immediately drawn to assorted deities (both peaceful and wrathful) that I saw in the paintings. They resembled creatures I had seen in my own visions and dreams. They were real. I wasn't crazy. At least that was a relief. They were spiritual guides that had come to me in dreams at an early age so I could begin a life-long process that would lead to enlightenment. I had to develop an inner life that was strong enough to deal with these incredible visions. Many of the visions reoccur today, but training I received from Rudi helped me to build strong enough *chi* to deal with cosmic entities.

When kundalini activates itself there's a light show that makes the Fourth of July look like a five-watt bulb. An intense, kaleido-scopic vision of the universe fills our heads. Some have likened it to an LSD trip. But it's more than that. Kundalini is an energy force that rises up the spine and connects us to the cosmos, a power-ful force that merges with the soul of the universe and makes it possible for our consciousness to go outside the realms of time and space. The marriage of kundalini and the universal soul gives birth to a river of energy that descends from the cosmos into our chakra system and brings knowledge, wisdom, love, foundation; in a word: a spiritual life. In the Bhagavad Gita, when Krishna reveals himself to Arjuna, it's like a thousand suns that suddenly appear in the sky. This powerful revelation is similar to activated kundalini.

To keep energy that strong from turning a person's system to ashes, a meditation practitioner must be rooted in the navel chakra. Light, color, and form are emanations of a higher force of energy. They can be used to develop strong chakra systems. One can't construct a building from the fourth story up. Without foundation, the inner life of a person and the world about him will crumble.

I receive emails and texts all the time from folks who tell me about fire at the base of their spines, about visions of light, color, and bardo-like creatures that come to them either in dreams or during meditation. The word kundalini is in every letter. Can I give them advice? "Yes," I reply. "You have to find a teacher, someone's who's mastered kundalini and is willing to pass on what he's learned." Rarely, if ever, do I hear from these people again.

❖❖❖❖

A student of mine saw blue light that surrounded me and filled the room in meditation class. "What do I do with it?" he asked me. I smiled and said, "Nothing. You don't have to do anything but let the light absorb in your chakra system." The color blue is a healing energy. I use it all the time when I do hands-on work with ill people. If you let the blue-light energy absorb in your heart chakra and the chakra below the navel and spread to the rest of your body, it will help you to rid yourself of many physical and mental problems. Don't think about blue or try to analyze the experience. That's the quickest way for it to disappear.

The universe sends us gifts and we have to know how to use them wisely. It's easy to forget that we've come to earth to learn important lessons. When asked what those lessons are, most people don't know and shrug their shoulders. It never dawns on people to transform suffering into a spiritual life and free oneself from a prison that houses souls that move from one lifetime of pain to another; it never dawns on them that the universe sends healing agents in the form of light, color, and sound to help the soul to evolve. Blue light is that kind of agent. If taken deep into the heart chakra, it could rid one of many blocks that keep him from a spiritual life.

Every human being suffers from one mental, emotional, sexual logjam or another. There's always pain in some bodily part and we delude ourselves into believing that the next massage, the next pill, the next workout, the next relationship, the next monetary score, the next thing we attain we will take discomfort away. It never does, at least not a hundred per cent. The Buddha said that "suffering is the fastest path to God", a truth that should remind us to transform our suffering into a spiritual life. Without physical and mental pain we'd never do a thing about ourselves. We'd live in well-insulated towers and spend our time complaining about flies and mosquitoes that come out late in the afternoon—a bored and tired existence that contributes little or nothing to the world in the course of a lifetime. Stagnant water is undrinkable, and stagnant people are repositories for problems that eat away at body and soul. We need reminders that there's karma to work out, and suffering is one of the best prompts to take action.

Rudi once said to me, "We either suffer like schmucks or we suffer with consciousness." One way or another, a human being is going to suffer. He might as well use mental, emotional and physical problems to build a spiritual life. Meditation isn't a religion or cult: it's a craft that helps us to repair ourselves. Anyone can master it. They just have to commit to a practice over a long period of time. The only thing we're up against is a lack of training. If we learn to quiet our minds and emotions, the rest is easy. Each person's problems reflect flaws in their own unique chemistry. I once thought kundalini meditation was a cure-all for students that attended my classes. Today, my thoughts have changed. I tell my students that I can provide a great deal of *shakti* and teach them how to meditate. But I can't do it for them. I need their help.

People ask me if it's necessary to live in an ashram, become celibate, eat only brown rice and vegetables, wear white and orange robes, become a disciple of some swami, and renounce their lives in the world. None of the above is necessary. The holiest temple on earth is life itself, the great teacher that reminds us every day what we must do to connect with spirit. There's a story about a monk who lived in a cave for twenty years, practiced meditation, celibacy, and ate a diet of grains and vegetables local villagers cooked for him, a monk who decided, after all those years in a cave, to go to the city and teach. He trekked from the mountains to the main gate of a large city, saw crowds of people move in and out of its portal, and had an argument with the first beggar he met in the marketplace. "I'm here to teach you about God," the monk shouted. The beggar laughed at the monk and asked him for a few rupees.

It's possible to have a spiritual life in both the cave and the marketplace. One isn't a better place to learn than the other. When we develop our chakra system and connect with higher energy, environment no longer matters. A spiritual life is possible wherever we live. Life continues as it did before. The only change is an internal one, and we manage to live each day with heightened consciousness.

❖❖❖❖

Each person is born with special gifts and uses them to attain varying degrees of success. Those gifts benefit us, but they can also be our limitation. If the ego and mind get involved, a spiritual teacher can easily become a caricature of himself: a person who controls students attracted by the glitter of orange swami costumes and charismatic, pseudo-spiritual poses that substitute real inner work for a position in the world. We have to become less, not more: free of ego, opinion, position and righteousness, free of anything that dams up our chakra systems. A saint needs to surrender his sainthood if he's to attain enlightenment, a wise man his wisdom, a fool his foolishness. We can't transform spirit into a wacky world that resembles animated films. Meditation classes work best when the teacher surrenders to a higher force and it nurtures everyone in the room.

❖❖❖❖

There's a banyan tree in Sarnath, India, under which the Buddha sat and taught his disciples. I've seen the same type of tree in Miami, all over India, and other places I've visited. Like a surreal piece of sculpture in nature's repertoire, its size, entangled trunk, age, extensive root system, and the powerful energy it emits startled me at first and made me realize how essential it is to be grounded if we're to attain anything in life. At times the tree appears to pre-date recorded history. "Ah, sir," Ramji, my driver in Varanasi, India, said when we visited Sarnath. He had a big smile on his face. "That is the Buddha tree." The tree itself looked like it imparted wisdom. It had the presence of a great teacher. I've often projected a rooted image of the Banyan tree in the chakra below my navel—a tree of life firmly planted there, its trunk and branches extended into the cosmos—an entity that draws nourishment from the soil and wisdom from the universe. When I need to focus, when my mind drifts away from my core, the "Buddha tree" always brings me back.

Nature produces startling works of art, be they landscapes, desert scenes, seascapes, banyan trees or thousands of other plants, animals and trees that take on unique forms. Its seasons change: hurricanes, snowstorms, tornadoes, rainstorms, sunny and cloudy days are often a reflection of the ebb and flow of thought patterns in the human mind. Trees are uprooted because they are ready to die. Animals prey on weaker members of herds; jungle and forest food chains feed thousands of large and small creatures. There's no waste, no gluttony, just enough food to satisfy hunger's nagging pains. Though life and death are locked in a daily struggle, there seems to be an unwritten law in nature, an invisible hand that keeps the universe in check—a sound in silence that human beings don't listen to. Life and death aren't intellectual concepts, but accepted realities in nature's scheme of things. Without them, nature becomes a stagnant force and the hand of spirit loses its grip. Like a banyan tree's deep-rooted presence, it reminds us there has to be balance. It's one of the great spiritual teachers on earth. All that's required of us is to listen to wisdom hidden beneath nature's blanket of silence.

CHAPTER 9

I'd often visit Rudi in his gallery on Seventh Avenue South. We'd meditate together, have some coffee, a slice of pizza, an apple or noodles Alfredo, and I'd listen to him talk about his life. His words came at me nonstop and most of them I don't remember. I wasn't interested in a superficial conversation with Rudi. In fact, I realized early on that I wasn't strong enough to converse with him. What I was interested in was the powerful energy force that flowed from his system, not his words, but the *shakti* that came with each sentence. He would talk and I would listen; he would continue to talk and I would work deep inside myself to absorb his energy. Each of my chakras opened and was strengthened by an internalization of my mind, breath, and the incredible force transmitted from Rudi. He talked about old love affairs, his mother, his business, friends he had to meet, astral traveling, the stupidity of the world, and the amazing spiritual growth that had taken place in his life over the years.

By the time the "*shaktipat* monologue" was over I could barely stand up. I felt like a slice of burnt toast. My entire inner life was different. Sometimes there were tears of gratitude in my eyes. I couldn't believe that God had blessed me with the opportunity to learn from a great master. It was never his words. It was the unspoken truth that sprung from the heart of this remarkable man who was a living incarnation of spiritual energy. The words were often mundane, but the love, the force of spirit, the commitment to God was beyond anything I'd ever experienced before. It tore my ego to shreds and my inner walls crumbled in his presence. I was left with nothing of myself except room inside to receive a flow of spiritual energy. He made me realize that the world wasn't to blame for my inner condition. It was I, Stuart, a frazzled young man, unhappy, and full of pain, a seeker after God who had always looked in the wrong places.

Rudi was relentless, a no-holds-barred transmitter of *shakti* who hadn't time or patience to listen to feeble excuses about why one procrastinated in the development of a spiritual life. "We live in a world rife with illusion," he'd say. So, why should we substitute a finite, surreal, almost dreamlike state of existence that has no permanence for a connection with higher energy? His very presence forced me to work on myself. At times, I'd approach Rudi's gallery like a battle-wearied samurai with love in my heart, gratitude, and a deep need to be with God. I was well aware that the battle wasn't with him, but with myself. His presence helped me to gauge my shortcomings. I preferred a shredded ego to non-stop chitchat in a mind that created more tension than I could deal with. There was so much poison inside me that needed to be transformed into spirit. It didn't matter what price I had to pay as long as I could sit with a great master and receive his *shakti*.

Early on I realized that my meeting with Rudi was no accident. I had spent twenty-five years of my life listening to myself and almost wound up in a sanitarium. It was time to open and learn from a master.

"Bring your crap to the meditation room where you can burn it up," he said.

There didn't seem to be an endgame for my tension. I was a lonely kid, spiritually gifted but frightened, a kid who looked at the world as if it was a stark-naked cast of charismatic characters that paraded past him. I wanted nothing to do with pretense and glitz. I had read Shelley's poem about Ozymandias when I was sixteen. In my mind's eye, I stood beside the poet in his "antique land" and looked with sadness at the grave of an emperor who had once conquered the world. Is life nothing more than an absurd theatrical piece, I thought, with a cast of animated characters that romp and play, that cheat and slaughter, love and hate in a farce directed by death?

When Rudi said, "the best way out of town is up," it registered so deeply that I used every class to free myself from psychological and emotional gridlock. I made one important commitment: to learn what he had to teach, no matter what the cost. My decision to live in his ashram on Tenth Street had nothing to do with the food or hangin' with a bunch of yogis. I had a singular purpose: absorb Rudi's *shakti* and learn from an incredible master. A time will come when I'll have to apply what I've learned to my own life, I thought. God, higher energy, the universe (whatever one wants to call it) will make sure of that.

"You don't have to like me," Rudi said. "I'm not running for Miss America. This isn't a popularity contest. You're here for only one reason and that's to open inside, take in my *shakti*, and use it to build a spiritual life."

He was easy to like, but difficult for me to hang out with. His energy was like a massive forest fire. When I was near him, my ego burnt to cinders. The less opinion and personality I brought to the table, the easier it was for me to spend time with Rudi. When he told me that the "best a guru can be is the servant of his students and a servant of God," I understood, for the first time, the true nature of surrender.

CHAPTER 10

Every month or so, either in Chicago, Portland, Miami or Pacific Grove, I hold a meditation retreat—a two-day intensive in which there are three meditation classes a day, each consists of hands-on healing, a lecture, and a regular session in Rudi's open-eyed double-breathing exercise. It's an intense and trans-formative weekend and those who attend often leave with a new sense of purpose, and the realization that inner work is essential for one's well being. The hands-on healing sessions always reveal deep inner blocks that surround the heart chakra. Fear, insecurity, and a lack of trust create layers of tension that block kundalini as it tries to rise from the base of the spine to the top of the head. It's almost a universal condition. We've all been hurt; we've all lived with imperfect parents that short-circuited the flow of love children need to grow up in a healthy way, parents who can't be blamed because they were raised by parents who also had imperfections, generation after generation of badly-wired people that keep the light in most children's hearts from ever going on. When I place my fingers on a student's heart center, I often feel like Joshua at the walls of Jericho. The transmission of *shaktipat* is like a surge of explosive energy, and bulwarks of tension that surround the chakra tumble down. Some people cry or laugh or feel a sense of relief they haven't felt since childhood; others just smile and say thank you. The pressure that people feel at the center of their chests or between their shoulder blades is a result of internal walls built to protect themselves from negative vibrations. It often leads to heart conditions, or even worse, strokes, heart attacks or deep emotional instability. We have no control over our emotions and they manifest in needy and distorted ways. It's like living in quicksand.

Meditation intensives dredge up stuff in people that gives them a real opportunity to change. They are, perhaps, the most powerful inner work that I teach. I use hands-on healing to break up blocks in my student's chakra systems into a force of energy that will activate kundalini. No two students have the exact same experience. Some of them open immediately, but others have resistance. They cling to familiar habits even if those habits are killing them. The biggest problem is in the heart. Walls of insulation surround the heart center and there's a lack of trust that's difficult to overcome. We've all been hurt at one time or another. From childhood on, of necessity we've built a fortress that keeps the heart center well protected. There was no other way to protect oneself from life's endless deception. In relationships, unconditional love has difficulty sustaining itself. Partners get used to one another, familiar, and take each other for granted. It's trite, but true, when they say familiarity breeds contempt. The magic is gone, the love has diminished and we look other places to fill the void. "When you meet a woman or man," Chris Rock suggested to his audience—it was an HBO stand-up comedy special—"on the first date, you don't meet her or him, you meet their agent. You find out who you are really with six months, a year, maybe three years later."

The energy of a meditation intensive breaks down barriers that surround the heart chakra, and lets our inner child breathe. It's important to sustain this openness beyond a two-day retreat, to shed ourselves of the ridiculous idea that only some external event will make us happy—a knight on a white horse . . . a ride into the sunset. Responsible inner work over long periods of time will get the heart open and keep it open. Intensives and meditation classes are just markers on a road to openness. They remind us that we have to work on ourselves if we want our inner child to be released from self-imposed prison.

Monthly weekend meditation intensives are important because of the strong and transformative energy that manifests in them. On Sunday night, I'm not the same person who sat down to meditate when the weekend began. There's less tension, more openness, and a vast ocean of internal quiet I take with me when I leave. My mind is focused in the *hara*, my heart is open, and the *Om* sound vibrates all the time. Though my life has changed, everything around me is no different than it was before. "If the objective world is a mirror image of my inner life," I've asked myself, "why is everything still the same?" Cars speed by, people argue, scream, get drunk, and fight with one another. Terrorists roam freely on earth, armies are at war, and politicians spout platitudes and nonsense. "If I've stepped off the karmic merry-go-round, how come it's still spinning?"

It has become clear to me that as long as I'm alive there will be karma to work out. Time doesn't stop, and whatever exists within its precincts falls short of perfection. Daily meditation practice gets me closer to oneness with higher energy in the universe; it has taught me that enlightened people live with open hearts, with joy and happiness, and it has helped me to accept that only God is perfect. The rest of us have to struggle with our limitations. The highest language of God on earth is love, yet we enmesh ourselves in emotional gook and false images of self-importance brought on by ego, and the words "I love you" often sound like static from a radio. There's no mystery to any of this. It's not some secret message hidden in a metaphysical library that only the "chosen" can read. The only mystery is why people don't work on themselves. They're born with minds and breath, but these tools get rusty from years of neglect and disuse.

❖❖❖❖

We hide behind invisible masks and costumes, false fronts that cover up false assumptions deep inside us. If we take a chance, it's with such caution that we keep loved ones from getting close to us. When I place my fingers between a student's shoulder blades or at the center of their chest (the heart chakra), many of them sigh, others shriek, others cry, jerk, laugh or bounce. The *shakti* is so strong that it breaks down inner walls. They let go of pain that's been buried inside them most of their lives. There's often resistance, but it's not necessarily a negative thing. A part of us wants to open and change, another part refuses to let go. We latch onto the familiar. If it incapacitates us, so what, it's still familiar. We have difficulty letting go. It's often a life-and-death struggle that ends a cycle we've clung to for years.

Shakti is like homeopathic medicine. It releases pent-up poison buried in our hearts that makes us feel worse until we flush it out of our system. Our stomachs may get upset, we may vomit, get headaches and feel pain in our bodies—symptoms of tension that's been released, poisons repressed and lodged in the heart chakra that could lead to strokes, heart attacks, and other diseases. Discomfort is a small price to pay for the release of venom that could kill us. Negative energy must be channeled to the *hara*, then brought to the base of the spine, and transformed into kundalini. Tension no longer festers in the heart, and we can embrace the people we love.

It's almost impossible to link a spiritual life with tension and pressure of daily living—family squabbles, the tedium of work, politics, financial pressures, social inequality, media and its non-stop barrage of horror stories, a montage of images beyond our control that seem real at the moment but fade quickly into the past. We're like characters in a Miyazaki animated film: ghost-like and unreal, we tread water in a floating world with nothing to hold on to but insecurity, fear, and a false image of self.

Meditation helps us to leave behind a complicated world, to go deep into ourselves and connect with spirit—a place where we can easily hide from difficult environments and forget that a spiritual life continues twenty-four hours a day. We forget that every thought, action, and situation we experience is a manifestation of higher creative energy. We can hide out in meditation class for only so long. The moment we leave, life will bite us in the ass. We discover how little we know and how much inner work we still have to do on ourselves.

An intensive is a powerful instrument for change. Attendees feel like a heavy weight has been lifted from their chests. They can breathe better, and there's a lightness of being not experienced in ordinary life. A question everyone asks is, "How do I sustain it? How do I live this way at home? I have a husband or wife, kids, a job, parents, and financial responsibilities. Everything detracts from inner peace." The answer is simple: we need to be reminded that we're not perfect, that we have a long way to go on the path to enlightenment. Life is the best reminder. It reveals our shortcomings and the amount of spiritual growth it takes to find inner peace.

People voice opinions about what they don't understand. They conceptualize the mystical, place it in a little box, and believe that meditation is for misfits and outsiders. Priests and rabbis never talk about chakras, imams and ministers haven't the foggiest idea what goes on in meditation classes. But they all have opinions. "You can take a shower to relax, read the Bible, the Koran, or run around the block," they've said to some of my students. "What are chakras? Breath? Mind? It's all stupid . . . ridiculous. It sounds to me like devil worship. Remember. There's only one path to God. If you stray from it, the penalties will be severe."

In the early 1990s, an orthodox Jewish man attended meditation class about three times a week. He wore a black hat or yarmulke, a tefillin, a dark suit, and other ritualistic items that adorn religious Jewish people. He worked hard on himself in every class. I knew nothing about his life, family, profession, where he lived, I only knew that he attended classes regularly. One day, after meditation, he came to me and said, "Since I was a child, I wanted to study Kabbalah. Not an intellectual study, but Kabbalah as living experience. What you teach is the closest I've ever come to it. Thank you." He paused for a moment. "I'm sad to say that I will have to stop coming to classes." "Why," I asked. "If my community ever found out that I study here, they would ostracize me, my wife and four children. We'd have nowhere to live." There was a tear in his eye. "Thank you, so much," he said. He gave me a hug. I never saw him again.

❖❖❖❖

We're welcomed guests on God's planet who easily forget that the earth doesn't belong to us. We extract vast wealth from the earth, resources that are sold to people who need them to drive cars, build houses, make jewelry, eat, drink. The earth provides abundance, but human greed creates imbalance. We denude the earth of its resources and complain when terrifying storms take lives, when forest fires and years of drought create havoc, when icebergs melt and water levels in oceans rise. We turn a deaf ear to scientists when they warn us about the effects of climate change. Self-interest blinds us to realities that stare us directly in the face.

The mad and the blind have a kindred spirit. One leads the other through life's torrential storms to a black hole located in remote areas of the human mind. They've learned nothing from history; they bumble about like fools, imperious and self-involved, only aware of what goes on a few inches in front of their noses. Oblivious to the tragic nature of avarice and greed, willing to sacrifice the many in order to fill the coffers of a few, they forget about Napoleon, Hitler, Bismarck, Ozymandias, Genghis Khan, presidents of hedge funds and banks, larger-than-life figures who screwed over the world for personal gain. There's no one alive today that lived in the sixteenth century, yet greed persists, egos and self-interest flourish, and the very planet we live on suffers from a continuous "winter of discontent." The "I am" today is lost in a bizarre world of superficiality and illusion, and we substitute wealth and power for happiness, a pop art mindset that can't see beyond the glitter of one's own ego.

❖❖❖❖

Positive and negative energy manifests as good and evil, right and wrong, and a host of other conflicted ideas that create turmoil. No question's answer has relevance when we're up against a new set of circumstances. How to act on ideas in daily life is a conundrum that few have figured out. Internal struggle makes it difficult for us to share our gifts with the world, gifts that never manifest exactly as we conceived them, ideas turned into half-truths when we try to communicate. There's so little internal clarity that both speaker and the person spoken to talk to each other through the mind's polarity.

When there's static on a radio it's difficult to listen to music. When the human mind is in the grip of extreme tension it takes a remarkable person to speak, write, paint, make music, or live their lives from inspiration that isn't bastardized by tension, a person who's alive in the moment, free of mental and emotional inhibitions, in touch with creative energy, and trusts that their ideas and inspirations have a place in the world —people like Leonardo, Bach, Michelangelo, Caravaggio, and Beethoven whose creativity defy interpretation, and touch on divine beauty. They could be irascible, pugnacious, and morally decadent in their day-to-day lives, but the moment inspiration takes over, for some strange reason they become channels for truth and beauty. It manifests as music, painting, sculpture, writing, architecture, and verbal wisdom that's given as a gift to the world. I've often asked myself: Do good and evil exist unto themselves? Are they primordial energies? Do they need the human mind to be transmitted? Do they exist without duality created by mankind? If spirit transcends good and evil and connects us to higher energy, if our hearts are open, then higher energy manifests on earth as love, happiness, forgiveness, and a host of other attributes that allow us to interact with people in a compassionate way. The opposite is also true: a rational, overactive mind that secretes polarity becomes a vehicle for righteousness, aggressiveness and dogma. If we are wracked with tension all the time, if we can't find happiness that sustains itself, good and evil aren't just words, they're a roller-coaster ride in a demonic sideshow at a circus of our own making.

❖❖❖❖

Can there be an active force of evil in the world, one that uses people to commit horrible acts of terrorism like 9/11, a devil-like force that makes use of black magic to destroy love, compassion and forgiveness, and creates such intense suffering that the human race has to tread water in some kind of brackish hell, a force that uses power-crazed and egomaniacal dictators like Hitler, Mao, and Napoleon to fulfill its evil destiny? If a force of that magnitude does exist, then it needs underlings to channel its power. It needs people whose egos, minds, and self-interest have a singular purpose: power, domination, wealth, and all of the accouterments that accompany them.

The morning of 9/11, I received a phone call from a student who asked me if the world was coming to an end. I had no idea what she was talking about. "Turn on the news," she said. I did. I saw passenger planes flying into the World Trade Center buildings—a surreal, almost hallucinatory vision of destruction I couldn't imagine in my wildest dream, a tragedy of epic proportion played out in front of my eyes, an incomprehensible and mind-boggling series of events that killed almost three thousand people. My first thought was, "What did we do to those people to deserve this? What could anyone do to warrant revenge of such a horrible nature?" When a disciple of the Buddha received a bite from a snake, the Buddha wanted to know what his disciple did to the snake. Everything is cause and effect, I thought. Rudi once told me, "We receive exactly what we give off." A force of evil revealed itself on 9/11, but it needed human help: the terrorists on the planes, the mindset of those terrorists—an almost messianic need to take revenge on America for reasons not known to three thousand innocent people who were slaughtered. It was a strange marriage of evil and the will of man.

9/11 reminded us that we're all human. People sacrificed their own lives to save the lives of others. The darkest day in New York City's history produced a sense of camaraderie I'd never seen before. There was a singular purpose: save human life. Race, religion, financial status, and sexual preference became secondary in the face of tragedy. It was a wake-up call that forced people to stare death in the face and discover that the great equalizer cared less if one was rich, poor, black, white, gay or straight. If there was ever hell on earth it had to be at Ground Zero on September 11, 2001, hell created by a force of evil so strong that nothing could stop it. Out of unimaginable carnage came empathy, love, compassion, and the deepest sense of humanity I'd ever seen in New York City—a lotus flower emerged from muddy waters.

That evening in meditation class, I asked my students to take all of the people who died at Ground Zero into their hearts. "Happy people don't fly airplanes into buildings," I said. "The very idea is an oxymoron . . . anathema."

It's over fifteen years later, and New York City has returned to the same greed-induced snake pit that existed before 9/11. Money has become God again, and it has transformed people into slaves of their work. The city is once again a pressure cooker environment that's stripped people of their humanity. Do we need another 9/11-type tragedy to remind us that money isn't God? Times of great trauma fill churches, synagogues and mosques with desperate people who ask God for help. People pray, cry, embrace each other, feel humble and make sacrifices. Terror inflicted by planes that flew into the Twin Towers brought us to our knees—a terror that reminded us that self-importance can't protect people from great evil.

In 1973 I survived a plane crash in which Rudi died. When I look in a mirror today I see Stuart, the living miracle. I never forget that every breath I take is on borrowed time. My life is no longer my own and must be used for a higher purpose.

If nothing else, the 9/11 tragedy should remind us that we're all human—something quickly forgotten when things quiet down. We've been swept away (once again) into lifestyles that were instrumental in the creation of 9/11. The most powerful tool on earth is forgiveness: if we don't forgive other people, who will forgive us? Revenge, war, and mass killing will continue until we learn to listen to each other and accept the fact that no one fits into anyone else's box. We all make mistakes every day, and forgiveness allows us to move on.

❖❖❖❖

It's not uncommon today to meet women and men who have been sexually and/or physically abused by their parents. Anger festers in their hearts. It negates the possibility of a spiritual life. An old girlfriend of mine ragged incessantly on her dead mother, an alcoholic and abusive woman she hated all her life. After ten years of sobriety she still blamed her alcohol problem (illness) on her mother. "I inherited it from the old witch," she said. "If you don't forgive her," I replied, "you'll never move on in your life. It's all in the past. Let it go." "I can't," she said. There were tears in her eyes. "The very thought of my mother drives me crazy."

Rudi's mother threw him down a flight of steps when he was two years old. He cracked his head open and spent six months in a hospital. He mentioned this to me on a number of occasions when I sat with him in his store. "But I've never seen anyone love their mother the way you love yours," I said to him. "You treat her as if she's a queen." "What choice do I have," he responded. "She gave birth to me. She's the vehicle my soul took to enter the world. If I don't forgive her, I dam up the works. My soul won't move on. Anyway, who gives a shit? It's all in the past. I can't hang on to what's dead. I can't let the past stop spiritual work I do today. Unconscious people won't keep me from God. The only way I can move on is to forgive her, to love her, to treat her as best I can. We can walk away from anyone and anything but our parents and children. They both require unconditional love."

A number of years before I met Rudi, his mother had had an operation to keep from going blind. The doctors told her that it would take time for her to regain complete sight. At home with nothing to do, she telephoned Rudi. "Albert," she said, "I want to come to the store. I need to work." At first Rudi told her to stay home. But she insisted. "I can't sit here anymore." "Okay," he said. "It's busy right now. I'll come and get you in a few hours."

"It broke my heart," he told me, "when I saw her cross Seventh Avenue South and Eleventh Street by herself. She was almost completely blind, but refused to wait for me. I'm sure that her need to stay busy helped her heal quickly. People need to feel useful. Even a car or a refrigerator or any piece of equipment has to be used or it will break down. Human beings are no different."

No one on earth is immune to mistakes. If we can't forgive each other, life's movement is gridlocked by the inability to open one's heart. They say in the Bible: "Let him who is without sin throw the first stone." Who on earth hasn't done something terrible to another human being? How is it possible to love if we can't find forgiveness inside ourselves? We are not judge and jury. We're human beings that bumble along from birth to death. If our hearts are closed, if there's no forgiveness inside of us, the world we live in turns bleak.

❖❖❖❖

My ex-wife and I separated after a five-year difficult marriage. I promised myself that I wouldn't fight with her again, certainly not in front of our daughter. I refused to let our daughter see us in one of those ludicrous "you did it" brawls that go nowhere. It would only cripple her.

My daughter has grown up to be a wonderful person: bright, ambitious, clear in her thinking, funny and charismatic. She once said to me: "You and Mommy never fight. Why don't you get back together?" I replied with a smile. "Do you like the way we both treat you?" "Yes," she said. "We don't fight. There's a kind of sweetness," I said. She nodded her head, "Yes." "Do you want that to continue for a long time?" "I really like that, Daddy," she said. "Both your mother and I love you," I said. "You have a deep place in our hearts. Why change what works? Would it be better if we fought all the time?" "No," she said. I gave her a hug and said, "You have the best of your parents all the time." "Sounds good to me, Daddy," she said with a big smile on her face.

We can't change people who don't want to change. We just have to let them be. Rudi's mother once said to me, "You get your energy from spirit, I get mine from diamonds." Her son was the most spiritually gifted person I'd ever met, and her image of God was a diamond. Should I lecture her, try to teach her something about kundalini yoga? No, I thought. I don't think so. I gave her a big hug and had a good belly laugh. My own mother was different, not interested in diamonds and material things, but on occasion, she'd get nervous and a little lonely. She telephoned me one day, and said, "You never call me . . . you never call me . . . why don't you call me?" I had called her the day before. She went on for ten minutes. It didn't upset me. I just said goodbye, hung up the phone, picked it up again, and dialed her. "Hi Mom, how are ya doing? Just thought I'd telephone you and catch up." She started to laugh. "You said that I never call you." "But not in ten seconds," she said. We both laughed. The tension dissolved and we spoke for a few minutes. "I love you, Mom," I said, and we hung up.

My father died when I was sixteen-years-old. The pain of his loss cut me so deeply it transformed my entire life. I hadn't thought much about God or spirituality at that age. They were synonymous with religion, and, as a teenager, the torturous hours I had to spend in a synagogue were enough to turn me off religion forever. I dreaded Yom Kippur and Rosh Hashanah—fasting, the drone of prayer, bad breath, and my sins dumped in the Bronx River, and a stuffy temple with men separated from women. It was a strange way for me to say thanks. I didn't get it. When the rabbi blew his horn to end the High Holy Days, all I could think about was food that I'd put in my empty stomach. I was too young to understand the significance of fasting and the importance of this holiday to religious Jewish people.

The day before my father died his nurse told me that people enter a state of total surrender just before they die, a state of deep quiet and inner peace. Though my father wasn't an aggressive person, I'd never seen peace in his eyes. Why did it have to take forty-nine years for him to attain this quiet? Why did it happen just before he died? The thought shook me up. None of my relatives had inner peace or quiet. My friends were a restless bunch, unhappy, full of themselves, and ambitious to leave the Bronx. I was no different. Religion and spirituality had never come up in our conversations.

When I re-entered my father's hospital room I saw a strange, otherworldly light, something one sees in Renaissance paintings of holy people. It was bizarre, almost bewildering to a sixteen-year-old kid who thought about nothing but girls and his own future. "With so many shitty people in this world," I asked my mother, "why does God take a loving father who is only forty-nine years old? He's a good man, a kind man . . ." Seeds of rebellion formed inside me. I wanted to leave home, to travel, and find teachers who could give insight into my quandary. I read books on Zen, Hinduism, Buddhism, and mystical subjects, anything that could provide insight into how one finds inner peace before the last fifteen minutes of their life. A library of information was available, but none of it provided the right answer. It took nine years to find Rudi. His meditation practice made it clear how my father's death had transformed my life. In many ways my father was my first spiritual teacher.

Rudi became the single most important person to me. He not only saved my life, he taught me how to connect with higher energy. It took nine years for me to find him. The moment we met, something changed in me. I had never experienced such depth of gratitude before. The love I had for him became unconditional. I trusted him in a way that I had never trusted anyone. "One day I won't be here," he told me. "I don't want you to drag me back to earth. Open to spirit, love God more than you love me, free yourself from this crazy world that's full of suffering. If you want to find me, look in your heart. That's where a teacher lives, and I will always be there." I discovered that Rudi, Nityananda, Kalu Rinpoche, my father, mother and daughter all live in my heart. There's room enough inside me to accommodate them and many other souls that guide me on a path to enlightenment.

❖❖❖❖

Rudi asked me to meet him at the Bloomington Indiana ashram. I was living in Texas at the time. I flew to Indianapolis and was picked up at the airport by a member of the ashram. After a meditation class, Rudi, three or four young people and I decided to get an ice cream cone at a local parlor.

We walked on a lamp-lit side street that was dark and deserted. It was a suburban neighborhood turned ominous by a group of drunk or drugged young men that walked behind us. "Shit! Look it those suckers," I heard one of them say. "We should kick some ass. The bald guy looks like Mr. Clean." Their laughter was of such a hostile nature that I was sure a fight would break out. Whatever happens, I thought, I've got to protect Rudi. Nobody's gonna touch him. I deliberately slowed my walk and prepared myself for a fight. The next few moments were fraught with tension. I had no idea what would take place. To my great relief, the tension dissipated. "Shit, man," I heard one of the drunken men say. "Let's get out of here. We gotta meet the girls over on the avenue."

That tense moment in Bloomington pales next to the thoughts I have about the airplane crash that took Rudi's life. He protected Beau, Mimi and me from death and embraced his own *samadhi*. I never forget that my life isn't my own. "When I leave," Rudi told me many times, "don't mourn for me, don't set up shrines. Serve God or higher energy or whatever you want to call it. That's the best you can do for me. That will keep me from having to come back here to clean up a mess."

I once asked him what happened the day we met. "I saw my son lost in the universe," he answered. "I pulled you in the door."

CHAPTER 11

When I wrote the book *A Lotus Flower in Muddy Waters*, the metaphor of a beautiful (and sacred) flower that's rooted in mud and emerges from a lake or pond to greet the sun reminded me of the predicament of most people. It was particularly relevant at Coffee Creek Correctional Facility in Oregon. While I led a meditation class attended by twelve to fifteen inmates, it became clear to me that the only person we are truly up against is one's self. The eyes of those women twinkled, their hearts opened, and I had found angels living in hell. I told them, "The past is dead and the future hasn't arrived yet. All we have is the present, and we can learn to use our minds and breath to open inside and transform inner chaos and confusion into love."

It struck me that every person lives in prison. It could be made of concrete, barbed wire and steel, or it could be a mental, emotional, sexual, economic, religious or racial cell block. We all have to contend with inner chaos that keeps us from being happy; we all suffer in one way or another. When I saw the twinkle in the eyes of the inmates during meditation class, the gratitude in their hearts, and their profound need to make sense of a crazy world, I wondered why there isn't more forgiveness on earth. Can't a person change? Can't we give them an opportunity to live active and meaningful lives? By the end of the meditation class there was a lightness of being that we all shared. The remaining moments before I left could easily have become a hug fest. Prison rules forbade it. We were allowed a short handshake, but strict Coffee Creek rules didn't remove the smiles from faces, the gratitude in hearts, and the love that filled the room.

❖❖❖❖

What gives life to one person could destroy another. There's no set formula for what works. There are no two people that are on the exact same path to enlightenment. But once we find what works for us, only a fool takes for granted what has given him or her a connection with spirit; only a fool picks apart the path to enlightenment. It's easy to find fault with paradise if we listen to the mind. "I hate pastels, archways, angels on clouds, the color of God's beard, the nonstop sound of *Om*, the Pearly Gates," and hundreds of well appointed heavenly objects not suitable to the mind's taste. Given the chance human minds can pick apart anything. Heaven itself becomes an absurdity. Nothing exists outside of time and space, suffering, and the daily struggle to delude one's self into concocting reality out of illusion. Time has a singular purpose: to take us to the grave. We live in an absurd world, replete with reminders that nothing is real, that life will surrender to death, and whatever we possess, whatever fortress we've built to ward off the inevitable will crumble in time. It's a scary proposition (to say the least), but one that lurks in remote corners of every human being's mind. So what is real? Theologians and philosophers have debated this subject for thousands of years. If there's an answer, I haven't, as yet, found it myself. I believed and still believe that happy people are enlightened souls who have learned everything there is to learn on earth. It might sound simplistic, but try and find a happy person. He or she is about as rare as a fifty-carat clear diamond.

❖❖❖❖

When she was ninety-three years old, my grandmother was pronounced dead by doctors in a hospital. Moments later, she breathed again, came to life, and described the soul of my grand-father and the souls of other people she knew that welcomed her to the cosmos. She had seen a spiral of white light that emanated from some higher realm. She took my cousin's hand and said, "God sent me back. They don't want me in heaven, and there's nothing for me to do on earth. I don't know where I belong." It was an existential statement of such profundity that I couldn't believe it came from the mouth of my orthodox Jewish grandmother.

Where do any of us belong? We invest countless time and energy in the struggle for material gain that is eventually taken away from us. Does that struggle make the earth a better place to live? Greed and gluttony are still in the forefront of human activity. Murder, terrorism, power shifts, human trafficking, slavery and political wiliness make headlines every day. It's as if there's no end to evil in our world. It gets worse all the time. I've often thought: what inspires people to create projects in a world that shifts and changes like the wind . . . a world that is consumed by death and its voluminous cast of characters? It's easy for me to bury fear and insecurity in a busy life and my inability to cope with finality: an ever-present force that will one day consume what I have accomplished. It's impossible for me to understand the unknown. My intellect isn't big enough.

What I needed to learn became clear to me at a Passover gathering of my family. My grandmother had just cooked a meal for twenty people. She took joy in the preparation of food and serving it to her loved ones. I said to her, "Grandma, sit down and take a rest." She replied with a big smile on her face, "I'm too busy," and disappeared into the kitchen. Her heart was as big as the spread of food she placed on the table. She had cooked that meal for the people closest to her, the people she loved and served all of her life, a family that was alive and well in her heart. Many years ago, on a Passover eve, my grandmother's love for her family was stronger than her fear of death.

❖❖❖❖

Death is as important to the evolution of humankind as birth. It teaches us to let go. We are masters of our fates until the moment the inevitable takes over, the moment we enter a place from which no one has ever returned, a place that creates fear and anxiety in us, and transforms every human act into bravery or Theater of the Absurd. We accumulate wealth and power, we struggle to make ends meet, we marry, divorce, have children, love and hate other people, have friends and enemies, houses and cars . . . and all for what? To build a fortress that provides false protection against the inevitable— the dark knight who divests the empire of its wealth?

It's an ongoing soap opera that spans epochs. The question arises: does life have any purpose other than a flurry of activity and a sigh of relief when we step into death's mysterious domain? Another question. Do we actually step into death's mysterious domain or is there only nothingness—a blank nondescript void that smells of finality? Have any of these questions been answered to the satisfaction of humankind? I don't think so.

There's no greater force on earth than love. But how do I love other people if I don't love myself? It has to start inside me: gratitude, simple joy, service, compassion, a sense of self-worth that comes when my heart opens and I live my life in the moment, the realization that nothing belongs to me. It's all a gift that needs to be shared while I live and to be surrendered the moment I leave this planet.

❖❖❖❖

The day before my mother passed I sat in deep meditation at her sick bed. The room filled with an otherworldly light and the soul of my father stood near us. He said to her, "I've been waiting. It's time for you to leave. It's time for us to continue our journey." The light dimmed and my father's soul disappeared. I said to my mother: "You have to go. You don't need to suffer like this anymore. I can take care of myself and so can Sharon [my sister]." She nodded her head, "Yes." The next day my mother passed. She joined my father, and they continued on their journey wherever it takes them.

I possess nothing, not even the most basic things: food, clothing, money, and shelter. They are nothing more than gifts that I've been given at a particular moment in time. If I'm attached to them, they will shackle me until I die. The most precious of all gifts is in the human heart, a gift that's often buried beneath layers of tension, a gift of love, joy and happiness that comes at our journey's end, a gift that enables one to finally step off the wheel of karma.

❖❖❖❖

In Denton, Paul Kelleher brought his wheelchair-bound sister into my antique shop every afternoon. She was born with a severe case of cerebral palsy. I had agreed to have a daily meditation with her. My first thoughts were: What did she do in a past lifetime to be born like this? Can I clear psychic and physical obstructions and heal her of the problem? I had had many experiences with past lives, both my own and other people's, and never took them seriously. "Who cares what happened three lifetimes ago," I'd say to myself. "I have more than enough trouble dealing with this lifetime. I don't want to rummage around in the past."

The first meditation session that Paul's sister and I had forced me to connect with her past lifetimes, but I came up empty. In subsequent meditation sessions, no matter how deep I went inside myself, there weren't any past life manifestations. Strange and disquieting visions came instead, almost Darwinian in the way they appeared: a vision of a fish emerging from water, animals evolving from one form into another, a sequence of lifeforms that went from single-cell creatures to the handicapped woman sitting in front of me. "It's her first incarnation," I said to myself. There was sweetness in her I rarely found in other people. She was a kind, love-filled young woman afflicted by a severe handicap, and the shock of birth had created her physical problem.

Prior to the first session, my thoughts were the following: go into her past lives, draw them to the present and transform them into energy that would activate kundalini. This meditation technique would source the problem and enable me to free her from its grip. When I discovered that it was her first incarnation I was forced to change the way I worked with her. "Treat her like any other meditation student," I said to myself. "Strengthen her chakra system, help her to build balance and foundation, and develop an inner life that's strong enough to deal with cerebral palsy."

Radiant and full of love, a child of God afflicted by a nervous disorder, but determined to change her inner life, she came every day to meditate and make the impossible possible. My heart filled with gratitude. Her spiritual need deepened in each meditation session, her chakra system got stronger, and she developed enough security to help her deal with the handicap. Although the problem didn't go away, her confidence grew, and she could live with cerebral palsy and make a life for herself.

"I have to return to Boston in a few days," she said to me. There was a touch of sadness in her voice, but also deep gratitude. I hugged her and said, "Look what you will take back with you, a new life, the ability to deal with your problem and do something wonderful in the world."

People ask me if past life regression can help in spiritual growth. "A return to one's past life isn't going to do much for inner growth," I've told them. "There's nothing we can do to change what's already happened, but a great deal can be done to change ourselves in the present. We see the past through a prism. The mind interprets what we glean from its own point of view. It's always a version of events that differs slightly from what really happened. Can we use those events to change ourselves? Yes, it's possible if we don't interpret them, but draw their energy into our chakra systems, a meditation technique that can free us from internal obstacles set up many lifetimes ago. The question is: how can this be done? It takes years of kundalini meditation practice to build a system that's strong enough to transform past-life experience into a force that helps us connect with spirit.

❖❖❖❖

When I was a kid in the South Bronx there wasn't a child in my neighborhood who didn't suffer from ADHD. The difference was that medical doctors and therapists called it nervous energy. Today they've renamed it ADHD. Drugs that are prescribed for hyperactive kids have become a billion-dollar industry that's created a new generation of legal addicts. Therapists dispense them with ease. They have forgotten that their profession is supposed to heal people and not turn them into junkies. For a therapist it's the easy way out. Write a prescription and the kid will become manageable. All creative impulse will deaden, and children will be transformed into zombie-like creatures that cause no trouble in school, in social situations, and while they are at home.

My neurosis (ADHD) stayed with me into my mid-twenties. Depressed for at least a month at a time I tried to calm myself with alcohol and weed. They'd relax me for an hour or two, then an overactive mind returned and took over. I tried different forms of meditation, Hatha yoga, anything to clear up my inner chaos.

Nothing worked until I met Rudi. He showed me a simple meditation technique I'd never heard of before. He told me to focus my mind's attention in an energy center (chakra) right below the navel. "The Japanese call this point the *hara* and the Chinese the *tan t'ien*. It will help you to develop foundation and balance, and a strength that's missing in your ordinary life. Your mind will get quiet and you will be able to keep your heart open."

After six months of practicing this meditation I began to see results. My neurotic self (ADHD) disappeared and I was able to get through days and months without depression. A renewed ambition forced me to work hard to attain important goals I'd set for myself. It's a simple technique that I still use today. It keeps my life in balance. There are no drugs, no therapists, no painkillers, no uppers or downers, just mind and breath . . . the tools of meditation. We're born with these tools and if we learn to use them properly, we can overcome neurosis, hyperactivity, ADHD, and many other things that bother us.

❖❖❖❖

A touch of fear is almost a necessity if one is going to make it through the day. It's like a bell in a fog-covered port that warns a ship's navigator danger is ahead. The problem isn't fear, it's one's mind that creates a monster out of fear. If we listen to the bell and proceed cautiously, fear serves us. We understand that there's danger ahead and we have to be careful how to approach a situation. If we focus on fear it creates anxiety that throws us off balance. It makes us easy prey for people that want to take advantage. If the mind concentrates on the navel chakra, an inner life develops that can transform fear into harmony and balance. We listen to fear's warning bell and proceed with caution and stop producing B-rated horror movies in our heads, movies that keep us from being able to function.

❖❖❖❖

I lived in Rudi's house on Tenth Street in Manhattan for a little over a year. At first, my surroundings were nothing short of a wonderland of antique Hindu and Buddhist statuary and paintings, art that I loved because of its deep spirituality. After three or four months of living there, the statues became a blur of copper, brass and bronze. I no longer saw them. I had been a loner most of my life and couldn't adjust to the numbers of people that lived in or visited his house. He kept saying: "You've got to use everyone and everything to get to God. These people are here to help you grow. If you don't learn to transform your insecurity into positive energy, you'll never be good for anything." It took three agonizing months for me to free myself of self-doubt and open to other people.

Rudi had made me a teacher of his meditation practice. When he left New York City on a business trip or to visit friends, I would teach the classes. During my three agonizing months of self-doubt, Rudi asked me to stop teaching. He also told me to go to graduate school and get a degree. "In what?" I asked him. "I don't care. Just continue your education." It upset me. Had I failed both him and myself? The last thing I wanted was to go back to school. The loner part of me took over. "Whatever you want," I said in a disgruntled voice and walked out of his gallery. "Transform your anger," he told me many times. "Turn it into a spiritual life. It's time that you mastered yourself."

I sat in half-lotus position on the floor in front of Rudi's chair and entered a state of deep meditation. "You're pissed at him," I chuckled, "yet using what he taught you to get over it." My heart opened. Nityananda (my spiritual grandfather) emerged from its center. He sat on Rudi's chair and said to me: "All Rudi has done is prune the tree. Why are you so angry? It's the first time in your life that you will grow from a strong and healthy base. If you listen to him and attend school, he'll be responsible to give you his most important teachings." I meditated for about a half hour, got up, returned to Rudi's gallery, hugged him, and said, "Thank you." He smiled and replied, "I didn't think you'd get it this quickly."

A great burden was lifted from my shoulders. Did I really have to teach? Was I ready to teach? Spiritual teaching, I thought, is a lot of crap if it's a by-product of ego. Later on in my life, I met so many ego-invested teachers of Rudi's meditation practice that I was grateful he pruned the tree and allowed my growth to be organic. When he asked me to teach again the transmission of *shakti* came from a much deeper place. I no longer needed to be a teacher, I no longer needed a position of importance to satisfy my ego. I had arrived at a place in myself where service to God was more important than service to an image I had of myself.

❖❖❖❖

"The mind is the slayer of the soul," Rudi repeated many times in talks he gave after meditation class. This teaching was like a foreign language to me. "How does the mind slay the soul?" I asked him. "You spend ninety percent of your time thinking," he replied. "The mind eats your energy, cannibalizes you until there's nothing left." It became clear to me that the nonstop chatter in my brain consumes me whole. It transforms a juicy creative human being into a dried-out thought machine that has all the answers and none of them at the same time.

When I'd people-watch in New York City, to my amazement I discovered that almost everyone's attention was focused on the mind. They were all a little dazed, somewhat spaced out, and consumed by thought. Their heads were like enormous helium balloons supported by frail, almost invisible bodies: sleepwalkers, somnambulists, ghoulish-type characters straight out of a horror flick where thought consumes a person whole.

My own thoughts were like montage sequences in a movie. By the end of the day, I was exhausted, not from physical labor, but from a mind that refused to shut up. I was a slave to my mind's excesses. But this problem can't be mine alone, I thought. It must afflict humanity across the board. Is the *tan t'ien* or *hara* a cure all for problems? It certainly helped me to quiet my mind and live with an open heart; it helped me to see life clearly and not be distracted by excessive tension. I try to stress this in every meditation class. "Keep your mind focused below the navel and use breath to expand the chakra." What I learned is that most people aren't ready to practice this simple exercise that Rudi developed. People need personal soap operas to fill an inner void that's been created because of a lack of spiritual energy. The answers to this quandary are simple, but it's difficult to get people to listen to them. They are ready to listen to the mind and follow its dictates diligently. "How does one deal with unconscious people?" I asked Rudi. "With patience, tolerance, forgiveness, compassion," he responded, "and let them be. Love them anyway. They are on their own path. You need all kinds of people to help you with your spiritual growth. The mind can also give birth to the soul. We just have to know how to use it properly."

❖❖❖❖

On a trip to Jaipur, India, I entered a gallery in the Pink City and was accosted by five or six money-hungry salesmen whose eyes were lit up by dollar signs. I began to laugh. "What's happening, fellas," I said. "We have best inventory . . . cheap prices . . . anything you want." "Can I look around?" I asked them. "Please, sir. Do you want some tea . . . coffee . . . coke?" "No, just let me look."

The artifacts weren't to my taste, but with each moment that passed the salesmen let down their guards. The dollar signs disappeared from their eyes, and the conversation veered towards Hinduism and Hindu divinities. They had a six-foot stone Ganesha in the gallery, poorly carved, but nonetheless a Ganesha, and I put a ten-rupee note in front of it. "It will bring you good fortune," one of the salesmen said. "Yes, I know," I responded. "Are you a Hindu?" "No, but I have deep respect for the religion. I was trained in meditation by a guru who studied many years in India." The salesmen grew silent. They looked at me with great curiosity. "Ah, sir, I can see that you are a spiritual man," one of the salesmen said. "You are a strong, but gentle person." Though I didn't purchase anything, every salesman invited me back when I returned to Jaipur and wished me good fortune on my travels. A number of them hugged me. I never saw them again, but how can I forget that half-hour I spent in their gallery? The unexpected is always the best teacher.

On another trip to India, I visited Calcutta for three days to meditate at Dakshineswar—a temple complex on the Hooghly River, where rich and poor came to pay homage and show devotion to Ramakrishna, his wife Sarada Devi, and the goddess Kali. My car pulled into the temple complex parking lot, and a crowd of beggars gathered round, downtrodden street people who on first glance looked like they would tear me apart to get a few rupees. My first impulse was to shower them with ten-rupee notes, but an immediate gift of money like that would attract a battalion of indigents. I would never get to meditate at the Dakshineswar temple.

I decided to hold off until I'd finished my spiritual pilgrimage. I stepped out of the car. The beggars made a path and let me walk to the temple. A few asked for money, but most watched me take off my shoes, climb the steps and enter a shrine built for Ramakrishna and Sarada Devi where I paid homage to the souls of these great masters. I thanked them for profound spiritual teachings, I thanked them for their protection that kept me alive during the darkest moments of my life. After a half-hour of deep meditation I walked onto the temple grounds, took a moment and looked at the Hooghly River, a tributary of the Ganges that flowed past the sacred temple. There were many white kurta-clad male Indian devotees of Kali and Ramakrishna in the courtyard, along with women in colorful saris, a few Westerners, cows and crows, and dove-like birds. A queue had formed to pay homage to the statue of Kali. I joined the line. When my time came to bow to the Kali statue, I asked for help to transform my tension into a spiritual life. I asked for a life full of love and compassion, a joyful life that I could share with people close to me, a connection with God and spiritual enlightenment. A voice inside me said: "You have had great spiritual masters in your life. They will guide you. Listen to their wisdom and the path will lead to God." Joy emanated from the center of my heart, and it flowed to every muscle, organ, bone and cell of my body. It was a high like no other high. I rose and bowed my head again and walked to the temple exit.

Rudi said to me many times, "Every step in one's spiritual growth is followed by some kind of a test." When I put on my shoes and walked down the stone steps of the Dakshineswar temple, a crowd of Indian beggars gathered around me. Many appeared not to have had a morsel of food in days. Hands reached in my direction, pleading eyes and voices, half-starved teenage girls that carried their own babies or baby sisters, lepers and cripples—an onslaught of humanity I couldn't have conjured in a dream. "They're going to rip me apart," I thought. "Don't reach into your pocket. Wait until you get to the car." My fear was that if I gave a ten-rupee note to one beggar, a hundred others would attack me. I walked slowly through the crowd. Not a person touched me, but I could hear pleas for money, for food, a stark undercurrent of human misery that afflicted these people. It was poverty beyond anything I'd seen before.

When I reached the car, my driver opened the door and I got in. "To the hotel, sir?" he asked me. "No. Wait a minute." I reached into my pocket and drew out a stash of ten-rupee notes, opened the car window, and threw them into the crowd. There was a scramble for the money. The driver repeated with a smile on his face: "To the hotel, sir?" "Tell me," I asked him, "do you know an orphanage around here? I think it's named after Ramakrishna." "Yes," he replied and we drove off.

I had been to this orphanage on a previous trip to Calcutta. It was run by a swami who was once a street kid, whose life had been saved by his guru, and who now devoted his time and energy to providing a safe haven for homeless, orphaned children—an incredible man who had found room to nestle hundreds of kids at the center of his heart.

We arrived at the orphanage in short order. The swami ran over, shook my hand, and gave me a big hug. "Oh, sir, it is so nice that you have come back." "I couldn't leave Calcutta without visiting you," I responded. "Do you want some coffee, tea, or Coca-Cola?" "No," I replied, "but I would love to take a tour of the orphanage." He smiled and said, "Follow me."

The moment we entered the girl's dormitory, a cluster of children surrounded me. They had bright, inquisitive eyes, loving faces, and they looked at me with wonder. I couldn't speak Hindi and they didn't speak English, but communication wasn't a problem. "What is your name?" I asked one of the girls. She just looked at me and giggled. "My name is Stuart," I said. There was no reply. "What is your name? My name is Stuart. I am Stuart." They began to catch on. "What is you na'?" One of the girls said. "Stuart," I replied. "What is your name?" I asked her. "Lila," the girl replied and giggled. I went around the room. Everyone laughed and told me their name. The swami laughed more than any of us. "My name is Stuart," I announced. A young girl came up to me. "My name is Devi," she said. "What is your name?" I asked another girl. "My name is Gita," she replied. Within minutes every girl had told me her name, and we laughed like old friends, like family, a chorus of angels in the backstreets of Calcutta. I picked up one of the girls and kissed her on the cheek. She gave me a big hug. Before I knew what happened, girls had climbed all over me: "My name is Lakshmi." "My name is Vishnu." "My name is Reema . .

." and on and on. The swami was radiant. Both he and I had tears in our eyes.

The situation defied all reason, a white guy from the Bronx that laughed himself silly in a Calcutta orphanage with a group of angelic orphans who just wanted to feel human warmth. They loved and trusted the swami and learned from him how to trust life. A girl sat on my shoulders and repeated, "My na' is Amrita . . . my na' is Amrita," and we all laughed. I will never forget the joy in the eyes of those kids. They were full of light and love and so willing to share it with me. Nor will I forget the remarkable man who devoted his life to helping those children. He was himself a child full of love, innocence, and compassion. His eyes twinkled and his laughter filled the dormitory.

We left the girls dormitory and walked together from one side of the property to the other. "There's the boys dormitory," he said, "and over there we will build a house for old people." "You love what you do," I said. "Oh, sir," he replied, "I was one of those children. I lived on the streets. If it wasn't for the kindness of my guru, I would be dead today." When we returned to the main office, I gave him a stack of five-hundred-rupee notes I had put aside for his orphanage. I thanked him for his humanity and we hugged. "You must come back, kind sir," he said. "The children love you."

The intense suffering of indigents near the Dakshineswar temple and the innocent bright eyes of loving girls in the orphanage . . . I never know what life will bring. These experiences, I thought, reflect the inner life of every person on earth.

❖❖❖❖

Much can be gleaned from people if we listen to them. If we don't intimidate them and we give them space to express their needs, life's learning curve moves in an upward direction. The word "surrender" is a pariah in our modern world. People associate it with giving up. No one wants to relinquish freedom. But "surrender" has other meanings: letting go, making room, deferring to another person, listening to them, and learning from them. If we refuse to listen to people, communication becomes an ego-filled battle of wills. Creativity is limited to what the mind knows, and nonsensical ideas often dictate rule of law and the way people live.

We are creatures of habit, but habits can change, and change opens new ways to view life. We can recreate reality every day and, like children, transform the mundane into a magical playground. The external world doesn't change. What changes is our inner lives, our perceptions of color, sound, taste, and touch that transmute the boring and familiar into an enchanted experience. The only person missing from life's garden of eternal delights is one's self, and a touch of consciousness changes that. The difference is one's inner life that allows us to take joy in the simplest of things.

"How does one do what you talk about?" people ask me.

It takes years to form the habits we live with every day. We're not going to get rid of them in a moment or two. The transformative work involved to change inside often discourages people. We live in a world where fast is never fast enough—a world of high-speed internet, McDonald's, Kentucky Fried Chicken, instant news, computers, cell phones, and sundry other inventions that make us demand immediate results for problems it takes time to fix. It takes an investment of time and energy to build inner lives that connect with spirit. I can guarantee one thing: time will pass. If we don't use it to center ourselves and develop strong chakra systems, age and disease creep in, and it becomes more difficult to master one's self the older we get.

The universe waits patiently for us to get our act together. It wants to provide wisdom and knowledge to whomever is ready to receive it. In a strange sense, it's like a perfect democracy. No one is overlooked if they do their inner work. The problem isn't a shortage of spiritual energy it's what we do with that energy in our lifetime. When the mind dictates our actions every day, there will always be conflict. If we learn to focus the mind in the *hara*, balance, harmony and inner strength will determine how we act. Our hearts can open and the lower elements of life will transmute into kundalini. It takes time to change habits and to fix a broken-down machine, a conscious use of time that changes us and makes it possible to live a spiritual life. We develop priorities and never again take time for granted. We realize that the only person who keeps us from inner harmony and balance is one's self.

CHAPTER 12

My introduction to yin-yang came in a meditation class with Rudi. When I focused about five percent of my attention at the base of my spine, an intense flow of energy moved through the sexual area. It was similar to lovemaking, but much stronger, more concentrated, and it activated kundalini. I repeated this exercise many times and still repeat it today. The force that moved from the chakra below my navel to the sex was a male energy that merged with feminine energy or *shakti* at the spine's base. The marriage of yin-yang awakened kundalini—an orgasmic energy that moved up my spine to the crown chakra. In its wake, I saw visions of gods and demi-gods, animal-headed people, and strange, otherworldly creatures, light, color, and many other mystical forms and shapes too numerous to mention. The force of kundalini touched on similar energy in me. It was my first taste of God, my first insight into how powerful spirit can be.

In his gallery a few days later, Rudi showed me a small bronze Indian statue of a standing bull that faced a lingam and yoni in union, and a rising cobra. I looked at it carefully for a long time. My God, I thought, the bull, lingam, yoni and cobra are symbols of the experience I had in meditation class. I had tuned into something primordial.

Repetition of this meditation exercise gave me insight into the importance of internal male/female union and the importance of sexual energy in the evolution of consciousness. An in-depth practice of Tantra changes lower elements of life into spirit that activates kundalini. It's like a clearinghouse that rids us of impurities, a place where the human is transformed into the divine.

I was fortunate to have a girlfriend evolved enough to engage in tantric yoga during sexual intercourse. She would sit on my lap, her legs wrapped around my waist and I would enter her. There was little movement and a deep meditative quiet. We both experienced a strong force of energy move from our navel chakras through the sex to the base of the spine. The energy's intensity increased substantially when I touched her forehead and then her coccyx. Her back arched and my back arched and we both experienced internal fire and kundalini energy that moved up the spine to the crown chakra. The secret was to remain still and not interfere with the alchemical process that transformed human elements into kundalini. At the moment of orgasm I focused twenty per cent of my attention at the base of my spine and drew *chi* through the sex to an already activated kundalini. The energy moved up my spine and opened the crown chakra, and my soul merged with the soul of the universe. It was a powerful use of sexual energy that helped me evolve and cleanse my system. Most of my attention had to remain focused in the *tan t'ien*. Without inner foundation and rootedness, tantric and kundalini yoga could tip the balance in a human being.

The tantric experience is the same in women as it is in men. The male/female force of energy unifies when *chi* moves from the navel chakra to the base of the spine. The experience of Tantra can be had through deep meditation as well as sexual intercourse if practitioners have mastered inner work and have developed a strong chakra system. It's kind of like alchemy. Our internal garbage (tension) turns into gold (spirit). None of this takes place if the male/female aspects of self aren't unified.

Tantra enables us to give birth to ourselves—an immaculate conception of sorts that initiates the soul's union with God. This idea will raise the ire of religious Christians, but there are profound similarities between mystical Christianity and the meditation I teach. Inner, outer, and higher energies form a triangle, and the tantric union of male and female gives birth to kundalini, our inner child that is connected to God and spiritual enlightenment. When we meditate with our eyes open we're linked to the external world. When we ground ourselves in the navel chakra, the heart can open, and there's love, compassion, and unconditional giving and receiving—a holy communion with the rest of humanity.

Finally, there's higher creative energy. The inner, the outer, and the higher form an equilateral triangle, a vertex of which is in the chakra below the navel. It's almost the exact same principle as the Christian precept of Father, Son, and Holy Ghost. The God-child lives inside every human being. Often hidden but always there, it waits patiently for us to develop enough inner strength to unify three points on a triangle: the inner, outer, and higher. It waits for us to live our lives at the center of God's creation, a place where there's no past or future. There's only this moment recreating itself through eternity.

When I first read the Old and New Testaments, the words were secondary to a secret language hidden between the lines, deeper meanings than historical context that became source material for religions that followed. I discovered that Hindu/Buddhist chakra charts and the Kabbalistic Sephirotic Tree were strikingly similar. Early adherents to these religions must have practiced similar forms of meditation.

❖❖❖❖

I've listened to preachers lull their congregations to sleep using words from the Bible. I've listened to sermons given by pastors and rabbis who haven't experienced a syllable of what they try to teach. It's difficult to know whom to trust and who serves up a finely decorated table full of lies. Without trust, one can never move forward, but whom and what to trust is a serious dilemma. My teacher, Rudi, once told me: "Serve God, not people. You never know from moment to moment what people will bring." Their words of gratitude and love often morph into the exact opposite, like a quick-change artist whose face is layered by masks. No matter how many are peeled off there's always another one beneath. Truth is beyond human comprehension and hidden behind a veil of intangibles. We're confronted with interpretations of truth created by people who have their own agendas and accept half-baked ideas from the mouths of the powerful because of their positions. We also accept them because we fear persecution.

The first person we have to learn to trust is one's self. If we stop being our own worst enemy and live each day with a deep sense of self-worth, then trust is possible. The parts of us that can't be trusted are right on the surface: ego-driven personality, righteousness, being judgmental—anything that creates false superiority in our minds. We're too blindsided by dishonest images of self to recognize the disguises we hide behind. Do we need that kind of crutch to justify our lives? Do we revel in deceit (no matter whom it hurts) to get our own way? I always wonder to what end: money, power, success, and a superior position, all goals that turn us into caricatures and drain real-life flesh and blood. Then what should we trust? For a person who's highly evolved and spiritually awakened, that's never a problem. They trust themselves, their relatives, friends, and even enemies; they trust life in all its diverse manifestations, and above all, they've accepted life as their guru. Whatever the guru brings to their plate (even the most difficult tests) will create opportunities for them to grow. It doesn't matter what life has done to us. What really matters is what we have done with what life has done to us. If we waste time complaining about how difficult things are and never use difficulty to develop strong inner lives, we'll spend the rest of our days wallowing in the stink of injustice.

The development of trust enables us to make friends with life. It enables us to recognize that there's a power much higher than the human mind, ego, emotions, and physical body—an intangible force that deposits anima into everything that exists. No matter how diligent we are in our attempt to make rational sense of higher energy, we will always discover that it defies reason. We can investigate sundry departments in life's university, but it will never reveal to us the entire course of study. If we trust life, it will give abundantly. Technological and scientific discoveries are made because the human mind finds secret treasures that manifest in life's river of limitless energy. We will continue to find these treasures as long as we explore the unknown. It's one thing to extract knowledge from this river and use it to make money, and another to recognize that infinite energy is a path to spiritual enlightenment. The former will diminish individual trust as the human body ages and dies, as the mind deteriorates, and the lust for money and power diminishes. The latter will never lose our trust, because the human soul is enriched by spirit and will merge with the infinite.

Once we learn to trust life and the power of infinite energy, the past and future disappear and we live our lives in the moment. We are no longer "strangers in a strange land," we are no longer existential road warriors that bumble along the back roads of the universe, road warriors that try to make sense of an absurd existence. We accept life's incongruities, laugh at them, thoroughly enjoy them, and allow the soul to continue on its journey. There's no clear-cut path to the infinite because each of us peeks out from their personal underbrush. But spirit is always there and wants us to embrace its energy. It waits for us to choose life over death.

❖❖❖❖

As a young man I prized my philosophical and religious insights into the nature of things. An existentialist at heart, I identified with the absurd in theater and literature and believed that death transformed every human act into a ludicrous statement gobbled up by time. Nothing made sense to me. My father's death unleashed a powerful inner force that demanded answers to some serious questions. Why was I born? What did I come into this world for? Is every act and goal an absurd undertaking? Is death the most powerful force on earth? Does anything exist beyond the ridiculous world I wake up to every day? Is there any more meaning to life than a loud and drunken guffaw from the belly of someone who can't make heads or tails of their own existence? Is all of humanity like Gogo and Didi in Samuel Beckett's play *Waiting for Godot*, a pair of fools that trip and fall over each other while they wait for some mythical person named Godot to arrive? Their lives are so hopeless they don't even know what they are doing in Beckett's play.

"What is this all about?" I screamed at the heavens.

These questions nearly drove me out of my mind. I left home and bummed my way across Europe, Africa, and America in search of answers that would justify my having been born. They never came. Years of an internal struggle taught me to like myself, to maintain balance in the middle of a storm, and to find a way to laugh at an absurd world. One of the benefits of age is that I no longer need answers to questions that are nothing more to me now than vague whispers in an ocean of distant memories. Will they come back to me? It's possible. I'll keep a lookout for them, but meanwhile, an aged and more settled me has found that I don't need those answers anymore. I need only a few things: to live my life in the moment, to enjoy the absurd and multi-masked entity that's called life, and to not let the nonsense of the world get me down. I realized a long time ago that if I make friends with life I will automatically make friends with death, and the absurd will lose its razor-sharp edginess. Why fear the inevitable? It's going to happen whether I'm afraid of it or not. So I accepted it, embraced it like I'd embrace a relative, and now live my life with an open heart. I freed myself from a monster I had created in my own mind.

❖❖❖❖

I surrendered the "guru" mantle and began to call myself (tongue in cheek) a kundalini aerobics instructor. I'd tell people that life is the guru. "I'm not your guru," I said. "I've been there, done that, and don't want to do it anymore. I'm a gadfly that's here to remind you of the effort it takes to build an inner life. It's impossible for any of us to know more than life and its co-conspirator, time. They will kick us in the butt whenever they have a chance. They will take us apart by organ, by bone, by flesh and by blood, by thought and by emotion until there's nothing left except the shadow of a person we once were. It's a fifteen-round boxing match that no mortal ever wins. Instead of making friends with this dangerous twosome, we attempt to rival them. We pretend to know better than they do and suffer the consequences. No philosopher or theologian—no matter how acute their minds, no matter how intently they analyze situations—will dissect life before life dissects them. The ego leads us to believe that we know more. It's an absurd belief, because life and time continue long after the ego shrivels up and dies.

The process needs to be reversed. When will people realize that the multi-departmentalized world they live in is a teacher of such magnitude and sensitivity that it doesn't matter what one's intelligence is? There will always be something to learn. Life is a mirror image of each and every one of us, and it reflects us at our best and worst. It teaches us exactly what we have to do to change and grow. We must listen to what life has to say, defer to it, and let it guide us through our karma. The moment we defer to life, both our internal and external worlds will change. We'll make friends with life and with ourselves (our two worst enemies) and use that friendship to develop a connection to spirit. And finally we'll be more conscious about the way we interact with other human beings.

❖❖❖❖

November 26, 2015—After a short walk up Fifth Avenue to Fortieth Street, I entered Bryant Park, a place I'd visited hundreds of times in the past. I'd never seen the revitalized version of the park with sundry small shops selling crafts and Christmas goodies and restaurants that surrounded an ice-skating rink. It was a scene from a 1950s movie. I expected the ghosts of Bing Crosby and Danny Kaye to make an appearance and sing an upbeat version of White Christmas. It was also a day on which the media blasted news of terror attacks around the world, a day on which there was talk of World War III, the Paris massacres, a bus blown up in Tunisia, a Russian plane shot down by Turkey, and the miserable, never-ending war in Syria and Iraq. On this day, hundreds of young and old people, some tourists and many New Yorkers, skated on the ice rink in the middle of Bryant Park. There was festive music and laughter, and an *I-don't-give-a-damn-what's-going-on-in-the-rest-of-the-world* fun-loving ring of innocence. Not a cop was in sight. Nor were there National Guard troops with semi-automatic weapons and hawk-eyed stares that scrutinized the park. Though CNN had reported that there were soft and hard targets terrorists could attack, and New York City was on their hit list, hundreds of people still mingled in Bryant Park without a care in the world.

It reminded me of my last trip to Israel, a ten-day visit in which I stayed at Elli and Aliza Malki's home in Jerusalem. A hundred miles away in Lebanon, Israelis and Hezbollah fought a vicious war, yet Jerusalem, a divided city in which Israelis and Palestinians lived together, was quiet, uneventful, as peaceful a place as I'd ever visited. I had lunch every day in Palestinian and Lebanese restaurants. I was greeted by Muslim owners like an old friend, catered to, and thanked for my patronage. Students came, and we had meditation classes. Every evening I turned on CNN and watched news of a war in southern Lebanon—surreal video, painful video, in which Arabs and Jews killed each other in a war-torn country a hundred miles from where I lived. Without CNN I wouldn't have had a clue that I was in a country at war. Sound and video-bites brought horror into Elli Malki's home.

At a talk and book signing in a New Jersey Barnes and Noble, a gentleman in the audience raised his hand and asked me to define hell. I thought for a few seconds then told him to turn on CNN. It doesn't get more hellish than that.

❖❖❖❖

November 26, 2015 (continued)—Today is Thanksgiving, a day of American grace that's supposed to be filled with gratitude, a day on which families gather and share with one another an abundance of food and good cheer. In a world replete with terrorists and nonstop newscasts of murder and slaughter in all corners of the globe, a world that seems to be coming apart at the seams, politicians and multinational companies have placed self-interest in front of humanitarian concerns, and Thanksgiving becomes a word that has little or no meaning in the scope of things. It gets lost in the din of bombs exploding and guns being fired, in the threat of subways and restaurants being blown up and massacres at rock concerts—religious intolerance that has turned innocent babes into murderous zealots. We live in a fear-based society. Terrorists understand the media and use it to promote their agendas. The nonstop reportage of CNN zooms in on diverse incidents across the world and saturates the human mind with evil. The questions I have to ask are: What have we done to bring this madness upon ourselves? Can we cure the problem by eliminating its symptoms, or do we have to ask ourselves what causes a young man to be radicalized? How can ISIS convince teenagers to be suicide bombers?

The superficial symptoms of this disease are carnage and murder, but the source of the disease is hidden in the hearts and psyches of young people who commit these acts. Is it religious fanaticism or a love-starved, angry young person whose inner life has been so scarred that the lack of compassion has transformed him or her into a lethal weapon? Eliminating the symptoms won't cure the problem. If a person has nothing to live for, an eternity in paradise sounds much better to him than the squalor of Molenbeek. An existential nightmarish future turns suicide into a good choice. These people are manifestations of a cancer that has ravaged the core of our society, a disease that won't be eliminated unless the society heals itself. They want to destroy a world in which there is little or no hope. Death is inevitable anyway. Why not become a martyr and spend an eternity in paradise?

Can a society cleanse itself of a disease that ravages its core, a disease that few admit to have, yet whose ominous presence surfaces and afflicts us with carnage? I can't remember one day in my life when there hasn't been war somewhere on planet Earth, and diplomatic convocations attended by heads of state, their appointees, or other persons of power, their polemics, rhetoric, ideas set forth and rational self-interest vomited up in futile spin to end conflict. Meanwhile thousands of young men and women are killed for little or no reason. No one attacks the disease at its core; no one ever plumbs the depth of humanity's psyche to discover the cause of the cancer. It's easier to formulate rules based on self-interest, and apply them to cultures that haven't the faintest idea what these regulations mean . . . and the war continues, the anger persists, and seventy-two virgins in heaven are an incredibly good option for indigent people. If we beat them down, it gets worse. There's more anger and less to live for. In prisons they radicalize other indigents who create havoc when they are released.

The labyrinthine maze and limitless quagmire created by religion and politics doesn't make any sense. If we work on ourselves and transform deep-seated anger and unhappiness into joy and love, it's a beginning. We have taken the first step to transmuting a society replete with murder, terrorism and destruction. It's no longer lip-service compassion, but a real effort to bring peace and harmony to our world, a real Thanksgiving for those people who transform anger and despair into love and empathy.

❖❖❖❖

It's not difficult for us to understand commonsensical language. The application of it to everyday living is another story. Being creatures of habit, years of conditioned behavior force us to make certain decisions. Life presents us with many choices, some beneficial, but most just fill a void. We think that "busy" means that we aren't wasting time, but busy being busy keeps us from real choices, from an investment of time in situations that nurture us and help us to grow spiritually. In the New Testament, when Christ tells his disciples: "Let the dead bury the dead. Follow me to life," he's pinpointed priorities. So much of life is the "dead burying the dead," situations that have no energy, but require our presence —family and friends that force us to attend events that waste our time and give little or nothing in return.

As a child I spent countless hours at the homes of relatives, tedious hours that nearly drove me to distraction, guilt-ridden hours that forced me to be exactly where I didn't want to be. I had no choice in the matter. At fourteen my first choice would have been pick-up basketball games in a local schoolyard, maybe a movie or poker with friends, or a baseball game at Yankee Stadium. I had priorities, but they were shelved to make room for my parents' wishes.

People put off meditation practice to some future date. There are always excuses: I have a date, a party, a movie, theater or concert; I'm tired or have a cold, or whatever comes to mind. They prefer not to be in meditation class. There are other priorities, most of them superficial and not important, but nonetheless priorities. There's nothing wrong with the choices they make. I'm in no position to tell people how to live their lives. The only guarantee I can make is that we all get older. What we do with our time between the present and the moment we leave the world determines how spiritually evolved we become. Do we use the time allotted to us to build an inner life or waste it on mundane and transient things? If we waste the time between birth and death on trivialities, we substitute the commonplace for an enriched inner life—a life that not only permits us to socialize, have relationships, earn a good living, go to theater and concerts, but enhances those things and gives us deeper insight into the ways of the world.

If the need for a spiritual life is real, there's never a problem with priorities. There will always be time for a meditation class; there will always be time to participate in situations that help us to evolve and grow. The glitter of the world becomes less important when compared to the light we see inside ourselves that tells us it's better to use our time for spiritual development than piss it away on the superficial. We don't have to become nuns or monks and sequester ourselves in monasteries. We just have to take advantage of circumstances the universe provides. If one's need is real, excuses fall by the wayside. We do what has to be done. When seen in this light, "Let the dead bury the dead . . ." isn't as harsh as one would think. It tells us to get our priorities straight and use them to follow a path that leads to enlightenment.

❖❖❖❖

I spent many evenings with Rudi. It was always a lesson for me to see how he interacted with people. We'd go to a party, say hello, how-are-you to friends, have a glass of wine or Perrier, and leave in about twenty minutes. I'd ask him why we left so soon. "What are we going to do there? Stand around and talk nonsense. It's boring. A party's best in the first twenty minutes and then it begins to wear on you." From one party, we'd go to another, and maybe another. He'd greet his friends, hug them, juice them up a bit, and we'd leave. After a few parties we'd go to a Chinese restaurant, have an ice cream or sorbet, and take a long walk through Greenwich Village. There was lots of talk about inner work and spiritual practice. It made me realize how insignificant social gatherings can be. Would I rather hang with people and talk about politics, theater, my job or their job, or walk through Greenwich Village with Rudi and receive spiritual teachings? The choice was clear to me. If I spent three or four hours at a party, when I left, rarely, if ever, did I feel rejuvenated. Much of my inner life had been deposited on a buffet table. Twenty minutes was the perfect amount of time to socialize at a party. It amazed me how Rudi could manage this without offending his hosts.

❖❖❖❖

The word "yoga" means union. Its practice attunes us to cycles, be they hourly, daily, monthly or yearly, cycles that bring order into what would otherwise be total chaos. Birth and death, marriage and divorce, friendships, social engagements, jobs—all of them have a beginning, come into fruition, and then come to an end. Everything in the universe follows one cycle or another. We take joy in the newness of things and have great difficulty letting go of familiar situations.

I attended a wedding of a close friend of mine. It was a sacred affair, held in a garden, and the pledges made were heart-warming and full of joy—two people who loved each other dearly and planned to live the rest of their lives together. They both had a love of music, theater, and literature, and enough in common to keep the day from ever becoming a bore. The marriage lasted ten years. I don't know the particulars of what happened, nor do I want to recreate some fictional account, but the last year of their marriage was diametrically opposed to what took place in the wedding garden. Anger verged on hatred. There was a bit of violence. As their love soured, friendship turned into a nasty struggle of me versus you.

My friend called me. She asked why things had changed so drastically. She sobbed throughout our conversation. "You had ten years together," I said, "ten great years that both of you can cherish. Not many people can say that. The cycle ended and heaven became hell. Remember those ten years. Be grateful to him for having shared his life with you . . . and move on. God created marriage and God created divorce, and each begins a new cycle; each affords you a remarkable opportunity to grow in your life. One isn't better than the other, and both represent a kind of freedom. Marriage is union, but if that union no longer works, we have to be strong enough to let go. Why hate a person you've spent ten years of your life with? Be grateful to him and remember the best moments, cherish them and complete the life cycle." "What about him?" She asked. "He's bitter and unhappy and he said that he hates me." "You can't live his life," I replied. "He's not unhappy because of you. He's just unhappy . . . period. Whether he's with you or someone else, he'll be unhappy until he makes an effort to change inside himself."

The fear of separation, of loneliness, of patterns that break down and lead to new patterns and new ways to live, the thought of not being worthy, of self-doubt, and the loss of a partner—these are natural fears that force us to re-examine ourselves, to find new depth, new understandings that make us grow as human beings. We defeat ourselves or we develop enough inner strength to bring to a new relationship everything we've learned from our recent divorce. Time will straighten out the jagged edges and renew a spark of life in us, and that renewed life will attract another person, a new cycle, a fresh start that brings with it a heightened sense of our humanity. We fall in love again. We become open and vulnerable and embrace another person with whom we can share our life. There's always an open door. We have to be wise enough to see it and not afraid to step in.

❖❖❖❖

Forty years of deep inner work have taught me that I know very little about life; it's taught me that I must spend every day learning what the universe has to teach. It's much wiser than I am. I rejoice in the fact that I have a long way to go and have only one job: get out of the way. Don't interfere with higher energy; don't know better; don't gloss over it with ideas and opinions that mean nothing when compared to spirit. On the other side of my tension is a spiritual life. On the other side of my tension is a connection with God. When I open my heart, when I embrace creation in its multifarious forms, be it animal, vegetable, human, or whatever, I realize that I am nothing. What I think about life has less importance than my ability to feel kindness and embrace the world.

CHAPTER 13

A spiritual life is twenty-four hours a day, seven days a week, at home, at work, on the streets, in trains, planes and buses, when we drive, eat, or spend time with our family. No matter what we do, spirit is present. The problems experienced in everyday situations remind us that we need to continue to build our chakra systems. We are not infallible, pure, and omniscient beings. We struggle with the pressure of daily living.

At meditation intensives, tension is dredged up that's been buried inside us for lifetimes. We transform our limitations into kundalini energy that rises up the spine and connects to the soul of the universe. When we return to daily life, regretfully, much of what's learned is left in the meditation room. People walk away from an intensive as if it has nothing to do with daily living. The real test of a meditation intensive isn't three classes a day on Saturday and Sunday. It's the day after, or two days after, when we have to deal with a slew of unconscious people. Did we build a bridge that connects the deep inner work of an intensive to whatever else we do in our lives? Did we relegate the intensive to another experience among thousands we've had from the moment of birth until today? Has the energy already drained from our system? As difficult and intense as a two-day meditation intensive is, the day after, or week after, is more difficult. The pressures of daily life test our spiritual growth. It's easy to forget what we've learned and fall back on anger, fear, unhappiness, and other superficial negative emotions. After the third or fourth class of an intensive there's a twinkle in the eye of everyone who attends, a glow that was missing when we began the weekend. Daily life should remind us of how essential it is to re-ignite our chakra systems. If we don't make that kind of an effort, the next intensive will begin with a dull glow . . . and we start over again.

People think a spiritual life is a part-time job. They think it's an adult education class one takes at a college to break up the week. They don't realize that every breath we take is sacred and every life situation offers us an opportunity to grow. They never ask the following questions: Can I distinguish between illusion and reality? Do my thoughts move like a pendulum from the past to the future? Do I live my life in the present? Is my heart open? Is my mind quiet? Is there forgiveness and tolerance, the ability to like myself and to love other people? A spiritual life begins with each and every person's inner need to connect with higher energy; it begins with the realization that life is sacred, that every breath we take is sacred, and the only thing missing from the mix is one's consciousness.

❖❖❖❖

The word *samadhi* has found its way into the English language, a word rarely spoken and not understood by most people, but a word so important in the evolution of consciousness that the soul of every human being strives to be one with it. *Samadhi* is the endgame of the soul's evolution . . . a state of oneness with God and the universe. The soul of a human being transcends duality and goes beyond time, space, life and death. The soul has freed itself from the cyclical nature of karma, from pain, suffering, illusion and delusion, fear and insecurity, and has merged with the universe. *Samadhi* transcends the limited comprehension of people whose concerns are strictly material and mental. Often written about by poets, theologians and philosophers, and experienced by highly evolved human beings ready to step off karma's carousel, it's the result of lifetimes of inner work and spiritual evolution. The following leads to *samadhi*: unconditional love, gratitude, forgiveness, tolerance, permanent joy and happiness, the realization that the soul of every human being must ultimately attain enlightenment.

Samadhi frees us from cycles of death and rebirth; it frees us from intense suffering experienced on a material plane. It's a door that opens onto a transcendental universe where the soul continues to evolve towards perfection. Like a rocket ship, kundalini propels the soul to realms of consciousness that exist outside the sphere of mind, matter, and emotion . . . and any other quantifiable manifestation of energy on a physical plane. There's no limit to spiritual growth, no obstacle that can't be overcome. *Samadhi* is an important step in the soul's development—a state of nothingness attained through the transmutation of tension into kundalini energy. This state of nirvana or satori brings total awareness of life's subtle manifestations as well as detachment from melodrama and freedom from karma that shackles us to the earth.

Nothingness frightens most people. They imagine it to be a void bereft of any kind of life, a place where brain-dead, zombie-like somnambulists roam in B-movie horror flicks. Does one have to give up that incredible "me" who vaunts success in the face of whomever one meets, that charming gadabout who knows more than anyone else; that over-inflated helium balloon that one pinprick from life sends tumbling to the ground? Whether one's rich or poor, at some point it all goes, at some point they have to contend with nothingness, they have to let go of whatever they think they are.

None of us are immortal, and there's the crux of the situation. Why should a lifetime of work be disassembled by the inevitability of death—a force so powerful it demands that we accept our own nothingness? How long can a veneer of personality hide deep-seated fears? Is there eternal life? Is the "now" the only thing that's real? These questions baffle the brain until we build an inner life that enables us to focus on the present. Polar opposites merge. Life and its nemesis, death, are eliminated from the equation. We no longer have to defend our position in the world, we no longer have to be anything. We "are," that's all, and have stopped "becoming." The mind ceases to play a volleyball game with itself. It no longer hits the ball from the past to the future and back again. It focuses on the internal vertex (*hara*). Gratitude opens the heart and allows joy to fill the emptiness inside. We have freed ourselves from internal obstructions, and the universe, not our polarized thought, guides our activities every day. "To live in the moment" isn't just fancy words written in a book, a poetic state that's out of reach. It's the end product of a highly developed chakra system that gives us enough strength to transform tension into a spiritual life . . . and experience our own nothingness. The mind's conflicted stream of thought vanishes when we focus on the *hara*. Fear is reduced to a manageable level and we're at peace with ourselves.

❖❖❖❖

"Thou shalt not worship graven images" is one of the Ten Commandments. People have refused to attend meditation class because there were Tibetan thangka paintings on the walls, photos of half-naked Indian swamis, and large statues of Hindu and Buddhist divinities in the room. They didn't want to worship graven images. Can a finely sculpted bronze statue of the Buddha be a graven image when its energy flow helps me enter a deep meditative state? It's no different with statues and paintings of Shiva, Krishna, or any other Hindu or Buddhist divinity. I've seen works of African and Pre-Columbian tribal art transmit a spiritual force that helped me open in myself. I question the Judeo-Christian concept of "graven images." There is no more graven image on earth than the human ego and its subsidiary forms: houses, cars, clothing, jewelry, food, spiritual righteousness, greed, and assorted other possessions that make us more important than our fellow men. Human beings transform money into an object of worship and fail to realize that its transient nature deludes them into worshiping a "graven image." Must a family of four possess a forty-bedroom house to get through the day? Do they need ten cars, ten houses, a thousand pairs of shoes, and a wardrobe that could clothe half the population of the Bronx? Personal wealth of that kind can produce only one thing: more personal wealth, and a new generation of children and grandchildren spoiled rotten by excessive luxury.

They say, "It's easier for a camel to go through the eye of a needle than a rich man to go to heaven." Let's put it another way: It's easier for a camel to go through the eye of a needle than a rich, poor or middle-class man's ego to enter heaven. Money isn't a consideration. My teacher, Rudi, was a wealthy man. He used it for a singular purpose: to nurture his students and provide an environment in which people could meditate and get closer to spiritual enlightenment. "When I saw Swami Nityananda roll out a potato sack and go to sleep," he told me, "I promised myself to spend every day of my life working to attain that kind of simplicity."

Great wealth doesn't protect us from loneliness and inner turmoil; it doesn't prevent fear of age, illness and dying. If money consumes the lives of people, if it's a drug that transforms innocent children into half-crazed financial junkies, there'll never be enough of it to fill the pit in one's stomach. It will never keep overblown and neurotic egos under wrap. It takes courage to change one's inner life, to accept that "less ego is more" and that a cup can be filled with just so much water; it takes courage to admit that the pain in one's gut comes from spiritual malnourishment. We've substituted junk-food energy diets for nutrition that has real substance. We invest all our time in transient goals, and create gods out of material things. The "graven images" we worship are just an extension of our egotistically blind pursuits. They're goals that will be consumed by time and death, that provide momentary highs in a world where ups and downs are the norm. It's an illness without borders. It afflicts people in cities, states and countries everywhere in the world.

We spend every moment of our life on God's playground—a magical place where joy and sorrow mingle, where the good and not so good teach us how essential it is to develop a spiritual life. All that's asked from us is heightened consciousness. In every generation a handful of people attain *samadhi*. They've detached themselves from illusion, from pain and suffering, and become one with the universe. They have learned every lesson the earth has to teach. Where do they go? That's a mystery we'll never understand, but they've shown us that the soul of a human being never ceases to evolve.

❖❖❖❖

Ask yourself, "Who am I?" Ramana Maharshi told his disciples, "and the masks you hide behind will disappear." When I ask myself, "Am I a man?" The answer is, "Yes, but only for a short time." "Am I white, American, and do I live in New York?", more masks that need to be peeled away. As I remove these masks and look at my naked self, I'm aware that I've hidden my true identity. I am nothing: not a man or a woman, not rich or poor, not white, black, yellow or brown, not a person with a country, not tall or short or handsome or plain. When these masks peel away, I'm left with an empty vessel that fills up with spirit, and all conceptual imagery vanishes. At best I am a human being, and even that will disappear in time.

At the source of creation is a peaceable kingdom in which I roam freely and learn from everyone and everything encountered on my magical journey through time and space. The only constraint is the human mind that attempts to conceptualize everything. It creates theories that explain the unexplainable and works tirelessly to figure out what can't be figured out. Even Einstein, perhaps the most brilliant mind of the twentieth century, shrugged his shoulders and thought that the human mind is not capable of grasping the Universe. At eighty-two years of age, Tolstoy, the great nineteenth-century Russian novelist, ran away from home. They found him in a train station. He lay half dead on the platform, and as snow fell, he muttered, "I know nothing about life." If you stop for a moment and think about it . . . what do any of us know?

Rudi called his book, *Spiritual Cannibalism*, a strange title, but a readily understandable one when we accept that life is a feeding frenzy. We consume animals and plants that have also consumed animals and plants of one sort or another; death consumes life and life consumes the unborn. Time eats up minutes and hours allotted to us on earth, and the universe, like a raging fire, consumes everything in its path. And strange as it might sound, deep-seated tension in people eats them alive. Cannibalism is a harsh word until we recognize that a sincere practitioner of kundalini yoga will be consumed whole by spiritual energy. They must surrender everything to achieve an all-inclusive oneness with the universe. There's no logic in it, no readily understandable program that makes sense in quiet moments at home. *Samadhi* isn't who or what I am in my own eyes or the eyes of others. It's an enlightened state attained after lifetimes of deep inner work and surrender. We no longer hide behind masks; we no longer have to ask, "Who am I?" We "are," that's all, and by living in the moment, we have stepped off the wheel of karma.

❖❖❖❖

Tension needs to be broken down. Like compost, it must transmute itself from poison into an organic life-giving energy. The proverbial "garden" in Rudi's teachings made me work to transform my tension into a force that activated kundalini. Even as a kid I was well aware of how full of shit I was. I had no idea how badly it stunk, or what to do about it. The double-breathing meditation technique that Rudi developed helped me master inner chaos.

I'd been told by spiritual teachers to focus my attention on the third eye or listen to my breathing or focus my attention on the heart center or chant this particular mantra, but I had never been shown an exercise that developed the entire chakra system. Rudi's meditation practice made sense to me. How could I keep my heart open if there was no internal root system; how could I quiet my mind if my heart wasn't open; how could I activate kundalini without strong inner balance and foundation? Sanitariums are full of people who've activated kundalini but hadn't enough inner strength to support its powerful energy.

There's also sexual energy, a force so intense it consumed my thoughts every day. "Could that energy be used to enhance my spiritual life?" I asked Rudi. "Draw the energy from the chakra below the navel to the sex and then to the base of the spine," he replied. This meditation exercise transmuted impurities into energy that activated kundalini, and my soul force rose up the spine and entered the crown chakra. Rudi's meditation technique not only quieted my mind, emotions and sexuality, it transformed energies that were killing me into a life-giving force. His simple double-breathing exercise took the mystery out of spiritual practice. Anyone can do it, I thought. We all have chakras, we all have minds, and we all breathe. We all have tension, and we all have touches of emotional, mental and sexual dysfunction. What keeps people from learning this?

People would come into Rudi's gallery and browse. He'd ask them, "Can I help you with something?" The answer was always: "Just looking." This scenario played itself out over and over again. I'd see unhappiness in the browser's eyes, anxiety, fear, and a dullness that spoke of strong, unmanageable tension. We live in a world that's "just looking," I thought, a world that can't see two inches in front of its nose. Six months of Rudi's double-breathing exercise would rid them of deep anxiety, fear, and remove the deadness in their eyes. It astonished me how blind people were. I asked Rudi about this. "People come to spiritual practice when they are ready," he replied. "You can sleep next to a saint and not recognize his saintliness." "It's the mad and the blind," I said. "Yes," he replied. "Time has a great deal of patience with us all. We're given hundreds of lifetimes to get ready. The mystery is why people can't see what is directly in front of them, why they can't recognize that the answer is always there. If we remove our blinders, the universe is ready to provide."

❖❖❖❖

We're led to believe that Buddha, Patanjali, Padmasambhava, Milarepa and other great sages lived in times when spirituality was the accepted norm and touched the lives of most people . . . a time very different than today. "Gurus" in the contemporary West costume themselves in orange and burgundy robes and resemble *siddhas* and *rinpoches* that lived a thousand years ago. They quote ancient texts and re-create shrines and altars that are museum-like replicas of an ancient world. Something is missing. We can't imitate what was, nor can we superimpose ancient rituals on modern-day mindsets that are conditioned by a different set of norms.

On a trip to India, I visited a Tibetan monastery in the Himalayan foothills and entered a temple where a group of lamas chanted sutras and prayed. Intermittently the sound of two *dungchens* (Tibetan horns) accompanied the prayers. The chants were hypnotic at first, and I sat in half-lotus position on a cushion right behind the monks and tried to enter a deep meditative state. The nonstop repetition of the sutras and the sound of the *dungchen* reminded me of my early childhood in a synagogue on Yom Kippur. I began to fall asleep. I was awakened when I saw two adolescent lamas throw spitballs at each other. An old Tibetan monk smacked them on their hands with a stick. The irreverent spitball throwers revitalized the energy in the temple and turned the endless drone of chants and prayers into something human. Other lamas laughed silently at the young monks who giggled when the old lama walked away. They resumed throwing spitballs at each other.

While I watched the young monks giggle I envisioned Buddha with a gentle smile on his face, Buddha who loved the antics of these spitball-throwing children who brought more energy to midday prayers than sutra texts. "Are ritual chants that lull us to sleep more sacred than laughter?" I asked myself. "Doesn't the Buddha live inside every human being?" There are Indian miniature paintings of a young Krishna who plays pranks on *gopis*, yogis, and adults. I said to myself with a smile, "Both Krishna and Buddha must find these spitball-throwing adolescent lamas sacred. They have to admire anyone who takes the boring out of ritual."

No one has to perform timeworn rituals to find that the Buddha lives inside all of us. So does Christ, Krishna, Mohammed, Moses, and every great saint, bodhisattva, *rinpoche*, avatar and spiritual teacher that's ever come to earth. It doesn't matter in what century we are born, if the chakra system is developed, we'll recognize that every person, animal, plant, fish and insect is a manifestation of God. They all live at the center of creation and must be loved, respected and treated with dignity.

When religious dogma or secular rules and regulations restrict us, our creative juices cease to flow. Trapped in another person's vision of the world, we must obey for fear of some kind of retribution. The moment we free ourselves from this prison, the laws of men are easy to obey. We no longer feel restricted by them. We can graciously "Give unto Caesar what belongs to Caesar," and never feel like the external world keeps us from living our lives in the moment. We've managed to take the esoteric and make it practical.

Stuart Perrin

CHAPTER 14

There are moments from my life, brief interludes that I want to share with the reader to show that the path to enlightenment can begin in tenements in the South Bronx. It's been a long journey that continues today. Much has been experienced and surrendered on my travels, but every moment has helped me to build an inner life that's strong enough to stay connected with spirit. I've interwoven these interludes with wisdom passages to create a tapestry based on my life.

❖❖❖

I studied acting in New York in my early twenties, a decision I made because of my strong interest in theater and film. I'd attend Broadway and off-Broadway plays in my high school junior year, and watch art films in an attempt to understand the reason these pieces were created. I had an inborn belief that works of art—novels, music, films and theater—were created for spiritual purposes. If I wrote a poem or novel or play, these creations would help provide insight into my inner life. Deeply insecure, I suffered from severe stage fright every time I had to perform a scene from a play or improvise in front of an audience. Acting class became a form of therapy. The time spent in scene study with other actors helped me to become less inhibited and a little more secure about my own person. As the craft developed, I still couldn't visualize myself in films or theater. It wasn't film or theater that bothered me. It was the competitive edge needed to succeed in the entertainment world—a shark's tank that attracted egos so strong

I couldn't imagine having to deal with them every day.

Mary Tarcai was my first acting teacher. Performers I'd seen on Broadway and television came to perfect their craft in her class. When I immersed myself in scene study and interacted with these people, it became clear to me that theater and film had nothing to do with spirit. It was a playground for business-minded tycoons that didn't give a damn about educating people or consciousness-raising. Their only interest was money. Every actor I met was either between jobs and a nervous wreck, or in a job that would end soon . . . and still a nervous wreck. After a lunch at Mary's apartment, she and I spoke in her living room. "Stuart," she said with a smile, "I don't think acting is in your future, but I'm sure that one day you will write books or plays." "You really know me," I said. "Yes," she replied. "You have something important in you that needs to be said." I have never forgotten that conversation.

Although I was obsessed with writing, my anxiety-filled inner life didn't allow me to put five words together that made any sense. In Ford Madox Ford's novel *The Good Soldier*, he said, "No one can write an important novel until they're forty-years-old." I was twenty-two at the time. I closed the book and threw it against the wall, went to my desk and began to write. I still couldn't put five words together that made any sense. It was a painful time, and I wallowed in deep depression and thought that a future of two-or-three-word thoughts on paper would drive me insane. It almost did.

I continued to study acting in New York City, but switched from Mary's class to one taught by Jim Tuttle. The first thing that Jim asked me was whether or not I'd be willing to invest ten years of my life in theater or film. "If you are," he said, "you will become successful." At twenty-two, I didn't know if I would be willing to invest that amount of time in anything, but answered, "Yes," and he took me as a student.

He taught in a very different way than Mary. Improvisation was his key to good acting: the ability to listen on stage and react accordingly. The words didn't matter. What mattered was concentration and one's presence in the moment, and the ability to respond to the emotional life of other actors. It was not only a good acting technique, it was incredible therapy . . . and we didn't touch a script for months.

I studied in Jim's classes for a little more than a year. I had also been introduced to hallucinogens: marijuana, hashish, LSD, and other powerful mind-altering and illegal drugs that changed my perception. They heightened the moment and made me realize that consciousness transcended my meager understanding. I would smoke a joint and spend two hours in the heart of the Buddha. Bach's *Mass in B-minor* and the masses by Elizabethan composers John Sheppard and John Taverner transported me into a world replete with seraphim and angels. The paintings of Monet, Pissarro, Van Gogh, Turner, and other masters of Impressionism and color touched on a source of transcendental light that ordinary vision didn't comprehend. They were scenes painted by extraordinary visionaries who saw spirit in everyday life. I'd smoke a joint, go to the Metropolitan Museum of Art, and revel in the light, form and color that hung on its walls—a silent revelation, personal and deep, one that transformed my view of the world.

"Reality goes deeper than matter and mind," I said to myself. "Beauty and truth touch on something that I don't understand, a mystical force that has made itself known to many great artists and musicians. If Turner and Van Gogh could see it, why can't I?"

Nothing else mattered but finding that truth, not money or relationships, nothing but an open door to a force of energy that would validate my life, a force that turned an absurd and mundane world of illness, death and dying, into real purpose for my existence on earth. Every time I smoked a joint, an area of my brain opened and gave insight into life's beauty. I'd hear my neighbors' footsteps, people talking in the living room, the TV, the honk of a car or truck horn, people on the streets, Miles Davis' trumpet, the songs of birds, water running, my heartbeat, the sound of my blood as it moved through my body: a symphonic tone poem in which every part of life had a voice and purpose, a symphony orchestrated by a force much higher than myself. Even conflict found a place in life's orchestra. There was perfection of sorts that continued as long as I stayed high. I was mesmerized by cracks in the ceiling, by the geometrics of windowpanes, by designs in rugs, by photo books of Old Master paintings, by the shape of a person's face, by anything and everything that came into view.

It was early evening at a friend's apartment. I had just smoked a joint. The TV was on. I watched an interview program. Engrossed in the conversation on the television screen, I said to my friend, "What a great script. Who the hell wrote it?" He laughed. "It's not a script. It's a video of an interview." I didn't believe him. "No, that's impossible. I want to meet the writer. What else has he done?" My friend ignored me. He continued to seduce a young woman who sat next to him. Their conversation sounded to me like dialogue from a play, a bit superficial and open to interpretation. The same words spoken by better actors would have different meanings.

All conversation is nothing more than dialogue from a play, I thought. People are so out of touch with themselves their words ring hollow, their meanings are inconsequential, their voices are an aberration, and their personas are phony cover-ups behind which they bury themselves in shadow-like caves that blot out the self. People are disconnected from their own words, and their conversation sounds more like bad playwriting than an interaction of thought and idea.

The joint's effects wore off, and puppet-like movement and duplicitous words that came from people's mouths had less of an effect on me. I was tired, a little brain-dead, and had lost touch with a magnified sense of reality brought on by marijuana, an indelible sense that nothing was real and that most people were cut off from their true selves. They communicated with what sounded like scripted words that revealed little about their inner lives, almost like conversation in Chekhov dramas. If "the world is a stage," I thought, then most conversation is dialogue from a third-rate play . . . and personality's a cover-up for the truth. Neither the speaker nor person spoken to has the faintest idea what's being said. It's a comedy of errors played by a troop of rowdy actors. No two words make any sense, and the performers keep tripping over themselves like untrained actors hired by a foolish producer to perform in a foolish play.

Tired of my thoughts, I tried to remember my experiences while stoned—a dim recollection at best, a *through a glass darkly* experience that disappeared into remote realms of my unconscious. All I wanted to do was sleep. "There's got to be another way," I thought. "If I continue to smoke dope, my mind will erode, dementia will set in, and I will be left with nothing." It took days for me to recover from an LSD trip and five or six hours from marijuana. The hangovers convinced me that there must be another way. How would I find it? Who could teach me to live my life in the moment?

❖❖❖❖

The Day of the Dead festival had begun in San Miguel de Allende, Mexico. The crowded streets were full of drunk and stoned revelers. Drums and guitars played, and costumed Indians, some in shamanic masks, paraded in a wild frenzy. Ten minutes after I swallowed an LSD capsule I watched a procession of demon masks and eight-foot puppets on stilts march to the sound of drums and guitars. I had the following thoughts: form and content in the external world break down when I see them clearly . . . there's no structure, and lucid forms move one into another . . . the moment is all there is . . . if I think about the past or future, my tension increases and neurotic Stuart comes to the forefront . . .

Some friends of mine joined the parade. Stoned and in a complete frenzy, they danced like possessed men and women on the streets. They waved to me and I joined them. Every nuance of thought disappeared. I moved to the sound of drums. I forgot about form and function, about life and death, about philosophic insights and psychological gobbledygook and immersed myself in the dance like a shamanic Indian that placated the dead and prepared the universe for his own demise. I was made privy to a world of gods and demigods, demons and angels, a world that transcended imagination and connected to the infinite. There were no more thoughts, ego, or opinions, nothing but a stream of energy that moved through me like a river without end.

"A river that has no beginning," I thought, "and flows through all eternity." The sound of an Indian drum was akin to the sound of my heartbeat—an ever-present inner voice that helped me move to life's rhythm, and I was one with that rhythm, one with the universe—a fearless voyager on a path that led into and out of the arms of God.

Men, women and children paraded in multicolored costumes and skeleton masks. They chanted pagan-like prayers in guttural Spanish to the god of death. Their arms flailed, they jumped up and down, with tears in their eyes and incantations on their lips, they pleaded with an invisible God to free them from a world of suffering and death—the same world that I wanted to escape. "If I am going to be drowned," I heard the writer Stephen Crane's words in my head, "why, in the name of the seven mad gods who rule the sea, was I allowed to come thus far and contemplate sand and trees?" Why was I brought so close to God and not given entrance to His gates? I asked myself. Crane's voice slowly faded behind the sound of drums, a visceral voice that haunted my dreamlike state and gave me no rest. It made me dance a life-and-death dance on the streets of San Miguel de Allende. "If I am going to be drowned . . ." But I'm not going to be drowned, I thought, not yet, anyway, not until I discover what mysterious force has given birth to a vibrantly beautiful world that's also half-crazed and absurd, a world populated by men and women and children who live distinctly different realities.

"I want to come down," I thought, "but no, not now, not ever. I don't want to come down and find myself adrift in mental and emotional sludge, in sensible mindsets that never make sense to me." If I could just stay focused deep within myself and excavate some semblance of truth.

It was the Day of the Dead—a special day on which logic no longer had meaning, and I danced a shamanistic ritual dance in the arms of a skeleton-clad Indian lady. She guided me through the streets of San Miguel, took off her mask and smiled, "You *loco, señor.* You a crazy Americano." We both laughed and continued to dance until my high diminished and a deathly tiredness took over. I stumbled into a café by myself and ordered a coffee. "What happened to the skeleton-clad Indian lady," I asked myself, "and, more importantly, what's happened to me? *'If I am going to be drowned, if I am going to be drowned . . .'* what have I learned in this short life? I've been given moments of clarity, insights into higher consciousness, but know nothing about either life or death. They say that, "Many are called, but few are chosen." I was born, wasn't I? I came into this world for some purpose other than nonstop inner turmoil. I was called, but for what reason: to suffer like a schmuck, to enslave myself to money and power, to mediocrity and delusional living, to the craziness in my own head? Am I going to throw away my life on situations that have no substance? There must be something else. There must be a higher purpose to justify the price people pay for being born, a bridge that connects the human with the divine."

I slept like a dead man that night. When I awoke the next morning, there was a moment of clarity. I'm trying to change what can't be changed and I haven't the strength to do it, I thought. How can a foolish young person redecorate God's playground? First I have to find peace with myself, to like and love myself, and feel worthy of the life I have been given.

❖❖❖❖

I resumed acting classes in New York. Without real ambition, I thought, and a strong desire to make something of myself in the world of theater and film—success, money, a bit of fame, and to work at a profession that had meaning—these classes would take me nowhere. The people who succeeded in the entertainment profession, the money-mad producers, directors and entertainers, the competitors for parts in mediocre films and plays, the highly inflated egos that made the film and theater world work— they all forced me to look at myself in the mirror. A daily diet of acting could rob me of deeper needs: to find balance inside myself, to find a purpose for my life other than the hyper-tense, shallow, ego-filled world that produced plays and movies. I wasn't talented enough to succeed, nor was I attracted by the glitter of bright lights and fame.

I quit acting class and focused my creative efforts on the written word. Mary Tarcai was right: my acting chops weren't strong enough. The written word gave me an opportunity to explore my inner life and find meaning in a twentieth-century world that had been denuded of depth and spirituality. It was lonely and quite solitary . . . Stuart versus a blank page. Did I have anything to say? Could I say it in a literary manner? I didn't know, but my desire to write was compulsive and slightly mad, and kept me working at the craft. I knew that there was only one person I was up against: if I mastered myself, the written word would find its way onto the page. I had to quiet inner chaos, develop self-worth, and overcome a fear of failure that had haunted me for as long as I could remember. My chosen path lacked stability. There was no money or fame involved, just words on paper that explored my inner needs: poetry, thoughts, ideas that I hoped would someday manifest as a book.

❖❖❖❖

My first visit to Paris was in the autumn of 1963. I was a twenty-one-year-old restless and deeply unhappy young man in search of wisdom beyond my years. A splendid city, old and giving, shadow-like and mysterious, and at times like a wise and well-seasoned streetwalker, it welcomed me into its arms and whispered gothic tales written by writers that huddled in catacombs and crypts. I was almost broke and without a clue as to where I would make money. In love with a splendid Austrian girl named Dagmar, we arrived in Paris after a summer spent hitchhiking along the French Rivera, a city where Rimbaud and Verlaine wrote poetry together, where Picasso, Hemingway, Giacometti, Lautrec, Van Gogh, Hugo, and hundreds of famous and not-so-famous artists, musicians and writers crafted their works and contributed to the evolution of painting, music, and literature. It was a city that inspired me to write my own poetry, and to visit museums like the Louvre, the Jeu de Paume, the Guimet, and to absorb wisdom I had found in original paintings and sculptures I'd only seen before in books. Tired of the redundant life I lived in New York City—restaurant work to support myself, sterile and tedious classes at Hunter College, brief affairs with women that came and went, superficial and unsatisfying spiritual paths that did nothing to quiet my inner turmoil—restless, unhappy, and defiant, unable to fit my round peg into a square social circle, adrift and angry, I thought Paris would help me channel my creative energy. I didn't mind being a penniless visionary poet inspired by Parisian streets, buildings, and boulevards, by Les Halles, Notre Dame and the Left Bank, by echoes from the past that seeped into my consciousness. I never doubted that Paris would help me to develop skills as a writer. I wasn't sure what I had to say, but I was confident that something would come.

I lived for two days in a youth hostel, then moved from one cheap hotel to another until I rented a room in a hotel on Rue de Four. Paris was *tout complet*. Tourists, students, hippies and assorted Bohemian types flooded the Left Bank. Adrift in Parisian currents, a hodge-podge of artists, writers, photographers, film-makers and musicians had come from all over Europe and the United States to make Paris their home.

The Hotel St. Surplice des Anges on Rue de Four was a five-franc-a-night fleabag that catered to every prostitute on the Left Bank. The nighttime orgasmic oohs and aahs were like a symphony of cheap pleasure that kept me awake until early hours of the morning. I stayed there for about a week. The French police searched my room two or three times at four in the morning to see if I had drugs. Though horny as shit and drugged by the nonstop sound of people fucking, I refused to let Dagmar stay with me at night. She had found an *au pair* job with an American family in the 16th Arrondissement. It came with a *chamber de bonne* in their apartment building. "Just wait," I told her. "I'll find another room on the Left Bank where we can live together."

My days were spent in the Louvre Museum where I absorbed myself in the timeless beauty of Old Master pictures. I tried to extract from each canvas a force of spiritual energy that would help me find a path into myself. I studied line and color and divine beauty captured by masters who lived hundreds of years ago, and discovered that their depiction of truth far exceeded the Christian subjects relevant to their time. It touched on the mystical—a divine beauty that could only be found in the hearts of people. Could art fill my inner void? Would another poem or a piece of music or architectural masterpiece fill that void with nothing but transient feelings? When I looked at paintings by Leonardo, Caravaggio, Duccio, Fra Angelico, and Giotto, they stirred the writer in me. They showed me that human beings could create on the highest levels. Beauty was indeed truth, as Keats wrote, but it didn't free me from voices I heard in my head and constant depression. Though New York was behind me and I now lived in Paris, I had brought emotional and mental bag-gage with me. I still hadn't freed myself from the one person who always made me unhappy. It became clear to me who that person was, and a change of environment, of living space, a new city, country, or continent hadn't rid me of the tensions that raged inside me. No matter where I lived, there I was, and I stared at myself in a mirror.

Early one evening, after Dagmar and I ate dinner at a student restaurant, we took a walk by the Seine and across Pont St. Michel to the Ile de la Cité. She took my hand, "What's the matter?" she asked me. "Oh, nothing," I replied. "It's that freakin' hotel. I haven't slept for days. People are fucking their brains out and keeping me up all night." "I don't think that's the matter," she said with a smile on her face. "What do you mean?" "Something is eating at you," she replied, "something I don't understand." "What's eating at me?" I asked. I was a little upset. "I don't know. But it's always there. Like the pit in your stomach can't be filled." "You fill it," I said and kissed her. "No, not me. My love isn't strong enough." "Then whose love?" "No one's love can fill that void," she said. "It's too deep, too strange, and it will haunt you and depress you for the rest of your life." I stopped walking. "Look at Notre Dame," I said. "It's so goddamn beautiful. It was built for God. Nothing today is built for God." "Maybe it's God that will fill you," she said. "Do you believe in God?" I asked her. She just smiled and said, "I don't know."

Does God live between the legs of strung-out prostitutes? I asked myself as I lay in bed that night amid a chorus of orgasmic sounds that filled the hotel's musty air. Dagmar's insightful patience with her moody lover-of-art boyfriend blotted out the gasps of horny johns and made me promise myself after breakfast the next morning, I'd look for another hotel room. First I went to Rue Dauphine and Rue Mazarine, but nothing was available. "*Complet, Monsieur, nous sommes complet.*" The entire Left Bank of Paris was *complet*. My search for a room was like a journey into the lower depths. It had led me to the Hotel St. Surplice des Anges where everyone was getting laid but me. "*Nous sommes complet, Monsieur,*" became an existential mantra that nearly drove me out of my mind.

On Boulevard St. Michel I met a Dutch artist friend named Wilhelm who did chalk drawings on sidewalks in Nice. One cloud-filled day in mid-July, I had met him on the beach. "Hey, Wilhelm," I said. "I'm freakin' broke. Would you mind if I color in your Van Gogh sidewalk drawing and make a little money?" "No problem, man," he replied. "Make as much as you want." That afternoon, I got down on my knees and with chalk Wilhelm provided, I colored in a faded drawing he had done a week before.

Within a few hours, I had a hat full of French centimes and francs. It was a glorious day. In the evening, I took Wilhelm and Dagmar out to dinner. "Hey, man," Wilhelm, said. He gave me a big hug. "How are you?" "Okay," I replied. "I'm looking for a hotel room. Do you know of anything?" "Yeah," he said. "Hotel du Centre on Rue de la Boucherie. A friend of mine checked out of there about half an hour ago." "Oh, shit!" I said to him. "See you later. The entire Left Bank is *complet*. I'd better get over there."

That evening Dagmar and I met at Shakespeare and Company. I told her that I had moved to a hotel just down the street. "Is the room big enough for two of us?" she asked me. "The room's small, but the bed will fit two." "Okay, good," she said. "I'm gonna quit my job." "Why?" "I've had enough. The husband came on to me this morning. It was disgusting." "What did you do?" "I was going to kick the creep in his balls, but he backed off. Anyway, I'm sick of being a nanny. I can easily get a job selling the *Herald Tribune*."

We lived together at the Hotel du Centre through New Year's. Dagmar sold the *Herald Tribune*, and I pedaled the *New York Times*. Between the two of us we'd make just enough money to get through the day. I attempted to write poems, but they all fell flat. There wasn't a line that I liked nor a paragraph I'd show to anyone else. The entire Paris cultural high began to slip away from me. I became Stuart again, and I couldn't spend one peaceful day.

The highlight of my first few months in Paris was the Musée Guimet—an incredible collection of ancient Hindu/Buddhist art from Asia. I would sit in front of a large Cambodian stone Buddha and meditate. My mind calmed a bit, and I experienced strength inside myself I'd never known before. The moment I left the museum, depression took over, and I became lost in a hail-storm of thought that crippled my inner life. I didn't know what to do, and Dagmar lost patience with my bouts of gloominess. "Nothing can touch you," she said. "It's like there's a door in your chest, and I can't find a way to open it." "I don't know what's in my chest, nor do I give a shit. It seems to me that I'm gonna sell these fuckin' newspapers for the rest of my life." "And me," she said, quite upset. "What's gonna happen to me?" "I don't know, Dagmar, I just don't know anything." "You know what I think," she said. "You should join a monastery, become a monk, and dedicate your life to God. You certainly have trouble dedicating your life to another human being." "I'll be back," I said. I walked out of the hotel-room door, down three flights of steps and wandered aimlessly to Boulevard St. Michel and across the Pont St. Michel to Rue St. Denis and Les Halles.

On a lamp-lit night, overcast, and chilly, a prostitute stood in every doorway. There were young and old women that sold themselves to truck drivers, teenagers and indigent laborers for twenty francs a hit . . . maybe a bit more or less after negotiations. The bars were full of laborers from all parts of France. Some trucks unloaded produce and other trucks unloaded sides of beef in a market that supplied most of the restaurants of Paris, grocery stores, meat shops and supermarkets. I didn't know what I wanted there. The prostitutes were of no interest to me, nor could I shop for produce or fresh meat without a kitchen in which to cook. What I craved was the energy of the place: a force so raw it couldn't be found anywhere else in Paris, a warren of uneducated people that worked nonstop to feed the rest of the city, an explosive and dynamic market that thrived while the rest of the city slept. It filled a void that art, music, and literature couldn't fill. What I hungered for was life stripped down to basics, a manifestation of spirit on a practical level.

I hung out in Les Halles for two or three hours, went into a café, had onion soup, two or three *demis* of beer and half a baguette, spoke to truck drivers, prostitutes, and market laborers until sheer exhaustion forced me to leave the bar and walk back to the hotel. Dagmar was asleep when I arrived.

I studied her beautiful face. Her turned up nose and cheeks were like a baby's. Perhaps she's right, I thought, perhaps there's a God-like force that will help me find inner peace. No matter where I go, I never leave myself behind. If I don't learn to master my chaotic and undisciplined self, nothing will ever be real.

I kissed her on the cheek and smiled. How does she know me so well and comprehend all the confusion that upsets the balance? Do I need God, religion, or someone to help quiet my mind and connect my consciousness with a higher force in the universe? I didn't know. I didn't think I'd ever know. "I'll be no good to anyone if I don't subdue the chaos in myself," I said to myself.

Francois, an artist friend of mine, told me not to worry about it.

"If you don't suffer, *mon ami*, what the hell will you write about?"
I knew my relationship with Dagmar wouldn't last. Regretfully,
I told myself this. I'll never forget this remarkable young woman
whose smile could light up any room. To this day, she lives in my
heart, and I'm grateful for the time we spent together.

CHAPTER 15

I've read many books on the lives of Hindu and Christian saints, hagiographies that reveal life-and-death struggles that make the comfort level of today's Sunday school religion a bit silly. The need to be with God can't be housed in a suburban, white-picket-fenced veneer of security. It's a gutsy undertaking that demands surrender on the deepest levels—a hunger so profound it won't be satiated by money, fame, power, or the trappings of mediocrity. We tend to relegate meditation to an esoteric box and forget we live on earth and are hungry for some kind of spiritual food. What we also forget is that chakras won't develop by themselves. The universe, so willing to provide wisdom and knowledge, waits patiently for us to develop an inner life that can receive its gifts.

One thing I can guarantee: we will all grow old. The alternative isn't to anyone's liking, but age brings little wisdom if we don't work deeply on ourselves. Time is an enemy if not used consciously, but time can also be an intimate friend. If we waste time, then it will eventually beat up on us and cause illness, fear and anxieties. If we make conscious use of time and build an inner life, time no longer pits us against the unknown. It prepares us to leave the world; it supports our effort to attain spiritual enlightenment. We no longer fear either life or death and we're given enough "time" to connect with the infinite.

A spiritual life isn't sedentary. The notion that one should sit and meditate twenty-four hours a day is a mistake. Nature reminds us that sedentary water attracts insects, algae and disease. No one drinks water from a lake. It will do nothing but upset

145

one's stomach, causing diarrhea and other intestinal problems. People are no different. If one lives a sedentary life, he will attract discomfort and illness.

Life demands that we interact with the external world, whether it's with humans, with nature, with pets, or something else that attracts us, something that demands we give it our attention. People need to love and be loved and to fill an empty internal void. It draws them out of themselves, and makes demands on their energy and time. The moment we desire something be it money, fame, love, or security, we have to interact with the world, and that interaction gauges our inner strength. Do we make childish demands like, "give me . . . I want that . . . it belongs to me and I'll take it no matter what pain I cause?" Do our actions reflect a selfish and immature need for attention—a grating voice that screams (sometimes silently): I'm an emotionally malnourished and immature adult who is still a seven-year-old brat? I'm starving to death for love and spiritual energy, but afraid to admit it. It's one thing to be full of joy and another to be eaten alive by tension. Both are energy, but one gives life and the other kills us.

Samuel Taylor Coleridge wrote a poem called *The Rime of the Ancient Mariner*, a profound and very accomplished study of the human condition. Though written in the eighteenth century, it's a metaphor for twenty-first century life.

Water, water, everywhere,
And all the boards did shrink;
Water, water, everywhere,
Nor any drop to drink

They are lines that speak to people in any age. There's abundance all around us, yet our systems shrink, and our inner lives become narrower. We're dying of thirst and won't take a drink. Opinionated and full of ourselves, there's no room for anything but twisted ideas of the truth, an unclear vision of the world that reduces life to Coleridge's metaphor—a tiny sailing ship on a vast windless ocean, a ship that can't move in any direction, and we live on that ship with an albatross around our necks. We also live at the center of God's creation. There's abundance all around us. The only thing missing is our ability to embrace it, to drink from its fountain, and quench our inner thirst.

❖❖❖❖

Power, be it political, economic, social, or just conflict among egos in day-to-day life, is a potent drug that transforms people. No one ever mentions humility and the incredible inner strength it takes to open one's heart and say thank you to life, strength that transforms conflict into love and makes room for other people to live and breathe. We're attracted like moths to headlights when charismatic and egoistic people enter a room. It's almost surreal: one person's presence fills up a space and hundreds of other people become like Lilliputian creatures that peek out at him or her from cracks in their own armor. They hang on to every word spoken, mesmerized not by wisdom, but by wealth, position, political office, celebrity; media-made leaders that are like characters in *The Emperor's New Clothes* fairytale and well-paid pundits who speak with certainty about things they barely understand. I've seen eighteen-year-old rock stars interviewed on television news programs by reporters that want opinions on the human condition. I've seen terrorist attacks on TV in Europe, America, and the Middle East, people shot in front of my eyes. I'm told to stay tuned for more news and blitzed with ads for lipstick, make-up, medicines, cars, and whatever else companies have to sell. I almost never hear a pundit or politician say to a television audience: what did we do to bring this horrible situation on ourselves? Does revenge really work? Does physical violence accomplish anything? Don't we have to change? Does human greed do anything other than create more greed? Where is the role of forgiveness in humanity's playbook? Patience? Tolerance? Compassion and respect for life and the struggles of people?

Humble people say to each other, "I am wrong. What do you have to teach me?" They've discovered that there are many ways to see the world. Humility comes from a much deeper place than the violence and vengeance used by political and religious power brokers to kill thousands of people. Death and destruction never solve the problem. They create a hopeless society in which vengeance seeds more death and destruction . . . and the problem never goes away.

There's a much bigger problem at work here: every person killed has family and friends. Their death leaves behind a void that's often filled with enough anger and despair to blind people's reactions. When you kill one person, it creates an empty pit in loved ones that lacks forgiveness. To kill one person is to kill the entire world, because each person is an embodiment of God's creation. When a Jew kills a Muslim or a Muslim a Jew, both of them channel a dark side of the human mind that never allows love and kindness to take root. There's no end to the madness until every Jew and every Muslim has been slaughtered. Some religious fanatics would call this an apocalypse. They relish the thought of total destruction and the end of the world. I think it's much simpler than that: happy people don't kill other people. People whose hearts are open tolerate religious and political systems that differ from their own; they tolerate racial differences and thoughts that conflict with each other. They let the world be. They've found the greatest treasures that exist on earth: an open heart, love, compassion, and everything that falls in their wake. They get up in the morning and say to themselves I was born here to have a wonderful life; I am worthy of loving and being loved; I am worthy of living with joy in my heart.

The question is, what defines wonderful? Is it Money? Success? Power? I don't think so. When I look into the eyes of successful people, I see the same unhappiness I see in other people. Politicians always look half-dead to me, and beneath the egomania emitted by celebrities and business moguls, there's almost always a twisted underbelly of arrogance and unhappiness. So what is the greatest treasure on earth, and why is it so difficult to find? I've said it before and it should be said again: "The only successful people on earth are happy people." To find a happy person on earth is like finding one particular leaf in a forest. We believe that external things will make us happy—a husband or wife, a child, a job, money, a house or a particular car, but people and things turn us on for a moment. When that moment ends we have to deal with ourselves. We have to learn how to keep our hearts open, we have to learn how to fill ourselves with spirit instead of ego, we have to learn that love, joy, and humility connect us to what's infinite in the universe. Everything else leads to the grave.

❖❖❖❖

After a meditation class in New York City, I asked my students how many of them were taught about chakras in elementary or high school, how many of them were taught about surrender, humility, how to use mind and breath, how to sit still and focus on the *hara*. Everyone in the room chuckled but not one person raised his or her hand. "Meditation redefines everything you've learned from childhood," I said. "It will not only revolutionize your thought process, it will reinterpret life. Most books you've read about meditation barely scratch its surface. They provide an intellectual understanding of a process that goes so deep inside a practitioner that the only way to grasp its essence is through experience. The mind is no longer the master. It interprets life, but doesn't live it." From our childhood on we're told to think things through, to work them out, to try to understand what is happening before we make a decision, a process that keeps us from being spontaneous. Society says: "contribute, give back, make an effort to help other people," but these words get lost in a massive din. People who have attained success are rewarded with honors, no matter whom they've hurt or killed as they moved to the top. We're taught to extract as much material gain as possible before we die. It doesn't matter what happens to other people. The goal is to win at all costs. When age and illness come to the privacy of our bedrooms, rewards are meaningless and our crippled condition forces us to re-evaluate life and think about what is missing.

"Has anyone taught you about reincarnation in high school?" I asked my students. They all chuckled again. "No one ever teaches us to come to terms with death and dying," I continued. "No one ever tells us that the fifty or eighty years we spend on earth are like a drop of water in a huge bucket. We think we own this planet, but, in truth, we're guests here, and guests shouldn't muck up the home of their host. We come to a place that's filled with divine beauty, a gift that should be cherished and should teach us to open our hearts and feel gratitude. Instead of dark thoughts and grisly bouts with evil, the answer can be found in the human heart—love, forgiveness, and tolerance—states of grace that equal the gift of life. If we don't learn this in our present lifetime we'll try again in the next incarnation until we finally open our hearts, become happy, and share this happiness with other people."

❖❖❖❖

The child in us can be resurrected from the deathlike state called ignorance. After years of deep meditation practice it now has foundation and maturity and can sustain itself through any kind of storm. We can step out of our cave and enjoy the sun. No rule or regulation, no dogma or righteousness will strip us of this newfound self. They say the kingdom of heaven is open to children. Yet the child in each of us has been buried beneath layers of tension, barely alive, barely able to breathe; it waits for us to free it from an internal prison created out of emotional and mental waste. When we manage to free that child, there will no longer be paths that lead to enlightenment, there will no longer be past or future. The entire universe will create and recreate itself around us, and the seven days of Genesis will transmute themselves into the "now", a new beginning that has been and always will be there.

❖❖❖❖

I began this treatise with a simple, commonsense idea. Meditation, kundalini yoga, and everything related to spiritual practice or religion have little or no value if they can't be put to practical use. They are nothing more than words or disciplines without meaning. Years ago a student of mine had been involved with another spiritual practice before she met me. She said, "When I studied with my teacher, I'd often sit and meditate eight hours a day, but the moment I left my house, the streets, the noise, the crowds of people, the pressures of my everyday life would freak me out. I wanted to hide out in a closet." It's easy to find safe and secure places that don't threaten us, but life is like a university. It has many departments, some safe, others easy, yet others extremely difficult, but all demand that we learn something about ourselves in order to get through the day. If we hide out in a meditation room (or any other venue we deem safe) and we're afraid to walk the streets, our fear has driven us into a prison. I've lived in cities and suburbs, in small towns and even on the top of a mountain, and I've discovered that no matter where people live they create cocoon-like safety nets that keep them from exploring deeper areas of self. They don't want to be bothered. Why change if I fit comfortably into the lifestyle in which I live? The answer to that is simple: crystallized worlds become static and replete with boredom. What was once beautiful and interesting transmutes itself into a robotic way of living. We become familiar with our husband, our wife, our partner, and our children, with the landscape, seascape, or cityscape, with our job, our friends, but familiarity often breeds contempt. We're not really angry with people and things in our life, we're upset because we've stagnated.

We live in a kind of burrow. Every day is the same—a safe, conditioned world in which each action is calculated to bring a certain result . . . and it never does. There's always something wrong, be it the children leaving the nest, the garbage not being collected, the air conditioner not working, crime, money problems, something that irks us, that keeps us from being happy. If liquor and drugs are a popular escape, if affairs and crime goose people and make them feel alive, and rids them of stagnation, boredom, lethargy, and a life that lacks creativity, something external to themselves that changes things and transforms routine dullness into a life worth living, we quickly discover that external stimulus doesn't fix internal stagnation. It turns us on for a few moments, but real change, real transformation of a crystallized inner life into energy that's not shackled and damned up by fear and insecurity requires deep inner work, a commitment to change—meditation practice that often takes years to convert comfortable ways of living into dynamic and creative lives.

Knowledge gleaned from books, meditation and yoga classes has to be used in everyday living. What we know is a hindrance if it can't be applied in a practical way. The real questions are: Does it work? Am I changing? Do I have less tension, anxiety, fear and ego? Can I build a bridge from the meditation class to my daily life? Am I stuck in a spiritual cocoon or can I transform every facet of my life into a temple? I've met many occult, metaphysical and esoteric scholars who are intellectually sound, know their facts, and can prove any point. When they speak about chakras, gods, demi-gods, ritual practice, they have unshakable knowledge about Hindu, Christian and Buddhist beliefs. But their classes are often like a dry, juiceless river of words spoken from intellectual mindsets that sound more like masturbatory projections than a person who truly believes what he or she is saying. Their voices often put me to sleep. I've also met people who talk "religious talk"—the right words expressed in some kind of false biblical or Vedic fashion, a sweetness that oozes phony love and spirituality, and has nothing to do with an open heart. It's more like a role they must play to convince followers that they're on the side of God. Real people are difficult to find, yet every person has internal tools that can be used to transform superficial knowledge into a practical application of spirituality. Like anything else in life, one has to learn how to do it.

❖❖❖❖

The most brutal war fought on earth is the ongoing battle that takes place in every human being—a life-and-death struggle that tests the strength of opposing wills. It's a war that's fought when internal cycles force us to undergo the experience of death and rebirth. Surrender doesn't come easy: the act of letting go to free one's self from old, musty ways of living that have turned us into robotic people. It takes strong willpower for an alcoholic to no longer succumb to booze. The same is true for drugs, whether they're of the prescription variety, marijuana, heroin, cocaine.

There's a deep inner need to be loved and to love, to become a whole person that can live a creative life and be happy, without daily routines that transmute our *joie de vivre* into a monotonous use of energy. There's a part of us that covets spontaneity, freshness, a renewed way to approach life's repetitive nature. If an actor doesn't recreate himself and find something fresh in a character he's played for the three hundredth time, the performance will be by rote, the character will become stiff, and cease to be real. "The world is a stage," Shakespeare wrote, and, yes, each human being plays a role in life's play.

There's a part of us that covets wellbeing and a part of us that succumbs to living death. We need them both, the first to inspire creativity and the second to remind us how easily joy and love can be snuffed out. They're antithetical forces that attempt to negate each other in a nonstop battle that rages from birth to death, polarized forces that will never come to the peace table until we find a way to transform them into *chi* . . . and merge the male/female principle. Whether we need to wage this war or not is irrelevant simply because it goes on no matter what we think—a life versus death struggle, a whirlpool of tension that keeps us all on edge, that upsets the inner balance and creates barriers between ourselves and other people . . . and never lets us live in peace. The external world reflects this internal battle. War will never cease until there's peace and harmony inside every human being. As long as one mind ticks on earth there will be disharmony. It's the norm . . . the way our thought processes work, a life-and-death situation in which the demon-mind pits positive and negative ideas against one another. It's easy to pick apart other people and recognize their internal struggles. It's easy to sit in judgment and pass opinions on what's wrong with them. It's more difficult to see inside one's self, to recognize one's problems, and make a serious effort to realign one's inner life and create harmony and balance. The real battlefield of truth is located inside each and every one of us. Until we resolve that mystery, until we learn to work deeply on ourselves, war will persist on earth, people will kill each other, and the internal battle between life and death will never cease.

❖❖❖❖

People often tell me that I look different when they see me. I'm not the same person I was three months ago. It makes me smile. "I'm really not the same person you met then," I've replied, "and I'm grateful that changes take place so fast. I hope that I'm much different now than when I woke up this morning." We are constantly changing, but it takes months for our minds to catch up. Whole new areas open inside us, the chakra system renews itself, and we're given the opportunity to get closer to enlightenment. Though the body gets older our inner life remains youthful, vibrant, and full of energy. There's a twinkle in our eye, a lightness of being, a highly developed forehead, heart chakra and *hara*. Throughout a meditation class major transformations take place, and students undergo radical inner change. By the end of the class, I'm amazed how different people look. They're lighter, easier, calmer, and more focused. They've opened to receive spiritual energy and it has given them a new way to look at life. Early on I learned to make friends with parts of me that I don't like. Without that unwelcome and disliked creature inside me, I wouldn't do anything about myself. I would take life for granted, I would wallow in a self-satisfied, almost crystallized world of pseudo-spirituality. No matter how much I grow and change, there will never be perfection. I have to work every day to evolve and get closer to God.

❖❖❖❖

An artist friend of mine grimaced when I told him that happiness is the goal of all humanity. "It's impossible," he said with a sneer, "to ever be happy or to sustain moments of joy for long periods of time." I understood his skeptical approach to a happy life. True happiness is so rare that even the thought of it borders on the impossible. The heart builds layer upon layer of insulation to ward off disappointment, aggression, and a battery of hurt that most people endure in one relationship or another. The mind calculates every interaction we have with the objective world. Doubt, skepticism, and an overly cautious self create barriers to love and true friendship, and the heart is buried beneath rubble that thickens because of dense layers of accumulated tension. Hidden beneath that rubble is our inner child, a part of us that wants to come out and dance in the sunlight: innocent, trusting, caring, and compassionate, but buried beneath layers of disappointment and hurt.

The heart is like a flower. It has a stem and it has roots, and it needs to be nourished by spiritual energy. Without roots there is no flower, without *chi* there's no rootedness in a human being. If the heart chakra refuses to open, we swim with our lips barely above large puddles of chaotic emotions and anxieties. Without love a human being suffers from spiritual anorexia—half-starved, he cries out for nourishment but hasn't the faintest idea where to find it. The heart shrivels up until it's encased in a tomb-like box devoid of light or spirit. The tension becomes so extreme it brings assorted physical ailments. During intensive healing sessions when I touch people on the forehead or the heart, I have to make certain that I drop the psychic poison released. It could easily do damage to my own chakra system.

To break down walls of tension that surround the heart, I have to strengthen the *hara* and connect with spirit. Layers of tension dissolve and allow the energy of kundalini to rise up the spine to the crown chakra. Only time, patience, and masterful training can quiet inner chaos. I've discovered, over years of practice, that one of the most difficult tasks on earth is to focus one's attention in the *hara*. Four years of disciplined deep inner work enabled me to get my mind quiet, but even now, three decades later, I still hear voices in my head. I just don't listen.

❖❖❖❖

Ego often inspires fledgling yogis to want to become gurus, an immaturity that fosters belief that they can sit in front of other people and transmit *shakti*. What appears to be simple to them is perhaps one of the most difficult things to do. Upwards of ninety percent of students who are made teachers either give it up or transform Rudi's meditation practice into some watered-down version of what Rudi taught. They dress in orange, chant, use Tibetan ritual objects, and play Indian guru to a chorus of innocent people who haven't a clue as to what is going on. Rudi always spoke about less being more. The moment the ego gets involved, the flow of *shakti* is distorted. One transmits an overblown version of self instead of the energy of God, and most students can't tell the difference. They absorb a river of "spiritual ego" that doesn't help them to build an inner life.

As a young, inexperienced teacher I realized my job was to open to spiritual guides in the cosmos and on earth and be used by them to channel *shakti*. My connection to Swami Nityananda was very deep. He would always come to me during class. I asked him for help to break myself down. I asked if he could transmit *shakti* to the people in the room. The energy in the meditation hall intensified, and my inner blocks were transformed into a life-giving force that nurtured people.

"*Shakti* transmission requires very deep surrender," I said to myself after a class was over. "Everything that I believe in or think about has to be relinquished. If my ego teaches the class *shakti* will cease to flow."

At a Big Indian ashram *satsang*, Swami Muktananda extolled the virtues of guru. "The guru is God," Mukatananda said, "and must be worshipped like one worships God. The guru is so pure that a fly won't land on his body." After the *satsang* Rudi said to me, "The guru isn't God. God is God. At best the guru is a servant. He serves both his students and higher energy in the universe."

I've never understood how *shakti* transmission works, but years of meditation practice have taught me that the less there is of me, the more spiritual energy can flow through. I don't even understand how I met Rudi. It was like some karmic accident that completely transformed my life, something that was meant to be, but makes no sense when I think about it. So I don't think about it. When opportunities arise, one must be smart enough to take advantage of them. If not, they disappear into the great maw of life. An angry student once left Rudi's meditation practice, a student who didn't like the fact that Rudi was overweight, he ate meat, had a sex life, and a laundry list of other things. "He needs this work and it might take ten thousand lifetimes for energy like mine to return again to earth," Rudi said. It's a hell of a long time to wait for something that man rejected in this lifetime, I thought.

It doesn't take great genius to find fault in other people. It takes a remarkable person to use what the universe provides to develop a spiritual life.

Spiritual teachings must be passed on from generation to generation, but not in a superficial way. One can't promote God or become a public relations outlet for a meditation practice that requires unconditional surrender and love. One enters a door that most people are not willing to step into. It's almost impossible for an ordinary work-a-day person to believe that the universe will use them like this; it's almost impossible to believe that the highest position on earth is to serve both God and man.

❖❖❖

It was six forty-five on a Wednesday evening. Rudi and I sat together in a deep state of meditation on the second floor of his loft building. Swami Muktananda had returned to India a few weeks before. Many of Rudi's students sat in the meditation hall downstairs. They chanted, *Sri Ram, Jai Ram, Jai, Jai Ram Om.*

Swami Muktananda left instructions on prop
wants to have a spiritual life. Chanting, vegeta
bacy were essential, and Muktananda told Rudi t
meditation, the very core of our ashram's spiritual p
my guru," Rudi said. "If I surrender my teachings, the
my sex life, it will all be replaced by a deeper connection
Rudi was the most irreverent holy man who walked
of the earth, a spiritual seeker who had little or no patience
bullshit even when it wore orange robes. He told me one d
"I've taken a vow of celibacy, but that doesn't mean I can't giv
someone else an orgasm." He also told me that he'd rather smoke
dope than chant, and dope was the one thing not allowed in his
meditation practice. One of Mukatananda's contentions was that
we shouldn't eat lamb or beef because cows and sheep don't eat
meat. In Dallas, at the World of Animals, Rudi told Mukatananda
that he was going to have a lion steak for dinner because lions
eat meat. It was a riotous three months of vegetarianism. When
we perused menus in Chinese restaurants to see what we could
and couldn't eat, I had to remember that I wasn't having dinner
with an ordinary mortal. He was Swami Rudrananda, the earliest
form of Siva, the most primal energy force in Hinduism, a Creator
and Destroyer who was born in New York City to remind us that
everything is a manifestation of God. "The world is a smörgåsbord," he once said to me. "I've come here to eat from every corner
of the table. I don't want there to be anything to come back for."
When Rudi and I emerged from our meditative state, I looked
at my watch. "It's seven," I said. "Time for class." His students
were chanting downstairs. *Sri Ram, Jai Ram . . .* He smiled and
said, "Let the fanatics finish chanting." The fanatics clapped and
swayed and chanted in overly loud voices. They continued to chant
until Rudi sat on his teaching chair, picked up a clapper, and hit a
large Japanese gong . . . and there was silence. We closed our eyes
and meditated in that silence for half an hour—no transmission
of *shakti*, no energy, just silence that put many of the meditators
to sleep.
I missed the intensity of Rudi's open-eyed, double-breathing
meditation, the direct transmission of *shakti* and the development
of the chakra system. When he told me that he'd rather smoke
dope than chant, it made perfect sense. In my early twenties, I'd

er procedure if one
ianism, and celi-
o stop open-eye
ractice. "He's
food I like,
to God."
he face
with
ay,

er pretended marijuana would
anted *Om Namah Sivaya* or
d me, even rid me of surface
ly on the chakra system; it
lways a letdown when I left
l with the chaos I found in
ular world that protected

d me to teach. I'd put on
a, go to the meditation hall,
clapper, sit in half-lotus position on a
and pretend that I was a guru. Insecure and
for half an hour, I had no idea what I was supposed
to teach. The day Rudi announced that we would return to the
open-eyed double-breathing exercise, a cheer went up in the ashram . . . a sigh of relief. My system came alive again and I could
feel spiritual energy in every organ, cell, and bone of my body.

❖❖❖❖

"How can I live in a material world and have a spiritual life at
the same time?" students have asked me over the years. On the
surface, these two realities seem diametrically opposed to each
other, but on closer examination, the act of surrender makes it
possible for us to live a spiritual life whether we're in a monastery,
ashram or in New York City. We associate the word "surrender"
with giving up, but the word has multiple meanings, one of which
is the simple act of "letting go." If we're full of ego, emotion, mind,
and other tensions, it's absurd to think we can invite spirit to live
in our personal asylum. It would be like inviting a guest to spend
a weekend in a filthy house. Surrender doesn't mean you become
some kind of wimp. It means you make room inside yourself
for spirit or higher creative energy to come and live. They say in
the Bible, "Ask and you shall receive." When the vessel is empty,
you can demand that God, or higher energy, fill it with spirit. A
pianist will spend hours a day on his craft. When it's time to play
the concerto, if he's mastered the craft, music will flow through
him. If his ego and thoughts don't interfere, the music will not
only flow through, it will touch on divine beauty and truth.

In times of tragedy and trauma, of great suffering and loss, people run to houses of worship. They plead with God for some kind of answer. In good times, they relegate God to a back shelf. Houses of worship become empty. Congregants assume that peace and prosperity will last forever. They forget that there's dialectic at work, a polar network of opposites that gives birth to one another. Good follows evil, and vice versa, in a succession of karmic events that dangles humanity from a string. Tragedy strikes when we least expect it. Nobody is prepared for the loss of a parent or a child, a husband or a wife, or illness that threatens imminent death. We presuppose that life goes on forever and death exists in a black hole none of us dare to enter. The fear of death is so strong that we blot it out and fool ourselves into believing that it happens to other people, not us. The mind doesn't understand it, the heart quivers with unhappiness. The only way to come to terms with this reality is to build a system inside that's strong enough to have a spiritual life. Life and death merge and become one entity. It is no longer a philosophical or theological abstraction, but experiential—a living example of unconditional love that transforms fear into knowledge, wisdom, joy and happiness—a union of all things.

It takes guts to engage in an internal dialogue with higher energy, to rightfully demand answers that help one evolve and get closer to enlightenment. The act of doing this defies everything we're taught from the moment of birth. We're taught to covet things, to glean what we can from life, to bury ourselves in an arsenal of material possessions—a strange, almost surreal altar built to worship ego. Humility topples this altar. It makes us realize how transient life is, it makes us realize we've buried ourselves in a stockpile of objects that will disappear in time. People strut their steps on life's ego-filled stage where performers assume the role of God. I have even met gurus who proclaim to be God. It's a scary proposition, because God is God, and the rest of us have to deal with our limitations. Who in their right mind wants God's job, anyway? The very thought would give any sane person a headache.

Two voices inside us vie for our attention. One chitchats in our heads and the other bellows from a deep inner place. Initially, it's difficult to differentiate between these two voices, but early on we discover the voice in our head encourages self-importance. It has a voracious need to be right all the time. It has none of the answers and all of the answers at the same time; it lashes out at people that test its limited perception. It tries to fit the universe into a conceptualized box in which there's very little room for knowledge and wisdom of an infinite nature.

The second voice demands inner growth. It must be fed by spirit and not illusion. It understands surrender and is open to life's possibilities, and never assumes it knows anything. That voice, and only that voice, must be satiated by higher energy. No impediment will keep it from a spiritual life. Alive and vital in its desire to grow, it will never accept superficial answers to profound questions, and it bellows from humanity's core.

CHAPTER 16

"We live in a circus, but no one goes to the circus to have a lousy time," I wrote in a book. That line has stayed with me over the years. When I turn on the news or read current events in a newspaper or on the internet, the violence, rage, greed, and hatred I see borders on madness. It's like getting a bird's-eye view of life in an insane asylum. It used to upset me no end until I realized that it's impossible for me to fix this world. The only person I can fix is myself. The rest is God's problem, and God (higher energy) provides an endless amount of time for the human race to get its act together.

As a young man I lived in Paris and bought books written in English at Shakespeare and Company. In a book of poems I purchased by Rabindranath Tagore, I came across a line I've never forgotten: "Madness falling from the sky," a line so applicable to life in our world today that newspapers and cable TV depict nonstop insanity that saturates the planet's senses—human beings trapped in an asylum on which a torrent of madness falls contemptuously from the sky. In the 1960s it was Vietnam, and today it's Iraq, Syria and ISIS. No one ever learns: war doesn't work . . . revenge doesn't work. All that happens is that thousands of people get killed and nothing ever changes.

❖❖❖❖

I returned to Paris in the mid-1960s and took up residence in a hotel on its Left Bank. I was twenty-four-years-old, adrift in a world of literature, yoga, quasi-spirituality, drugs, and a deep need find my way out of a labyrinthine mental and emotional swamp I'd lived in since my early teens. Obsessed with the written word, yet unable to write anything but visionary poetry that I never published, I lived in a hotel on Rue Dauphine, an eight-francs-a-night *chambre de bonne*-type room on the hotel's top floor—very light and airy, small, but comfortable—and much better than any Parisian hotel room I'd ever inhabited. A few blocks from Pont Neuf, from Odeon, from Saint Germain des Prés, from Boulevard St. Michel, and the Louvre just across the Seine, at the bohemian heart of a city where painters, musicians and writers had lived and worked at their craft for hundreds of years, I'd smoke a joint, meditate, and walk over to the Louvre where I spent hours in front of Renaissance religious paintings. I'd enjoy a *café crème* and *petit pain* for breakfast, then attempt to write poetry or read a classic novel or study the Bhagavad Gita and Vedic texts translated into English, a monk-like existence that forced me to examine my inner life and try to come to terms with the chaos I saw. I studied fine sculpture and paintings, focused on great novels and poetry, tried to absorb what writers and artists of every age had to say, but there was an internal abyss I couldn't cross. All of that study brought no inner peace. I was still angry, unhappy, and unfulfilled by my efforts to write. When George Whitman invited me to read my poetry at Shakespeare and Company, my world opened a bit. I met other writers and artists. We'd gather in bars at night and get drunk or smoke dope in hotel rooms and talk about poetry and literature, but none of that reduced my internal confusion. Regardless of how much culture I tried to absorb, a hole remained in my gut that nervous energy and insecurity couldn't fill.

The Parisian street scene was a combination of madcap entertainers, storytellers, ballet dancers, mimes, sidewalk artists, and other acts that compelled me to take long walks from Rue Dauphine to the Contrescarpe or to Montparnasse or Montmartre or to the Arc de Triomphe to be entertained by talented street performers. Like an elegantly dressed high-end prostitute, the city seduced me wherever I went. I believed that Paris would inspire me to write a book that was hidden in a place deep inside myself. It would help me tap talent that I knew was there—a work of literary fiction that would bring personal satisfaction as well as success in the world. I had never been averse to benefits accrued by large sums of money, but the thought of time spent in ether-ridden and soulless corporate environments, the very thought brought on a severe case of nausea. There had to be another way. Perhaps theater or film or perhaps that undiscovered book hidden in my gut would bring a touch of fame and fortune. It was a mystery to me. No business or profession inspired me to sacrifice myself to its calling. It wasn't weakness. It was more like the deadness in people's eyes, the burnout, the sickness, and for what, to work twelve hours a day with shark-like and ambitious folks ready to step over each other to attain their goals. It had little appeal to a twenty-four-year-old writer who had come to live in Paris. Would the "City of Light" help me write that book? I didn't know, but I would do everything in my power to find out.

Obsessed with Oriental mysticism, with the art and culture of the East, I retained the thought: I must go to India to find a guru. Every day, I'd spend half an hour to an hour in my hotel room chanting *Hare Krishna* or *Om*. I'd sit cross-legged on the floor and make half-assed attempts to meditate; I'd smoke a joint and watch my mind wander into cosmic realms where astral and Bardo entities welcomed me; I'd eat in macrobiotic restaurants and spend time at the Musee Guimet where I'd sit in front of a Cambodian statue of Buddha and ask it to help me find my spiritual path. It was more than passing fancy. My need to be with God transcended every other need. "Could I go to India?" I'd ask myself. "What would I find there? Did I really want to be a monk? Did I want to live in an ashram and devote my life to God?" Driven by intense inner needs that conflicted with each other, I couldn't make two plus two equal four. I was a seeker after truth and a master of nothing, and most of my goals were out of joint. Horny as hell and in need of a girlfriend, I'd internalize these problems, and rarely, if ever, spoke about them with anyone.

I lived with a mistaken belief that literature should tap the mystical. In my reading I discovered that much of what was called literary fiction in the mid-twentieth century was a formless attempt to put words together that had little or no substance. Writers created a new language that had nothing to say. It was like reading books written in some kind of hieroglyphic. The mystical had almost no place in novel writing in which sterile and formless words had taken its place. I looked for the same spirit in modern-day works that I had found in Old Master paintings and ancient Buddhist and Hindu art. I came up empty. The spiritual was relegated to a no-man's land where life and death co-mingled in dreamlike landscapes that had nothing to do with twentieth-century reality. Suspended in that dream space, I didn't know where to look for inspiration. A few writers peeked through. One was Henry Miller whose books combined a street-smart vision of the world with profundity, and a raw, gut-wrenching exploration of his own life that I could relate to. In one of his books, he said, "A writer writes because he has something to say." I believed this, but discovered that in most contemporary books, writers wrote without having anything to say. They wrote for money or fame or they just wrote a book for the sake of writing a book. Mediocrity was the rule of thumb: literary pop art that dulled the mind and senses, and sold millions of books.

❖❖❖❖

Late one night I walked through the backstreets of the Parisian Left Bank with a stoned American friend who had a greater obsession with Oriental religion than I, a friend who kneeled on the pavement and threw his arms up in the air, waved his hands, and cried out, "O sacred Kundalini in the sky!" He had tears in his eyes. He bowed and hit his forehead on the pavement and lay face down with his arms stretched above his head and chanted a Hindu mantra. When he finished, he sat up and said to me, "I'm going to India. I need to find a teacher. I need to do something besides talk about spiritual things." He left Paris the next day. I never saw him again and always wondered if he found what he was looking for.

In the Rue Dauphine Hotel, my next-door neighbor was an American writer named Hal. He was about my age and he held mini-soirées in his room. He'd invite four or five young artists and writers to spend a few hours over tea and hashish, and discuss art, music, and literature. It was at one of Hal's soirées that I met Marian. A group of young people had already gathered when I entered his room. The smoke was thick and the smell of hashish even thicker. Everyone was stoned except for a beautiful eighteen-year-old German girl. Tall, almost statuesque, she stood out from a crowd of drugged-out hippie types like a blond goddess on a brief visit to earth. She reminded me of the actress Ursula Andress. I was immediately taken with her. The conversation turned from Picasso to Satie to Pollock to Miro and back again to Picasso—major advances in modern art and its internal depiction of the human condition. Form no longer mattered. What mattered was insight into the human mind, abstraction, and color, an internal search for a new kind of beauty and truth. It was an interesting conversation, but even more interesting to me was Marian, the German girl, who was silent, but whose very presence said a great deal to me. At the end of the evening, I asked her if we could meet tomorrow for lunch. She smiled, and said, "Yes." That was the beginning of a three-year relationship.

"Hey," Hal said to me as I got up to leave. "Next Tuesday evening, I've invited poet friends of mine to come here and read. Can you read your poems?" "Okay," I replied. "Thanks for the invite."

❖❖❖❖

Marian and I met in my room the next day and went out to a small, inexpensive restaurant and spoke about our past lives, our ambitions, and tried to get to know one another. She was born on Sylt, a small Frisian island in the North Sea, not far from Denmark, and famous for its nudist beaches. A Valkyrie of sorts, she had strong Germanic beauty, steely blue eyes, long blond hair, and a statuesque figure, sexy and vivacious, a young woman with ageless beauty. Her parents had moved to Chicago when she was very young, and she had lived most of her early life with an aunt on Sylt. "I moved to Chicago when I was twelve-years-old," she said. That explained her almost perfect English. "What are you doing in Paris?" I asked her. "I wanted to see Europe, to travel, to just get away from my parents and be on my own." She's eighteen, I thought, with a sense of independence you rarely find in a girl her age. That night she stayed with me at the Hotel Dauphine, and the next day, and just about every day after we hung out together. We'd go to museums and talk about the works of Van Gogh, Monet, Manet, Pissarro, and other Impressionist and Post-Impressionist painters that had great influence on modern art. I could never quite figure if she liked art or she liked me and would tolerate my deep interest in literature and painting. It didn't matter to me. In the first few months of a relationship one could do nothing wrong. The sex was frequent and great, and we both took interest in each other's life.

On Tuesday, I went with Marian to Hal's soirée and met a number of American and English poets. Hal asked me to read a long poem I had written called *Amphitheatre*. It received great response from the people present. "Hey, Stuart, where the hell have you been?" an African-American poet named Ted asked me. "Here, in Paris, minding my own business," I responded. "I'm gonna put on a big cultural event with poets and musicians, and I'd like you to read." "Cool," I said. "Just tell me when." "I'll be in touch," he replied.

For most of my young life I'd been introverted and moody, and had difficulty with people that thrust themselves into the spotlight. I believed that quality should be thrust into the spotlight. For whatever reason superficiality and brazenness brought influence and success, and real artistic endeavor had become secondary to personality and hustle. Whether it was in film, theater, music or art, contemporary masterpieces were rare. Artists and filmmakers that critics called masters (auteurs) were often prime characters in an Emperor's New Clothes fable. Publicists hustled them into the limelight. Paris was no different. The art and literary scene there forced me to focus on Old Master paintings, on ancient Hindu and Buddhist art, on the writings of nineteenth-century masters like Dostoyevsky and Tolstoy, on poets like Shelley, Coleridge and Keats, on places where I could find both beauty and truth. When I couldn't translate what I found deep inside myself into a poem or a story, it didn't matter. I had faith that someday I would find a door that opened onto a world of divine beauty.

Marian discovered that I could be introverted and moody. I was used to being alone; I had always struggled with my own demons and it was difficult for me to make room for another person. My non-structured, almost gypsy-like life never considered a career or future. I was insecure about my chosen paths, both literary and spiritual. I had yet to master either of them and saw no immediate success. Keep at it, I thought, without the foggiest idea where that thought would take me.

Marian had a stoic side: cold and withdrawn, she'd disappear into a place within herself that was difficult for me to enter. She didn't care a hoot for money or luxury, being eighteen, a sense of ambition had yet to enter her consciousness. We lived on what little we had, and neither of us complained. "You know my greatest fear?" I asked her. "What?" "That I will become a monk. The spiritual thing is so strong in me that it often takes over." She laughed. "You like sex too much to bury yourself in a monastery," she said. We didn't fight at all and usually made love at least once or twice a day. When I'd get moody or withdrawn, when I'd sit and meditate or chant *Hare Krishna* or *Om*, when I tried to write a poem or a short story, she'd leave our room, go to a *tabac* down the street, order a café crème and smoke a cigarette or two. "It's what you are," she told me, "and I love that you do this strange work on yourself. You're different than any man I've ever known."

Raymond Ajavon was a Dahomey-born black African actor friend of mine whose father, a journalist, was assassinated for having written and published the truth about Dahomean politics. Raymond and his mother had to flee their native country and take asylum in France. He told me about an American filmmaker who was looking for a lead actor to cast in a film that would be shot in Paris. "You the perfect type, *mon ami*. Audition for him. He will pay you money." He gave me the filmmaker's name. I knew of this filmmaker. He had made a film in New York that won a number of awards. It starred a French actress who had lived in Greenwich Village at the time and was a quasi-friend of mine. This woman now lived in Paris and we had met a month before. I telephoned her. "Yes, you are the perfect type," she said. "I would have told you when we met, but didn't know you are an actor." "I have some training," I told her. "*Bon,*" she said. "I will tell the director and let you know when there's an audition."

The audition went well. I received two callbacks and was told by the producer and director that the part was mine. We would start shooting in a few weeks and they would get me a script. We would have to sign a contract. The producer's office would prepare it. If I had an attorney, I should show it to him. There was enough money involved that Marian and I could live in Paris for almost a year. Two weeks went by and I heard nothing from either the producer or director. I called my French actress friend, but she didn't know anything. I had no idea how to get in touch with either the producer or director. They always contacted me. It was a strange two weeks. Expectations were high and the thought of a decent amount of money was in my head. When I bumped into the producer and director in a café on Boulevard Saint-Germain, they told me that production would begin in a few weeks. They had hired Pierre Clementi, a well-known and up-and-coming French actor, to do my part. "He has some time between projects," the producer said. "But the character's a twenty-five-year-old American hippie who lives in Paris." "Yeah, we know. We just had to do some rewrites." I don't know if they ever made that movie. I never saw it in the theaters. Marian told me not to worry. "Something else will come along." I didn't know what. The money I possessed slowly diminished and I didn't want to sell newspapers on the streets. I didn't blame the producer and the director. They were looking out for their own interests. I was an unknown. Pierre Clementi had a serious reputation as an actor in France.

A few days later, I met the African-American poet Ted in a café. "I've set up the event," he said. "It will be on Sunday in two weeks. I really want you to read. Your poems are great and people need to know about them." "Okay," I replied. "Just give me the address and time and I'll be there." "Be sure to bring that *Amphitheatre* poem you wrote. I just loved it."

The event took place in a large studio in the 6th Arrondissement. It was well advertised and packed. Marion and I sat in the front and Ted came up to us. "Hey, man, how ya doin'? Look, it's like this. Leroy is here and Stokeley," and he named a few other African-American celebrities. "I don't want you to read." "That sucks," I said. "Why the hell did you invite me to read in the first place?" He didn't answer. He got up and joined a group of black men and women at the other side of the room. Ted was the master of ceremonies. When he recited a poem about chocolate soldiers, Marian and I got up and left. "It's that same freakin' world of ego and self-importance that I hated in New York," I said to her. I was very angry. "I can't stand it." She didn't respond. A few days later my anger subsided. I realized that the poems I wrote were spiritual by nature. They weren't revolutionary, anti-American or anti-anything. They were the outpourings of a young man in search of God. Why should I give a shit about those people? My spiritual life was more important than a poetry reading in Paris. If it was fame I wanted, I had better take up another profession. "Let's get out of Paris," I said to Marian. "I've always wanted to visit Marrakech. What do you say? Let's go. We can live there without being bothered by all this bullshit. It's much less expensive than Paris." A week later, we packed our things and hitchhiked from Paris to Spain, took a train to Alicante, a boat to Ceuta, a bus to Tetouan, and another bus to Casablanca and Marrakech. We were in Morocco.

CHAPTER 17

It's easy for people to believe that evolved spiritual beings are born that way—avatars come to earth to uplift transient beings and teach them about the ways of God. The Tibetans believe that *rinpoches* and *dalai lamas* are incarnated beings that have lived many lifetimes. Bodhisattvas also return to earth to relieve the suffering of human beings. As highly evolved as a *rinpoche* or the Dalai Lama is, they still undergo arduous spiritual training. They're taught to master rituals and ceremonies, sutras and iconographies, and the most rigorous aspects of Tibetan Buddhism.

In Rudi's meditation practice there are no reincarnated lamas, no avatars, or great saints born from lotus flowers. The people are born in places like East New York and the South Bronx, people who come from ordinary backgrounds, but somehow find each other, learn from each other, transcend the commonplace and walk a spiritual path. No royal family surrounds the king; no chosen successor takes over the throne; no gilded lineage of *siddhas* comes to earth to enlighten the masses. Rudi bequeathed to his students a double-breathing exercise that anyone can learn. What separates ordinary from extraordinary students is the amount of work they invest to develop a chakra system that's strong enough to connect with God. It's easier to convince oneself that a weekly visit to a church, a synagogue or a temple is enough time invested to have a spiritual life. I am a Buddhist, a Christian, a Jew, or whatever, but does the "I am" go deep enough inside a person to connect with higher creative energy? Does religious ritual pierce an internal carapace behind which most people hide? Does it just coat us with a veneer of sweetness that assuages guilt, fear, and insecurity without ever getting to the root of the problem? These are questions that true seekers have to ask themselves when they are alone and forced to be honest about the depth of their spiritual practice, questions most human beings are afraid to ask. Their answers are avoided like the plague. Instead, people substitute superficial solutions that relieve symptoms, but never get to their source.

❖❖❖❖

Chakras aren't just an esoteric or thought-provoking idea you read about in books. They're primal energy centers that evoke inner change. If the chakra system is congested and overrun by tension, internal circuits disconnect and creative energy ceases to flow: it stagnates, becomes lethargic, lugubrious, and daily life becomes immobile. Ego's tumescent presence takes over and what we're left with is a false image of self. Human beings have strong resistance to change even if what changes makes their lives better. The most difficult of all things to change are one's ideas, opinions, prejudices, and sense of rightness. We hold on to what's killing us and refuse to let go. It's a familiar, recognizable trait, something we feel comfortable with, and it protects us from the unknown. If we're ever to rid ourselves of inner turmoil, change is essential— not just change of environment, friends, and jobs, but internal change that renews the way we see life. There's always a part of every human being that's a little crazy. We need it if for no other reason than to remind ourselves that we haven't been enlightened yet. High attainments crystallize when they become ends in themselves and gnaw at the very core of our being. Either we use them to grow, or we allow inertia to paralyze our inner lives.

Each chakra must undergo transformation. The *hara*, for instance, is often overlooked in most meditation practices. It's an area so essential to spiritual growth that when undeveloped, our systems are never in balance. We're taught to vomit up our tensions on the world, to argue, to prove a point, and to never let anyone best us in a situation. It's no different than a bowel movement. We feel relief for a moment, but the next day we have to go to the toilet again. The tensions released on friends and loved ones don't resolve any problems. The moment we learn to focus our attention in the *hara*, anger dissipates, fear dissolves, anxieties begin to disappear, and we feel inner calm.

The heart center is very similar. The seat of emotions and much disquiet, like a whirlpool it pulls us into a turbulent river of disaffected feelings, and keeps us from ever being happy. The moment we transform emotional imbalance into joy and love, the entire inner life of a human being changes. We discover that happiness is life's foremost treasure. To be happy the mind has to be quiet, the heart open, and the *hara*, like a full-blown lotus flower, becomes a Buddha-base that supports our entire inner life. The noise in our head diminishes and we receive higher knowledge and wisdom, and the words we speak channel that wisdom when we interact with the world.

The most important transformation takes place in the sexual area where all elements undergo an almost alchemical change that activates kundalini. As mentioned earlier, the male/female principles merge, and the soul of a human being connects with the soul of the universe and spiritual enlightenment takes place. Transformation is the key. When the inner life of a human being changes, the external world will also change. One is just a reflection of the other. We're trained from an early age to believe that change in the outer world will benefit us and make our lives easier. It never does. The outer world is a reflection of our internal life. If we want real change then we must transform our inner problems into harmony, balance and love.

The universe is ready to provide answers to whatever questions we ask. It has a vast resource of wisdom, and dispenses knowledge to whoever is ready to listen. Most questions have little or nothing to do with a spiritual life. They're about money, success, marriage, children, and a host of other conundrums that people think will bring happiness. People concern themselves with earthly attainments and the role they play in life's ongoing soap opera, they concern themselves with what they possess and with whom they possess it. Little attention is paid to spirit. It's almost a non-existent factor in the lives of most human beings, something shoved into a corner, discarded, and an embarrassment on many occasions. God has died a slow death in a secular world and hasn't been revived yet. No one has time to pay attention to Him. They're too busy chasing money to focus on their inner lives; they're too tense to recognize that they've lost themselves in a whirlwind of delusion. They've even forgotten what questions to ask. It's like a strange joke. Knowledge, wisdom, a deep understanding of life, a purposeful life that's full of love and joy has been lost in a deluge of mistaken goals. Human beings are blinded by the glitter of material things. They can't see two inches in front of their noses. It's like the mad and the blind in a dance to the death. What stops this dance? Trauma, recognition of one's own mortality, burnout, illness, and the death of a loved one: dramas that stop us in our tracks and make us reconsider the way we live, a moment in mayhem's pulse when nothing makes sense and all our attainments amount to a six-foot grave. We discover our mortality, and there's nothing that any of us can do about it.

Very few people begin meditation because they want a spiritual life. They usually start because of personal difficulties: tension, relationship or money problems, the lack of a relationship, mental or emotional discord, sundry reasons other than a need for a spiritual life. The need for a spiritual life comes once they get over the initial problem. When confronted with a decision of whether or not to continue meditation, most people leave. A spiritual life isn't on their agenda. Those that stay because they want a spiritual life will discover that meditation prepares them to receive wisdom and knowledge. They are the "chosen"—a small group of individuals who open deeply enough inside themselves to let the universe guide their lives. Higher will and human will dance together to the beat of the heart, and this sacred marriage gives birth to teachings that are passed on from generation to generation.

❖❖❖❖

Disharmony in daily life mirrors imbalance inside people. It also mirrors mental and emotional conflict that's projected onto life's screen when we attempt to figure out what's wrong with the world. It's a game of checks and balances that no one wins because the focus is on symptoms, not their causes. The external world is a peaceable kingdom that human dysfunction turns into a jungle. The real illness is located deep inside every person—a force so powerful that it disrupts the natural order of things. It not only creates external conflict, it creates illness that decimates both mind and body. Like Shakespeare said, "Something is rotten in the state of Denmark." But something can't be rotten in the state of Denmark if there isn't rottenness in the people that live there. Not only its rulers, the entire country (or world) is infected with a cancer that eats away at the core of well-being, a disease replicated by political acts, war, social injustice, religious injustice, family dysfunction. That metaphorical cancer can't be cured unless people do something about their inner lives, and there's the old Shakespearean "rub." Little is done to alleviate inner turmoil, and a great deal is done to manipulate a shadow world by use of reason. No wonder people are always at odds with each other. The healing process can't begin unless we take full responsibility for our actions. It requires internal change and a transformation of negative energy into kindness, love, and compassion—an almost impossible thing for people to do without training. The chakra system needs to be realigned, and healing will be systemic when the heart opens and there's a glint of joy and happiness. It doesn't mean we live forever. What it means is we've transformed the metaphorical cancer into a positive energy, and we no longer radiate fear, insecurity, anger, and a solipsistic need to transform the world into our own distorted image.

Self-healing is difficult to accomplish. The reason is simple: we're up against a chaotic energy force that creates all the problems, the human mind. Magnified out of proportion, caustic, unhappy, yet full of life and ready to do the outrageous, the mind buries us beneath delusive layers of tension and creates mysteries we will never understand. The interior life of a human being is a mirror image of the entire universe. The seven basic chakras are like planets that evolve around the sun. The meridians are like stars and moons, and spirit is like a sun-source that nurtures life. If our inner life is out of balance, if it's congested by tension too extreme, the flow of spiritual energy will clog up and create illnesses of every conceivable nature.

Relaxation is a temporary fix that does nothing to uproot problems that are buried deep inside us. When there's pressure at home or at work, a whirlpool of repressed anger often surfaces, a force of nature too strong to keep under control. We lash out at people we love and forget to rein in our emotions. We subject them to verbal and mental abuse. Nothing relieves the pressure we feel in our gut. Neither logic nor reason can bring our system back into balance. We analyze our problems to the nth degree, listen to pundits pontificate about the development of inner strength and how to find success, about how to meet our goals, and how to heal ourselves with love and affection. Rarely, if ever, does anyone teach a technique that can dredge up tension and flush it out. Pundits and quasi-gurus give advice. They coach us and point out weaknesses and deficiencies, but most people need more than that. Without chakra development the complex inner life of a human being, often mysterious and wracked with tension, is too chaotic for them to keep from being eaten alive by mental, emotional and sexual energies.

❖❖❖❖

I've done hands-on healing practice with people that have physical problems ranging from headaches to cancer and AIDS. Over the years this work has given me deep insight into the cause of illness. Tension erodes cells and organs in the body, and tumors feed off impurities that thrive in a weakened immune system. Dietary cleanse is essential for the body to renew itself: vegetable juice fasts, colonics, enemas, and wheat grass, anything to reduce impurities that feed tumors. The next step in the healing process is inner work. If the mind and emotions become quiet and *chi* develops in the *hara*, internal strength is built that helps to overcome serious illness. Illness can be intense, unexpected, and drain vital energy needed for healing.

Under Rudi's tutelage my first attempt at hands-on healing was a powerful introduction to intense, negative energy secreted by carcinogenic tumors. I placed my finger on his patient's forehead. Tension was released of such an extreme nature that I fainted at her feet. I tried to draw the negative energy into my *hara* and transform it into *chi*, but the energy was too strong and it flooded my entire system. I wasn't strong enough to absorb it. Rudi smacked me a few times and made me walk around the block to revive myself. "You can't absorb negative energy that intense," he said to me when I returned to his store. "It's stupid to try. You've got to drop the tension as it comes into your system. You're not strong enough to absorb it." He smiled and looked at me for a moment. "You'll be a healer," he said to me. "You were just inoculated, given the disease, and it has strengthened your chakra system. You'll be able to heal people in the future."

Years of deep inner work developed my chakra system, and when I performed hands-on healing I was able to draw the negative energy into my *hara* and through the sexual area to the base of the spine. The kundalini burned up all the impurities. I discovered that sexual energy is key to healing because energy drawn through the sex undergoes a major rebirth. The lower elements of life are transmuted there into a force that activates kundalini—a fire at the base of the spine that will burn up impurities secreted from tumors, heart conditions, or any other illness. The healing process extracts negative quantities from diseased areas of the body and replaces them with positive energy. Tumors feed off impurities in the immune system and when those impurities are eliminated, tumors will dry up. Old habits must be reversed: the food people eat, their friends, associates, the place where they live, anything that attracts physical, mental or emotional toxicity. A major life change is essential to keep the problem from returning. At first it's difficult, but once a person gets used to a more conscious lifestyle and discovers that they remain healthy, every choice made will support the healing process.

When I first had healing sessions with cancer and AIDS patients, I had to absorb negative energy emitted from the disease into my chakra system. I brought it to the *hara* and transformed it into *chi*, and it took hours for me to detoxify. Afraid that I would come down with the disease I realized the patient must heal himself. I can absorb only so much poison before it will flood my system. I changed my method of working. When I placed my hand on the diseased part of a person's body, instead of absorbing negative energy into my chakra system I channeled it to the patient's *hara*. Once it's transformed into *chi*, I thought, the energy moves through the sex to the base of the spine and feeds kundalini. The process hasn't changed. The difference is that the psychic muscle system of the patient is now doing the work. With my help, the patient could heal himself. The results were remarkable and I learned a new way of hands-on healing that not only improved people's conditions, it kept me from getting sick.

A person's fear of death is tantamount to everything. He or

she wants to add another year or two or ten to their lifespan. They never think about a spiritual life, about connecting their consciousness to energy that's infinite in the universe. They want to return to a lifestyle that created the tumor in the first place. The transient nature of life makes no impression on them, and they believe that once they are healed the illness won't return. Being one step from death's door has taught the patient nothing. They continue to live in a delusional world that embraces pain and suffering, and they ride karma's merry-go-round until death finally takes them. The miracle of life is lost in forgetfulness, and people assume they will never get sick again. Time is wasted, ego glorified, and little or no attention is paid to spiritual matters. Life has lost its creative spark. It becomes a frantic effort to prolong time (even if nothing is done with it) and all of time's encumbrances.

The fear of death should make every breath sacrosanct, every act a miracle, life so precious that we never take anything for granted. If we're afraid of life we're going to be afraid of death. The reverse is also true. If we love life, death will turn into a friend. When the heart opens and the chakra system connects with infinite energy, both life and death merge in a joyous dance. They cancel each other out. We eliminate fear, and time ceases to be a burden. We embrace *samadhi* in much the same way we embrace the miraculous world we live in.

Most people who worship at the altars of money and power live Mickey Mouse lifestyles, fabricate an absurd existence from material things, and never ask themselves the question, "Who am I?" or courageously receive real answers. I've often asked myself the question, "Can we ever be truly healed?" After many years of spiritual practice, I've discovered that the answer is "yes." It's a tricky answer because "yes" has nothing to do with how long we live. It has only to do with whether or not we are happy people. If our hearts are open, if there's love inside us, we've been healed from the most insidious of all diseases: fear of life and death, and internal pain that won't allow human beings to live their lives to the fullest.

❖❖❖❖

A spiritual teacher should never determine how his disciples live. His responsibility is to transmit teachings in the form of *shakti,* and nurture students so they build enough confidence in themselves to find their path through life. The teacher must recognize each student's uniqueness and nurture that uniqueness so it finds a place in the world. As Rudi once told me, "You can be a second-rate Rudi or a first-rate Stuart." Any attempt to clone students creates robotic spirituality; it creates people that are shackled by dogma, ritual, and another person's vision of God without the freedom to explore life and to find personal paths to enlightenment. There's one danger in all of this—lack of gratitude, forgetfulness, rearranging history to bolster one's image, and shine in the eyes of others.

Finding a unique path doesn't mean we forget where we've come from. It should deepen one's gratitude; it should make us more respectful of people who made an effort to help us in our lives. When Rudi broke with Swami Muktananda, he never denied the thirteen years he spent under Baba's tutelage. He was grateful to Baba, but he knew that it was time to leave, time to move on, that he no longer needed to be treated like a shaggy dog that begged for scraps of food from his master. He had gotten everything he could get from Muktananda, and he had to follow his own path.

When Muktananda first came to New York, Rudi treated him with the respect and dignity that one treats a great spiritual master. There was more gratitude than I'd ever seen in my life. Baba's needs were taken care of; whatever he wanted was granted to him. In return, Rudi's life was turned upside down, and he never received an ounce of respect from Muktananda or members of his retinue. "What does it matter?" he said to me. "Whatever I surrender to him will be replaced by God's energy. Baba is helping me to grow."

Though a young spiritual student at the time, my allegiances were clear. I knew Rudi's meditation practice would help me get to God. I didn't understand spiritual politics. It struck me that Muktananda either detested Rudi or was deeply jealous of a dynamic Westerner who could not only transmit *shakti,* he could transmit deep love and compassion to his students. Muktananda transmitted strong *shaktipat,* but it lacked heart, and I never felt comfortable in his presence. He had picked apart Rudi's ashram, and, with horror, I watched many of Rudi's closest students inform Rudi that he was history. "You never serve people," Rudi said to me. "You don't know what they are going to do from day to day. The only constant in the world is higher energy. If you serve God you will never be disappointed." He surrendered his students, his ashram, and meditation practice. He even offered Muktananda his business. "A void has to be filled," he said to me, "and what better way to fill it than with higher energy."

Three months after Rudi broke with Muktananda, on a trip to India we decided to visit Ganeshpuri and pay homage at Swami Nityananda's shrine. The drive from Bombay to Ganeshpuri was about three hours. When we reached the village, our car drove past Muktananda's ashram. Three of Baba's disciples came onto the road and stopped our car. They opened the door and grabbed Rudi by the arm. "You have to see Baba," they screamed at him. "You cannot disrespect him." "Did Baba send you to get me?" Rudi asked them. "Yes," they shouted. "He wants to see you." They tried to pull Rudi from the car. He pushed them away and told the driver to take us to Nityananda's shrine. I never found out who was responsible for that outrage. Nor did I care. It made me sick to think that a swami of Baba's stature had so little self-respect. Rudi no longer needed to play astral games with Muktananda, he no longer needed to be treated like an untouchable that lived in the West. He worked harder at his spiritual life than anyone I'd ever met, and deserved respect for his efforts. If Muktananda was too self-involved to recognize that he'd lost his greatest student, there was nothing Rudi could do about it.

No teacher could shackle Rudi's iconoclastic energy. What I love most about Rudi's spiritual work is that it gives one room to explore their own life. He never told anyone how to live. He understood that if one surrenders deep enough inside, the energy of God would guide them on their own unique path.

❖❖❖

Mudra is an aspect of meditation practice that can't be taught. It develops as a student's inner life expands and spiritual energy transforms their hands into healing instruments. Examples of mudra can be seen in paintings or statues of the Buddha or Christ.

The movement or position of a meditation practitioner's hands will open energy fields in different parts of the cosmos. This can be diagrammed and explained, and names can be given to each hand position, but intellectual understanding of mudra will not make it experiential. There are chakras at the center of the palms of both hands, in every finger joint and the tips of each finger, and these chakras draw energy from the cosmos. They will instigate hand movements and bring higher energy to the system of a meditation practitioner. *Shakti* will enter each of the seven main chakras and strengthen them. The slightest movement of the hands will change the energy field.

Healing hands are the highest expression of mudra, Bodhisattva-type hands that are instruments of God and can be used to help people overcome emotional, mental and physical problems—hands that no longer belong to the meditation practitioner, but are gifts of God given to those who can transmit *shakti*. The mastery of mudra is an organic process that no time clock can predict. When we've advanced in our spiritual work it becomes integral to a meditation practitioner's repertoire and helps them to absorb and transmit *shakti*. When the mind convinces us we're ready to practice mudra, each movement upsets internal balance. The hands become string puppets controlled by thought not spirit. Mudra's purpose is to uplift the soul of a human being, open new sources of creative energy, and revive an inner life that hungers to be with God. If used in healing, the hands become divine instruments that save lives.

If we sit in lotus or half-lotus position during a meditation session, our soles are pointed upward and they will draw cosmic energy into the chakra system. When we walk, stand, or sit, our soles will draw energy from the earth. In Chinese medicine there is a meridian in the feet for every organ of the body. I've often had reflexology, a form of massage that works directly on the meridians in the feet. The pain is sometimes excruciating. When I asked the reflexologist why, she said, "There are obstructions in your kidneys, your liver, and stomach, and the pain you feel is because I'm working through those blocks. If there were no blocks in those organs, there would be no pain in your feet."

We are an amalgam of finely tuned meridians that have weathered badly because of a lack of attention. They're like short-circuited electrical wires in a house. Body and mind have broken down, and need to be restored. It's necessary for us to find an electrician who can rewire the house and turn on the lights. The opportunity for spiritual growth presents itself to most people, but the question is: are they wise enough to take advantage of the gift or do they let age short-circuit their wiring and decimate body and mind? That question often goes unanswered. Most people don't recognize opportunity when it's directly in front of them. Their well-constructed and highly insulated realities have to crumble before they get serious about spiritual practice. Money and success are nothing more than a band-aid. The moment there's a fissure in the internal house's foundation, money and success become meaningless, and people look for spiritual guidance to help resolve their quandaries. It's only through deep inner work that spirit reveals itself and we can use it to repair the damage done by an unconscious life.

❖❖❖❖

At the core of every religion there's a mystical element that resembles the meditation technique that Rudi developed. If we exhume hidden textual doctrines, layers of meaning beneath the surface guide one into realms of enlightenment. We'll discover that a word isn't just a word, it's a pathway to knowledge, a symbol or metaphor that can unravel profound insights we could dwell on for days. Has there ever been a more revealing chapter in a book than the Old Testament's Exodus? The "chosen" people are slaves of a ruthless master. Is this a metaphor or an historical fact, or both?

If taken as metaphor the image suggests that we are all slaves to some kind of intolerant master. It could be political, religious, a job, a marriage, economic woes, illness or self-righteousness: some internal or external condition that keeps us from being free—a metaphorical Red Sea that needs to part and give us room to breathe. The illusion of freedom is just as much a prison as overt slavery. A prismatic lens that blinds us to our real needs and creates a wall that keeps the rest of the world out. They take the form of class systems, religious enclaves, ideas of right and wrong, and personal images we have of self: who we are, what we want out of life, our importance, a plethora of distortion that never permits life's lens to focus. The walls of our prison are built from invisible materials. We suffer from self-inflicted emotional and mental wounds that create an internal Red Sea. The force of kundalini is like the rod of Moses. When it's awakened from a deep sleep, kundalini will rise up the spine, dissolve inner blocks, and create a pathway to enlightenment. It will part our personal Red Sea and let the "chosen" (us) become one with spirit or, as the Old Testament puts it, enter the Promised Land.

The Old Testament is full of metaphorical images that are applicable to life today. The walls of Jericho, the burning bush, Noah's Ark, the Jordan River, Sodom and Gomorrah, the idea of Genesis, and a thousand others, all of them appropriate to twenty-first-century life. They can be seen as silly metaphors or even science-fiction stories when looked at with rational eyes, but as poetry, as symbols, as a mysterious vision of stratified layers of consciousness, they touch on the human condition in a profound way. We just have to see beneath surface meanings, look past chronology and into Kabbalah's mysterious interpretation of biblical themes. I've been asked many times: Is there a "chosen" people? I've answered with an unequivocal "yes," but I would not stigmatize the Jewish religion with this impossible nomenclature. There's another way to look at it. The entire human race has been "chosen" from birth and every individual has an opportunity to become one with God. "Chosen" doesn't distinguish between religions and races, but gives whoever is born a clear path to enlightenment. Whether or not they take this path is another question. The opportunity is there; the tools are inside us, but mind and emotions get in the way and create impenetrable blocks that reduce the number of "chosen" to a few who have learned to master inner chaos. When the masks peel away and our inner child is freed of karmic encumbrances, when that child is happy and full of love, it shares a joyous state with other people and becomes a compassionate human being who has managed to unshackle himself from images of mind and ego, from an internal "wall of Jericho" that comes tumbling down.

❖❖❖❖

Before I met Rudi, I had rejected social norms and lived in a gypsy world of my own creation. Money and success meant nothing to me. "Make enough to pay your rent, eat, and get through the day," I'd say to myself. "Focus on writing, art, literature, and different ways to meditate and connect with spirit." Shelley's poem about Ozymandias had a deep effect on me: a traveler in an ancient land who points to a grave: *Here lies Ozymandias, King of Kings.* The absurdity of ambition, the grave, all made egocentric aspirations vanish from my life. I wondered why human beings struggle for power and success. There was also a knot in my stomach—an insane jealousy of people who could succeed in an economic and social climate I feared to enter. "You can't surrender what you haven't experienced," Rudi told me one day in his store. The truth of that statement touched a deep inner chord. "Why am I afraid of money and success?" I asked myself. "Why do I cringe when I'm around successful people? I've rejected something that exists outside my realm of experience." "You can't be free of money until you have it," Rudi went on. You can't be free of anything until you've experienced it, I thought.

Rudi turned my view of a spiritual life upside down. Rejection was a false premise and differed from deep surrender and detachment. My ideas about money and success were immature and stemmed from fear in myself to deal with a practical world. They had to change. It wasn't money that I wanted, but freedom from money and success. I would never have that freedom until I vanquished my nemesis. The path to financial success was replete with absurdities. Would I devote my life to the manufacture of some absurd object that people bought? Does a person, at an early age, decide that glue or umbrellas or cigarettes or paper clips or house paint or some other mass-produced and mundane item will become so important to their existence that it will consume their precious time and energy? Do they dream of lollipops falling from heaven, fur coats marching down Broadway, a place in paradise for jock straps and haberdashery? Can a ten-year-old kid's thoughts and dreams ever focus on a lifetime in some office cubicle, or as a real estate agent, or a financial scam artist who hustles money from people who have gained their trust? It would be like taking a pop-art path down a surrealistic road. I didn't want to live in a self-imposed prison fabricated from an insane need to make money. Then I thought, just jump in. Does it matter what you do? It will change as you change. Something positive will emerge . . . and it did.

It started in New York City where I ran a house painting and contracting business for a year. Though it never produced a great deal of money, it produced more than enough to cover my expenses. When I moved to Denton to run Rudi's ashram, I was confronted with a set of financial pressures I had never known before. Mortgages had to be paid, a group of people had to be fed, and a host of other bills manifested at the end of every month. "A diamond is a product of fifty-thousand years of the earth's pressure," Rudi said to me with a smile, and he asked me to buy a strip mall that bordered the ashram. "I've got six hundred dollars to my name," I told him. "Anyone can do it with money," he replied. A month later I bought the property. I borrowed money to make the down payment and developed businesses to pay the mortgage: a successful restaurant, a bakery, a candy factory, and an antique store. When Rudi's mother offered to sell me two truckloads of Asian art I said to her, "Rae, do you know where I live? It's the heart of the Bible Belt." "Think about it," she replied. I thought about it for ten minutes and called her back. "Let's do it," I said. It put me in debt for almost two hundred thousand dollars. Necessity forced me to develop ambition. The money never interested me. If it did, I'd still be in Texas running an ashram, a wholesale bakery, a candy factory, a real estate development firm, and whatever else came in their wake. Instead, I moved back to New York City. My need for a spiritual life transcended my need for money. I had learned what I had to learn in Denton, and it was time to move on. I opened a gallery in New York City, and the Asian art I bought from Rudi's mother stocked it.

New York City was a different kind of dragon's nest, but one in which I made a great deal of money. The Asian art business was kind to me. I developed connections with collectors all over the world and built a strong clientele. I disliked being a merchant, but I did it anyway and discovered that I could build good rapport with clients in every economic bracket. What I liked best about the business was finding art, intrepid treasure hunts in Asia, Europe and America often felt like the film *Raiders of the Lost Ark*. They turned up wonderful paintings and sculptures that could be sold to my clients, and helped me to support the ashram I had developed on Thirteenth Street and Broadway. Almost a hundred people studied there within five years of my having returned to New York City. The classes were always free and open to whoever wished to attend. By the early 1990s meditation students of mine formed groups in cities throughout the United States, in Europe, South America, and Israel. Whatever money I made poured into the situation. I not only had to support the New York City meditation center, I had to travel and teach in centers all over the world . . . and somehow run my business. It got even more expensive when I moved into a four-thousand-square-foot loft on Fourth Avenue and Tenth Street. Once again, necessity transformed my lack of ambition into an internal force that needed to be successful. I had no other choice. But money never conflicted with my spiritual development. I didn't have an egomaniacal need for power and self-aggrandizement, but I knew that I would never be free of money until I learned how to make it. That was my true test—a major step that worked out karma. Ambition necessitated a state of detachment. Success and money no longer frightened me. They had only one purpose, to serve people in need of a spiritual life. Like my teacher Rudi said: "You can't get free of what you haven't experienced."

Spiritual training I received from Rudi enabled me to combine material ambition with an inner life. One supported the development of the other. Pressure reminded me that I had to grow every day. It forced me to tap energy so deep inside myself that the impossible became possible, and I discovered how closely the material and spiritual worlds were connected to each other. I could run an international business, have well over a hundred students, visit ashrams on four continents, and teach meditation classes six days a week in New York City. The real test was to keep my mind quiet, to stay balanced inside, and to live every day with an open heart. It took six years of meditation practice with Rudi and nine years running an ashram in Denton to create an inner base that kept me connected to spirit.

The Taoists believe in the "path of no path," a profound recognition that once you have a spiritual life, all of religion, dogma, success and failure, and other polarities dissolve into the magical kingdom of spirit. They are no longer crutches to lean on. Genesis isn't some "Big Bang" that happened a million years ago. It's the "now" recreating itself every moment of the day . . . and all one has to do is open their eyes to see it.

CHAPTER 18

Before I met Rudi, much of my time was spent in Europe and North Africa. Marijuana and hashish helped me to explore my inner life. I used that exploration to write quasi-mystical poetry or prose that transcended a mundane, day-to-day existence that focused solely on money and success . . . an existence that plagued me when I lived in New York City. Lost in my own whirlpool of imagination, taken with visionary art and poetry, I looked for Rimbaud's fabulous cities, Blake's Jerusalem, and Turner's land and seascapes. Twenty-four-years-old, intense, often stoned, unhappy, very alone in my reveries and incapable of discussing this quandary with anyone, I brooded over life's many mysteries. Beauty transcends the commonplace, I thought, and artists draw inspiration from internal connections they have with a truth that has no place in the ordinary lives of people—a reality that is as much a dream as the dreams I have at night. Their sensibility touches on the mystical and manifests as light, form, and color on canvas. Vehicles for truth and beauty to manifest on earth, they were born to create visions that make the unexplainable concrete; their creations give us insight into a world of spirit made manifest as landscapes, portraits, still lives, abstract canvases, music and three-dimensional forms. They lay bare the human soul and remind us that there are higher concerns than material wellbeing.

❖❖❖❖

Marrakech was a magical city founded in the eleventh century. Elements of its ancient past still lingered in backstreets and market places in the Medina. It was a city more biblical than modern when I lived there in 1966. Tiny streets wound in and out of each other like a warren filled with burnoose-clad and *djellabah*-clothed Moroccans that bore no resemblance to the twentieth-century life I knew in the West. Oum Kalthoum's voice could be heard from every radio, a haunting voice that followed me when I walked past silver and gold markets, textile markets, brass-pots-and-pans markets, rug markets, a market for anything handmade under the sun. I expected Aladdin and his gang of thieves to accost me as I rounded every corner. I had never seen anything like it before. It appealed to my sense of the exotic—a romantic sense that was tired of a conceptualized pop-art depiction of life that scraped the surface of human understanding.

Place Jemmaa el-Fnaa (The Square of the Dead) was more alive than any park or playground I'd ever visited in New York. It was like a scene from the Arabian Nights. There were acrobats, fortune-tellers, scribes, storytellers, dancers, magicians, snake charmers, and a host of other acts in a nonstop performance that went on from mid-morning until dusk. One particular act drew my attention: two Berber men dressed in sultan's costumes sat on either side of a long Moroccan parlor rug they had decorated with flowers, rosaries, and a host of doves that fed off seeds that covered the carpet. Each man sat in front of a hookah. The acrid smell of hashish floated through the air. The men inhaled smoke from hookahs, chanted long passages from the Koran, and bowed to each other. This went on for hours. It was some kind of sacred mystery rite that seemed rooted in the Middle Ages.

I'd visit Jemaa el-Fnaa three or four times a week. I'd sit in a café, order a mint tea, and marvel at the flow of diverse humanity that moved past: Berbers, blue people, black and brown people, colorfully-outfitted water sellers, veiled women, oxen and camels that led carts, desert people and mountain people that dressed in robes and exuded a deep-seated spirituality to a kid who was born in the Bronx. Jemaa el-Fnaa's exotic nature tantalized me. I'd smoke *kief,* and spend hours engrossed in real-life hallucinations.

My favorite act in Jemaa el-Fnaa was a black African family of men and boys who danced and played drums. They wore long white robes and tasseled fezzes, beat hypnotic rhythms, and danced nonstop for long periods of time. I became a familiar face in their circle. They'd invite me to join their group. They'd always offer me sweets, mint tea, and a *kief* pipe. The hypnotic drumbeat and *kief* kept me stoned while I listened to the music and watched them dance. An old drum player sat down next to me. He took my hand and said, "Flushing." I looked at him with a puzzled expression. He continued in English: "Me know Flushing. World's Fair . . . me dance there." He had a big smile on his face. "You know Flushing? Me . . . there . . . me . . . there." He was proud of himself. I smiled and said, "Me know Flushing, too," and thought, for God's sakes, my mother lives there. She moved from the Bronx to Flushing four years ago. The old man offered me another cake, some tea, and *kief* to smoke, got up, and continued to beat his drum.

Marian had a more difficult time in Marrakech. Blond and quite beautiful, tall and with chiseled features, her long hair and exotic looks attracted a queue of Moroccan men that followed her on the streets. She couldn't walk out of the house alone. Every morning my neighbor Mohammed, who was a police officer, and I met on the roof of my house. We'd drink mint or hashish tea and smoke a *kief* pipe together. Mohammed proposed marriage to Marian. He offered to buy her a house in Marrakech. Marian and I had a good laugh about it. Mohammed and his Egyptian wife invited us to their house a few times a week to eat couscous. They had two kids and were good neighbors. His marriage proposal never interfered with our friendship. Nor did his wife seem to mind. "How many wives can a Moroccan man have?" I asked him. "As many as he can support," was the reply. "Incredible," I replied. "It's very different in the West." The thought of Marian married to a Moroccan policeman and living the rest of her life in Marrakech afforded us both many fun moments. Nothing ever came of it, and Mohammed remained a good friend. "My dream job," he once told me (we spoke in broken French), "is to mix *kief* and tobacco every morning for the King. If I could get that job I would move to Rabat in a minute."

Marrakech's pace of life had a timeless quality to it. The days seemed like months to me and the months like years, and at times I couldn't remember if I had ever lived anywhere else. "How does it feel to be a stranger in a strange land?" Marian asked me. She never felt at home in Marrakech. She had an independent spirit but it was almost impossible for her to leave the house. The Moroccan men clustered about her like mosquitoes. A blond, Germanic woman, and quite sexy, she received more marriage proposals per minute than most women get in ten lifetimes. I was once offered three camels for her by a man in Jemaa el-Fnaa. "I'm getting fed up with it," she said. "It's like the men here have never seen a woman before." We will have to leave soon, I thought. At least in Paris she can take a walk by herself.

Marrakech's biblical cityscape reminded me that there was a God in this world. Life didn't have to be a cut-and-dry, conceptualized daily battle with material things. In Jemaa el-Fnaa there was an old Berber man who sat in half-lotus position with five or six piles of oranges in front of him. He never moved until all the oranges were sold. His patience defied all odds, and the amount of money he made enabled him to return to Jemaa el-Fnaa the next morning. When I sold newspapers on the streets of Paris, I made just enough money to pay for my life and return to work the next day. I identified with the old Berber man. The only difference was that he sat in half-lotus position and never moved. There wasn't an ounce of tension in his face—a kind of serenity that meant one thing to me, he and Allah were on the same page. How many people did I know in the West with that kind of serenity? I asked myself. Who in Manhattan would radiate nobility of soul if his occupation were that of a street vendor whose entire inventory consisted of fifteen or twenty oranges? He'd be labeled "beggar" and relegated to homeless shelters. There's not a drop of serenity in the eyes of New York City mendicants, or clochards in Paris. They're downtrodden people no one wants to befriend. They don't sit in half-lotus position on sidewalks.

❖❖❖

"We don't fit in here," Marian said to me after we'd taken a long walk through intertwined Medina streets. "You're right," I answered. It upset me to admit that. I wanted to blame her long blond hair, beautiful face and shapely build, but knew that it had nothing to do with the problem. "I love Marrakech," I replied, "and often think about spending the rest of my life here." She laughed at me. "You're a romantic at heart," she said. "No matter what you do in Marrakech, no matter where you go, no matter how many Moroccan people you meet, you'll always be a stranger ... a tourist ... someone who is an accepted and even highly-touted oddity because you come from America." She poured herself a cup of tea. "It's foolish to think otherwise. You're not a Muslim, a blue person, a Berber, a performer in the streets. You're like a peeping tom, enticed by an exotic culture that will never be your own." "Why not?" I replied angrily. I didn't want to hear any more and walked into another room, sat down, and tried to quash my anger. I've dreamt of a place like this for years, I thought, and she's telling me I don't fit. Could I meld with Moroccan culture? Could I adapt to their customs and religion? I didn't know. No matter how long I lived in Marrakech, would I always be seen as an American? If I put on a *djellabah* or a burnoose, if I went to a mosque and prayed, if I learned Arabic, if I smoked enough *kief*, maybe I'd fit in. Does any of this really matter? All my life I've felt like a stranger in a strange land.

I took a long walk through the Medina and intentionally got lost in the labyrinthine streets that wound one into another. It was a game I often played with myself. Can I find my way out? Can I get to Jemaa el-Fnaa? I turned a corner and discovered a camel auction and watched for an hour or so. I stopped at a small café and ordered a glass of mint tea and a bowl of *harira*. Though I'm lost, I laughed to myself, I've found a way of life in a city that's been hidden in time for over a thousand years, a city that has no immediate plans on catching up to the twentieth century. Is this what Rimbaud meant when he wrote about fabulous cities? I didn't know. I didn't even care. Maybe I'll never find my way out of this tapestry of interwoven streets; maybe I'll never find Jemaa el-Fnaa or a street that I know leads to my house. Marian thinks I'm crazy, but I just laugh, and tell her it will give me something to write about.

❖❖❖❖

My precarious lifestyle is rooted in confusion, I thought. There's no sense of purpose or even enough security in me to sit down and write a book. I'm a writer who doesn't know how to write—a nerve ending exposed to sundry stimuli, and each of them causes deeper confusion and keeps me at odds with myself. Insecurity overshadows *joie de vivre* that surfaces at odd moments, a desire to live that's trapped in self-induced states of depression. In a word, I'm a screwed-up kid. Even Marrakech's exotica doesn't stop depression's crippling vise. It stifles me for days at a time. I meditate for an hour every day, chant mantras, and read the Bhagavad Gita, but nothing penetrates the invisible shield I've set up inside myself a black hole that sucks joy from my life and keeps me at odds with the world. "Wherever you go," I said to myself with a chuckle, "there you are. The environment changes and the food and clothing people wear, the languages they speak, but the one thing that doesn't change is Stuart Perrin, a seeker after beauty and truth who can't live one peaceful moment." Restless and intense, the one thing that eludes me is a spiritual life. No matter how hard I try I can't connect with God. "Maybe God doesn't exist," I thought. "Maybe the world is like Godot, and I'll have to make do with an absurd existence until death comes and gives respite." I've yet to find one real answer . . . just a Pandora's box full of questions. "You're too young to comprehend life's mysteries," Raymond Ajavon said to me in a Paris café at three one morning. "You're too young to do anything but worry about the future. A solid plan, *mon ami*, for one's future at twenty-four is like living with blinders in an airless box from which there's no escape. The juice is taken out of things, *mon frère*, the adventure, the ability to renew oneself and take in landscapes full of possibility and experience."

❖❖❖❖

Marian and I left Marrakech after a four-month stay. Practical considerations impinged on remaining there any longer: money was short and our relationship became edgy. It was impossible for her to go out by herself to buy a bottle of water, some bread, a pack of cigarettes, or to sit in a café. She couldn't leave the house without me. "I'm a freakin' prisoner here," she said. "Like a pied piper for horny Moroccan men. I can't walk by myself on the streets." She discovered that I was a loner, self-involved and used to long, solitary walks, hours of struggle with my writing, an hour a day meditating, and incapable of giving her the attention she deserved. "I live a monkish kind of life," I told her, "and I'm not sure how to change." "I don't care," she replied. "Just take my hand sometimes, kiss me, show me that I have value." "It's simple," I thought. "Why can't I do that? Would a relationship interfere with my ambition to have a spiritual life?" It showed how immature I was; it showed that I lived in an either/or world that made other people suffer. "Let's go back to Paris," she said. "I've had my fill of Morocco."

Almost broke, with barely a clue as to where to make money, we left Morocco a week later. There were enough French francs to take a bus to Ceuta, a boat from Ceuta to Algeciras, and to buy *kief* in Morocco to sell in Paris. I also had two hundred and seventy-five dollars in a Parisian bank account. "Maybe there's work at Billiancourt Studios," I said to Marian. "What kind of work?" "Extra work in movies. Crap like that." "You ever do that?" "Yeah. A few years ago, I worked in two American films."

Mohammed and his friend Youseff drove Marian and myself to an enormous farmhouse in the country. It resembled a small Medina, many intertwined rooms off a passageway that wound for at least half a block. The owner, Karim, a friend of Youseff's, took us to a green-grayish room with a small round low table at its center. We sat on pillows that surrounded the table. A young boy brought mint tea and cakes on a salver. "*C'est, mon fils,*" Karim said proudly. The boy poured water onto our hands, and served the tea and cakes. Karim stood up. He walked over to a chest, took a few plastic bags filled with hashish from a drawer and put them on the table. His father entered the room, an elderly man, perhaps eighty or so, with dark skin and thin gray hair. He shook Youseff's, Mohammed's, and my hands, threw a small prayer rug onto the floor, and began to pray. When we finished the tea and cakes, Karim handed me a pipe, the bowl of which was filled with lit hashish. It had a sweet, but pungent smell, and when I took a puff, I could feel a strong buzz in my head. I passed the pipe to Mohammed who took a puff, and he passed it to Youseff. "You like?" Karim asked me in French. "Best quality." "I like," I responded. I bought two bags from him, not a large amount, but enough to turn into about five hundred dollars when we got to Paris.

Our landlady Fatima and her husband threw a farewell party.

Mohammed, his friend Youseff, and I drove to the *Mellah* (the Jewish quarter), where bootlegged wine was made and sold. We all wore *djellabahs*. Each of us put two bottles in his belt beneath the *djellabah*, and we returned by car to my house. The laws were different in Morocco than America. If you were caught with *kief* or hashish the police would smack your hand and send you on your way. Wine was another matter. The Koran forbade Muslims from drinking alcoholic beverages, but the fear of severe punishment never stopped any Moroccan I knew from drinking. Halfway through the evening, I was the only one stoned on kief. Fatima, her husband, Mohammed, Youseff and Marian were all sloshed on bootlegged wine. We laughed and danced to Berber music and Fatima, now pretty drunk, impersonated Charlie Chaplin with a mustache, hat, man's jacket and pants. She asked me to put on a caftan and a veil, and to impersonate a Moroccan woman. Why not? I thought.

It was a wonderful party that defied everything I'd ever heard about Moroccan people. It was all in good fun. No disrespect was shown to anyone, though Mohammed made a last-ditch effort to get Marian to marry him. No one (especially Marian) took him seriously. Exhausted and ready for sleep, Marian and I said good night and went upstairs to our bedroom. We left Marrakech the next morning, took a bus to Casablanca, stayed overnight in a hotel, and traveled the next day to Ceuta.

CHAPTER 19

Though drawn to wisdom I found in books like the Bhagavad Gita, the Old and New Testaments, and the Vedas, drawn to beauty I discovered in paintings by Renaissance masters, by Impressionist and Post-Impressionist painters, to music by Bach, Mozart, Beethoven, William Byrd and Thomas Tallis, my problem was simple: I couldn't find that same beauty in myself. Internal chaos gripped me like a vise. There was always something missing. "On the other side of me," I'd think, "is a spiritual life." Time and again I heard that love would change my life, but no one ever spoke about the need to love one's self; no one ever told me that without self-worth I couldn't receive love from others.

I didn't realize then that it was my responsibility to transform negative energy into *chi*. In my early to mid-twenties I had no idea that something like *chi* existed . . . much less inside myself. I had never even heard the word. My knowledge of the chakra system was so superficial that it remained a mysterious term I had glossed over in books I read about Hinduism and Buddhism. It was all a big mystery to me, a door I had never opened, but one that would eventually lead me out of the depressed state I'd lived in for so long that I thought nothing else existed on earth.

It was easy for me to blame the world for my misgivings. There was so much wrong with it that I didn't have to be a genius to pick life apart. In my early- and mid-twenties I'd thrive on its imperfections—a nonconformist, the first and last angry young man, a rebel with a cause, a voice that personified a generation of misfits who wanted to change the world. Like Munch's painting *The Scream*, the pain went so deep inside me its echo carried to the bottom of a great canyon filled with internal muck. It was a voice that gave my life purpose but never a moment of inner peace. I had a score to settle with an unjust world. I continued to listen to that voice until one day I crashed into a wall constructed from contorted images of Stuart, the one person on earth I couldn't escape. It reminded me that my problems were subjective and buried deep in the unconscious.

"You can escape anything and anyone but your own self," Rudi told me. I don't want to escape me, I thought. I want to transform my inner chaos into a joyful life. I knew, at some point, I would have to stop running from the one person who imprisoned me. I'd look into a mirror and laugh. "You're that person," I'd say to myself and shake my finger at the reflection. "You're the only person who keeps you from being happy." It never occurred to me before I met Rudi that I had to be responsible for my own spiritual development. I believed enlightenment was something that just happened; spirit was a divine muse that inspired poetry, painting, music and architecture. It would enable me to soar above the earth and commune with gods and angels. It had nothing to do with the rudiments of daily living. I'd chant and pray, write poetry, listen to music, and look at art, and I'd commune with spirit and avoid everyday responsibilities, a definitive separation between the mundane and the transcendental. One had nothing to do with the other. As long as I got stoned and maintained a link to the spiritual, the material world became a shadow, sub-stance-less, unimportant, an imposition that dulled the cosmic glow. It never occurred to me— why was I born on earth? What is my purpose for being here? What is the meaning of karma?

Minstrel and troubadour songs inspired me, and I listened to recordings of medieval and Elizabethan madrigals and motets. "God lives in the magical landscape paintings of Salomon van Ruysdael, John Constable, Turner, Pissarro, Monet, and Sisley," I'd say to myself on my all-too-frequent visits to the Metropolitan Museum of Art in New York City. Like William Blake, I wanted to write poetical songs that celebrate an invisible world God has created. The everyday and practical affairs of life didn't meld with my consciousness. Minor inconveniences like money, food, a roof over my head would take care of themselves. Later on I realized that heaven and earth weren't separate entities, that I had karma to work out, responsibilities to take care of. I knew that I'd never be free of them until I accepted life as my teacher and no longer rejected practical living. My escape into masterful works of art, into poems or novels or great music lasted for short periods of time. What about the rest of the day? Did God not exist when I was at work or with a girlfriend? Could I compartmentalize the universe in cubbyholes of my own liking? I didn't think so. It seemed as if most people lived that way. "But am I like most people?" I asked myself. "It doesn't really matter. What does matter is the deep unhappiness I feel inside myself." I'm both emperor and child in *The Emperor's New Clothes* fable, I thought, a buffoon and a wise man conjoined in the same body, and neither fits into their costume. Like Shakespeare said, the world is "out of joint." But it was worse than that. The world wasn't out of joint, it was I who was; it was I who had created a cock-eyed image of the world in my own mind.

"What's missing?" I'd ask myself.

A concert pianist spends years developing his craft. So does a master artist, a plumber, neurosurgeon, writer, lawyer, actor, photographer—any professional or artistically-inclined person who attains success can't reach a career pinnacle without mastery of craft. There's nothing more difficult to master than one's own inner life, and nothing more complicated, more unique, more mysterious, more unforgiving, more resentful and more immature than the internal workings of the human mind. We can take university classes in just about any subject on earth except the mastery of Self. One wonders when the educational system will discover that half-baked loaves of bread make lousy sandwiches; that students who learn by rote are a disservice to their profession. The soul needs to be nurtured, the humanity of a student developed—a whole person must graduate from college, not an automaton with a degree who brings no depth to his or her chosen profession.

Universities crank out students on educational conveyor belts, not soulful people who've learned that compassion adds another dimension to life. It's not only the educational system's fault. Students mustn't accept trite answers to profound questions, especially when those answers affect their lives. Rudi once told me: "A great student can turn a mediocre teacher into a great teacher." A great student will demand that a teacher turn himself inside out to come up with real answers. He will force the teacher to disrupt the dinner of gods. If the question is important enough, no apology is necessary. It's written: "Ask and you shall receive." If asking isn't enough, then demand an answer. If your demands go unheeded, try another tactic. More importantly, we have to know whom to ask. There's no sense beating a dead horse, it's never going to move. There's no sense proposing questions to people who have no answers. The best a teacher can do is train students to find answers inside themselves. Rudi's meditation practice taught me that every important book written could be found inside me. Along with those books came answers to most of my questions—a way to learn that superseded mindsets of stodgy educators—a resource I've carried with me most of my life.

❖❖❖❖

Important spiritual teachings are not in the public domain. They're transmitted from generation to generation in a manner that defies ordinary means of understanding. There are no public relations firms that promote its wellbeing, no erudite committee of theologians and scholars that chooses enlightened people. I have never understood how the process works, why one person evolves more than another and what karmic circumstances are involved. It's a mystery that will force the greatest minds of any generation to come up empty. Somehow spiritual teachings are passed on, somehow guru and disciple meet and help each other attain enlightenment. Call it pre-ordained, karmic, pre-determined. Call it whatever one wants, it's essential that those teachings exist in our world, it's essential for people to become vehicles for their transmission. It has nothing to do with religion or dogma, with what one believes or doesn't believe. It's non-sectarian and non-denominational, and it transcends anything the mind can understand. It's the final step before spiritual enlightenment, a pillar that keeps the world from falling off its axis. Scholars have attempted to figure this out since time immemorial. Books have been written on the subject, treatises and articles, but no one has ever explained the mystery of spiritual transmission. It defies human understanding; it defies any attempt at rational thought. It exists, that's all, and it will find those whose need for spiritual enlightenment is tantamount to everything else.

Suffering on earth is a perfect democracy. It spares no one and touches the core of every human being in one way or another. No matter how often we ask, "Why me?" there's never a sensible answer. Who, in their right mind, would come to a place where pain and grief are the norm? What terrible crime has an infant committed to be sentenced to a lifetime of misery? It was born, that's all, and it brought joy to its parents. It reminded them of innocence lost to a lifetime of grief. Are we naughty children being punished by a wrathful God? The very idea is naïve. It blames a higher force of energy for an insane condition brought on by people. Once the human mind gets involved, once intellectual knowledge supersedes the wisdom of the heart, conflicted points of view determine the governance of this world, and misery and grief walk hand in hand on a path that goes nowhere.

The wise and the not-so-wise have spent an eternity trying to figure out what life is all about, and no one ever reaches a conclusion. They're not supposed to. They'll invent new and improved gizmos and proclaim a modern age that's far superior to life a hundred years ago. But basic questions remain the same: "Who am I? Why was I born? Why all the pain and suffering? Why do I have to listen to a crazy voice in my head? Why do I age? Why do I get sick? Why do I die? What's the purpose of all this?" These are questions that plagued people a thousand years ago and still plague them today, questions that have never been answered to anyone's satisfaction.

Most people sweep them under the rug. They can't be bothered by theological and philosophical questions that have puzzled humanity from the beginning of time. People have neither the time nor the patience to heal themselves of problems they've accumulated over a lifetime. Attention spans today range from about five to ten seconds, an edgy, overly neurotic, impulsive state of disrespect that keeps people at odds with each other. There's no room to explore, to learn, to make mistakes, and to grow from them. Either you got it or you don't. In meditation class no one is more important than anyone else. You bring an honest or dishonest version of yourself and work to improve. The only thing asked is a sincere effort to grow. If people were perfect, they'd live in seraphic realms and not on Earth. They wouldn't have to attend meditation classes.

❖❖❖❖

"I live in the light of my guru," I've heard people say. "That will protect me. That will make it possible for me to have a spiritual life." It's almost an insult to the guru. The student's on vacation while the teacher does all the work; the student works on his or her spiritual tan while the guru is burnt to ash by God's energy. The very idea is wrapped in laziness. The best way to serve a spiritual master is to build one's own connection with God. Absorb the teacher's *shakti* and develop a chakra system that's strong enough to sustain a spiritual life. Even the holiest of saints couldn't nurture people who don't make an effort to commit themselves to some form of deep inner work.

"I don't work on myself because I'm already enlightened," I've been told by many people. "How do you know that?" I asked. "My guru told me. He said that everyone is enlightened. We don't have to do anything but be." It's difficult not to laugh when you've seen nothing but fear in the eyes of someone who just told you they are enlightened—a murky almost mildewed expression that is part of their mental makeup—a veneer of sweetness that, when it weathers, will peel like deciduous bark from a tree. "Yes, you are enlightened," I answered. "We all are, but most people's consciousness is miles away from their enlightenment. They live in a shadow cast by a false idea of spirituality. Enlightened people don't know they're enlightened. They don't speak about it, they just live that way."

❖❖❖❖

1987—It was late morning in early August and I was in my art gallery. A man in his mid-thirties walked in the door and approached me. "I am R.," he said. "Are you Stuart?" "Yes," I replied. "How can I help you?" I invited him to sit down. My assistant, Kristina, brought us both a cup of coffee. "I'm going to Peru tomorrow," the man said. "It's important that you come and bring all your students." "Oh!" I laughed. "Yes. We're celebrating the Harmonic Convergence. There will be tens of thousands of people in Machu Picchu to meditate for world peace. It has to do with the alignment of planets, a moment in time that might not happen again for thousands of years." "When is this?" "It's been scheduled for August sixteenth & seventeenth."

There were many esoteric things he spoke about that I didn't understand. They had to do with the Mayan calendar—with the grand trine, with astrological theories and predictions made in a book by Tony Shearer that was published in 1971. I listened patiently to R., and tried to take it all in. "It's a tipping point," he said. "If we all converge in a profound two-day meditation, it will change the vibration of the planet. Peace will finally come to our world." "Do you really believe this?" I asked him. "Yes. Why else would I be talking to you about a trip to Machu Picchu?"

I was silent for a moment. Then I said to him, "What happens the day after? What happens on August 18 when tens of thousands of people leave Machu Picchu?" He didn't respond. "There will never be peace on earth until there's peace inside each and every human being that lives here," I said to him. "As long as one mind ticks, there will be conflict in our world."

There was silence for a moment and I went on, "I meditate every day, hopefully my students meditate every day. And I've built a system inside myself that's strong enough to live with compassion. This requires commitment to a spiritual life. It requires the guts to overcome myself and clear a path to God. Do you think that two days in Machu Picchu is going to transform the world?"

He didn't answer. "The most sacred spot on earth is wherever one finds oneself. If we mess up that spot, visits to holy shrines and sacred mountains aren't going to make an ounce of difference. Wherever one happens to be, that's where God builds His temple. It's our responsibility to treat that temple with respect, dignity, and awareness. If we don't . . . well, you see the Earth . . . people screw up all the time."

I wanted him to say something, but there was only silence. I said, "A peaceful planet is almost an impossibility if we don't find peace within ourselves." He didn't respond. He rose, shook my hand, and left the gallery. I never saw him again.

❖❖❖❖

I went to the Church of the Nativity in Bethlehem. It was the early 1990s. I marveled at the wonderful Byzantine mosaics and the architecture of the building. When I inadvertently walked down a flight of steps into a cave-like grotto, the energy became so intense I had to sit down to meditate. I had no idea where I was or why the energy was so powerful. I meditated for about fifteen or twenty minutes before a group of Romanian tourists entered the room. Their guide spoke to them in English. It turned out this grotto-like room was the birthplace of Christ . . . the scene of the Nativity. Without Rudi's meditation training that sacred catacomb would have been another stop on a tourist map. I would not have been sensitive to the powerful event that took place there. The experience was unexpected, and it opened new areas of consciousness inside me.

Decades of meditation practice have made it possible for me to enter holy sites and benefit from their energy. Knowledge of how to breathe and where to focus my attention, along with the ability to tune into divine energy and absorb it into my chakra system, enables me to open to sacred spaces and benefit from being in them. They're not just esoteric turn-ons that last for a few moments then become vague memories. My experience in the Nativity Church in Bethlehem deepened my respect for Christ's wisdom. It helped me understand that the "Son of God" is analogous to a divine child that lives inside me—a child that is resurrected every time I sit down to meditate. It created no desire in me to convert to Christianity. In fact, I had no expectations or desires at all. That's why I had a remarkable experience in the manger. I was prepared to take advantage of the unexpected. I didn't question it. Instead I used the powerful energy to deepen my inner life.

❖❖❖❖

I had never read the Old Testament as a chronological history of the Jewish people. There are too many symbols and metaphors in the book that touch on spiritual transformation. The Temple Mount in Jerusalem is one of them. It's the place where religious Jewish people are convinced that Abraham obeyed the will of God and offered to sacrifice his son Isaac. It's also the place where

Muslims believe Mohammed ascended to heaven. The paragraphs about Abraham and Isaac have deeper significance to me than an historical moment written about in the Old Testament. When my artist friend Mordecai Moreh told me that the Hebrew word for breath is *ha* and God had changed Abram's name to Abra-*ham*, my intuitive understanding of those paragraphs took on greater meaning. Breath is life, I thought, and Abram was infused with spirit (*ha*) that brought about his enlightenment. The power of breath in meditation is used to expand the chakras. The *I Am* is inhaled into the heart or the *hara*. With each exhalation we surrender to *That*—the universe, God, higher energy, whatever one wants to call it.

Abraham became for me a symbol of faith and unconditional belief in a higher power, the doorway to spiritual enlightenment. Isaac and Jacob have symbolic and mystical meanings that are analogous to two powerful centers in a human being: the heart and the sex. Isaac embodied trust, total surrender, the belief that life itself can be offered up to the will of God—a subtle metaphor that touches on the human heartbeat—its rhythm being the rhythm of life. At the moment of death, the Heart (all of life) must surrender itself to faith, a pathway to God.

From the loins of Jacob, thirteen tribes of Israel were born. The mystical teachings of Jewish lore were passed down from generation to generation, and spirit sustained itself on earth.

The Old Testament is a profound exploration of the inner workings of a human being, a guidebook on a journey that takes one from Paradise Lost to Paradise Regained. Like the Bhagavad Gita or the New Testament, it's a book written for all mankind, a book (if read properly and clearly understood) that reveals important insights as one travels a path that leads to spiritual enlightenment.

❖❖❖❖

When Swami Muktananda visited the Big Indian ashram in the early 1970s, over a hundred people sat in the meditation hall. They chanted *Sri Ram, Jai Ram, Jai Ram, Jai Jai Ram, Om.* Rudi sat on the floor next to Muktananda's teaching chair. I couldn't take my eyes off him. He was the only person in the room who didn't chant. His head swiveled, his body shook, and his focus was in the chakra below his navel. With every breath he took, he drew in Swami Muktananda's *shakti*. He didn't give a damn what anyone in the room thought . . . including Muktananda. He wanted one thing: a connection with God. Before Baba's *satsang* he told me, "Muktananda's energy-force is strong enough to break you down and open a path to enlightenment. Don't chant, Stuart. Just draw in the *shakti* and let it break up your resistance. You know how to work on yourself. Use this knowledge. Take in what Baba really has to teach and use it to connect with God."

I didn't chant once throughout the entire *satsang*. I absorbed both Rudi's and Muktananda's *shakti* into my chakra system and transformed my inner life. At the end of the *satsang* I felt like a different person. I had gone through a major death and rebirth. My spiritual training made it possible for this to happen. Rudi taught me how to use mind and breath to absorb *shakti*, how to will myself to another level of consciousness.

❖❖❖❖

Rudi's wisdom cut through New York City's distractions and brought depth of understanding to whoever had the temerity to listen. He once told me, "The dialogue between a human being and God is a personal dialogue that differs with each individual. It's best to keep quiet about spiritual experiences. Let them germinate, let them mature, let your interactions with other people be a by-product of how deeply you are connected with higher energy."

Silence is a gauge of my inner evolvement, I thought, when I left Rudi's shop. When I brag about my inner life and try to impress people, I always come up empty. It's false bravado, an ego-need that stems from my own insecurity, something I have to discontinue because it always drains me of energy and attracts negative situations. My internal dialogue with God sounds like static on a radio. Nothing is clear. My thoughts take over, tension increases, and it's difficult to interact with friends and relatives. I have to re-center myself; I have to reconnect with higher energy and let it guide my life.

It has been written, "In the Beginning was the Word," an esoteric sentence that has no meaning if we analyze it. What do we really know about beginnings? Can a word be the source of all Creation? Can each word we utter be a new beginning: the universe creating and re-creating itself through sound? Does our internal dialogue with God transmit spiritual energy? Can each syllable re-create the world we live in—a nonstop barrage of thought that took me nowhere and interfered with the ongoing dialogue I had with the universe?

Just listen and learn from Rudi, my thoughts continued. Don't be intimidated by the intensity of his energy.

"You'll need no other teacher but me," he said to me one day in his store. "Does that mean it's all there for me?" I asked him. "Yes," he replied. "Just get secure enough in yourself to take in my *shakti.*"

❖❖❖❖

The only voices I'd ever listened to before Rudi were in my own head, and they made me half-crazy. "There are people in the world that know more than you do," I said to myself. "It's time to listen to somebody else." Rudi's wisdom surpassed anything I'd ever heard before—street wisdom, survival yoga—a primal voice that bellowed from some ancient place and transformed New York City into a sacred temple. I had no choice but to learn from him. Even at the unripe age of twenty-five I realized that this opportunity might never come again. "Take advantage," I said to myself. "Trust him. All he wants in return is for you to grow closer to God."

I never trusted people before, not family, friends, girlfriends, or teachers. Most conversation was superficial nonsense and a waste of time. When Rudi spoke, everyday words took on a magical glow. A higher force came through him and turned our immediate surroundings into a sacrosanct place. He once said to me, "How am I different than anyone else?" I laughed. There was a golden aura of light that surrounded him. One moment it was Rudi who sat in his chair; the next I saw the astral form of Swami Nityananda or the Shankaracharya of Puri, or an infant or a two-hundred-year-old man or just light, color and nothingness, a void into which cosmic energy flowed. "How is he different?" I said to myself. I didn't know how to answer the question. "Just work deeply inside, absorb his *shakti,* and transform your non-trusting, skeptical, and insecure self into a human being who embraces higher energy."

CHAPTER 20

Alicante, Spain—Concrete walls enclosed a group of men imprisoned for many different reasons. A cell became my home away from home for almost a month. Steel doors clanged, and an internal voice told me my life had reached the bottom. I had been locked up because Spanish customs found hashish in my pocket. The prison food was inedible—stale bread and ink-flavored coffee for breakfast, the same foul-tasting dishwater they passed out for chicken soup was served every lunch and dinner. It was so bad that candy bought at the canteen almost passed as gourmet. In three weeks I must have lost fifteen pounds. My tiny cell was comprised of concrete walls, a steel door, and an open toilet that stood across from a wooden planked bed with one blanket. "You've reached the bottom of a long downwards spiral," I said to myself when I first entered the cell. The only possession I had was a Penguin edition of the *Bhagavad Gita*. Every morning, afternoon and evening, I'd read it for at least an hour. Marian was in the woman's section of the prison, and I didn't see her until we both got out.

The inmates made it bearable for me to get up in the morning— a cast of characters that the finest playwright couldn't assemble on stage. We met every morning and late afternoon in the prison yard. There was Mohamed, a twenty-eight-year-old Moroccan Muslim who had rowed across the Straits of Gibraltar with three friends and landed at a Spanish army base. Franco's soldiers greeted them with rifles, pistols, and machine guns, and they were carted off to prison, a scene that could have been written into an Abbott and Costello movie. "*Je suis un espion*," Mohamed said to me in French. *"Un grand chef de l'intrigue. Regardez-moi. Je suis comme James Bond."* We both laughed. The Spanish government indicted him for spying. He and his luckless friends would be tried in about a month. They rowed to Spain for only one reason: to get to France where they could work and send money back to their poverty-stricken families. They had already spent two years in prison without a trial. Mohamed and I had long conversations about Islam, Judaism, and other spiritual paths that honored God. He was a deeply religious man who prayed five times a day and meant no harm to anyone. A conviction would put him and his friends away for at least twenty years.

Old man Santiago was a white-haired, white-bearded inmate in his early seventies. He sat alone at a table in the dining hall. Franco's Civil Guard had busted him at least seven years before I arrived at the prison. Drunk and rowdy, he stood on a tavern table, and announced to the Spanish people that he wouldn't piss on Franco if he were burning. I didn't blame him for his point of view. In the United States it would go unnoticed, but to make that kind of proclamation in a fascist country had to bring trouble. A quiet old introvert of a man, he barely spoke to anyone; deeply troubled and alone, he was lost in an existential nightmare he brought on himself one drunken night in a cantina. He'd walk around the prison yard and mutter words in Spanish. He would raise his arms towards the sky, shout incomprehensible sounds, and burst into crazed laughter. Not one person came to visit him the three weeks I was there. His mind half gone, his will to live quashed under the thumb of a repressive government, he reminded me of a character in Charles Dickens's novel *A Tale of Two Cities* or Alexandre Dumas's *The Count of Monte Cristo*. Hasn't the world learned anything? I thought. Those books were written in the nineteenth century. I couldn't fathom seven years in prison without a trial, without a lawyer, without a hint as to one's fate.

Hans, a German drug dealer who had spent the last ten years of his life in and out of prisons all over Europe, was another inmate I befriended. His father was one of the first Westerners to live in Lhasa, Tibet. He paid regular visits to the Dalai Lama, studied Tibetan Buddhism, and was initiated into Tibetan mystery rites and sacred teachings that had been passed down for over a thousand years. Hans and I talked for hours about Buddhism and Hinduism. "I learned by rote," he told me. "My father, whom I saw in three-to-five-year intervals, told me stories about Tibet, but always kept the mystery teachings to himself. I wasn't ready to learn them. It's been over ten years since I last saw him. Frankly I don't even know if he's alive." About a week and a half into my incarceration Hans said to me, "I've got over a million dollars worth of hashish stashed in Malaga. I've got to bring it to Sweden. Do you want to help me? We'll sell the stuff and split the take." His offer took me by surprise. "I've been in this place a week and a half," I said to him. "It's enough. I don't want to return to prison ever again. You could have ten million dollars' worth of *kief* stashed on the moon. I don't give a shit. There's no amount of money that's worth being locked up in a place like this." He just smiled and said, "Okay." It was the last conversation I had with Hans. He became distant and avoided me. At times I wondered if the Spanish police had made some kind of deal with him: find out about this American kid and we'll take time off your imprisonment. I didn't know for sure, but the whole situation was weird.

There were many other inmates. Everyone had a story, but I became friendly with Clive, an Englishman whose cell was next to mine. He was a fun-loving soldier in the British army on leave in Spain from a Gibraltar army base who got drunk and a bit rowdy on a train ride from Granada to Malaga. He drank wine with Spanish travelers and flirted with a few women; a general cut-up, he swore to himself that he would have a good time. A few members of the Guardia Civil were on the train. They asked Clive for his papers. "I'm botherin' no one," Clive said to them. "I'm just havin' some fun in your country." "Your papers, señor." He gave them his papers. "English, eh?" they said in Spanish. "A soldier stationed in Gibraltar." "So!" "We don't like you English. You have no right to be in Gibraltar." The police officer pushed Clive. "Take your hands off me," Clive said. "Get off the train," the officer replied. He grabbed Clive by the arm and Clive slugged him in the jaw. "It was a big mistake," he said to me. "The freakin' cops pulled out guns and put me in handcuffs. I've been in this stink hole of a prison for a little over two years." "What about the British Consulate?" I asked him. "That's my problem. The Spanish and English governments are in a bullshit battle over Gibraltar.

Who owns it . . . crap like that. I'm a sacrificial lamb in some kind of idiotic political game the two countries are playing with each other. The Brits haven't the power to get me out." "You mean if the Brits give Gibraltar to Spain, you'll get out of prison." "Something stupid like that," he responded.

Once a week, the British commissary in Gibraltar delivered a gourmet food package to Clive. He'd always invite me to join him at lunch and dinnertime. He'd have cheese and smoked fish and assorted other goodies that were edible. Prison life had made Clive a sick man. He had serious kidney problems that the doctors didn't attend to. The pain could be acute and he'd be up all night. I heard him moan and scream for help. No one came. One night Clive's pain was so unbearable that he screamed for at least two hours before a guard came and took him to the infirmary. I never saw my English friend again.

I spent many hours alone in my cell. Without a person to talk to my mind made futile attempts to figure out why I couldn't get relief from its depressed state and apply my spiritual insights to everyday life. My thoughts dwelled on enlightenment, on success as a writer, on a dialogue between God and myself. When I looked at the concrete walls of my cell, at a steel door, a toilet that stared me in the face, a plank bed to sleep on, and my lack of freedom, there was a disconnect between thought and reality. I wanted to enter "fabulous cities," to soar above the misery and discontent I saw in life and create wonderment with my time and energy, but I was locked away at the bottom of an emotional and psychological dung heap: alone and frightened, and incapable of change, my inner life was paralyzed, static, uncomfortable with ideas about God and spiritual awakening. Karma has a stink of its own, I thought, that's so rancid I can barely survive its onslaught.

There's something important I have to learn here, something that will change me, that will give me the strength to implement my ideas and turn them into reality. Do I start with drugged-out cosmic visions? I smiled a cynical smile and thought, no one gives a damn about hashish highs, about "fabulous cities," or a vision in which time consumes all of existence, no one gives a rap about thousands of suns that manifest in the sky. No one cares about Stuart on a magic carpet ride through time and space, his drugged-out ideas, his escape into Never-Never Land, his mind that has never opened the door and allowed him to escape from a personal prison. If I am one with God, why is it that I'm plagued by inner chaos, why is it that my tension is so extreme that it could land me in a sanitarium? Why is it that I'm here, in this prison, why is it that poetical thoughts do nothing to change my reality? I'm like a tree without roots, a skyscraper without foundation. I'm like the sound of a bell that lingers in a distant sky, homeless and adrift in karma's undercurrent. There has to be a place the poetical mind can call its own, a place where the magic carpet can make a safe landing. I don't know where that place is. I don't know if I'll ever find it. At least this prison cell has forced me to take a good look at myself. The only answer I've come up with is that I must change; and somewhere on this ridiculous planet, there's a compassionate soul who can teach me how to do it.

❖❖❖❖

When I was released from prison, the first thing I did was kiss the ground. I was so grateful to be out of that hellhole I ran with abandon through the streets of Alicante. I went into a café, had a glass of red wine and a sandwich, found a hotel in Malaga, and spent the next week in negotiations with my bank in Paris, the German Consulate, and the Spanish prison authorities. I discovered (depending on the crime) a prisoner's freedom could be bought for very little money in Spain. In the case of Marian, it was two hundred and twenty-five dollars. I had two hundred and seventy-five dollars in a Paris bank account. After all the details were completed and Marian got out of jail, we took a train to the French border and hitchhiked to Paris.

❖❖❖❖

In the early 1970s, I contacted the warden of a federal prison in Fort Worth, Texas. We set up an appointment and he agreed to let me teach meditation classes to inmates. I went to the prison and taught twice a week for five years. I had never forgotten the inmates in Alicante—the vapid, almost hopeless energy of people lost in an existential cage. The classes in the Fort Worth federal prison system led to classes at Rikers Island and Sing Sing in the late 1980s and early 1990s. Today, there are meditation classes in Coffee Creek Correctional Facility in Wilsonville, Oregon, and Soledad prison in California.

Many of the inmates relate to the meditation practice that I teach. They've discovered that real freedom is freedom from self. It's easy to recognize that kind of freedom when you live in prison . . . and the changes it brings to one's life. It's wonderful to see light in their eyes, smiles on their faces, and the simple gratitude they have for someone who cares enough to help them make it through the day. You can't bullshit them. They've heard it all and will laugh in the face of a con man. When the talk is from the gut and rings of truth, they listen with respect and dignity . . . and many of them return for the next meditation class and the next. They come with gratitude and hugs, and there's joy in the room. Prison is just another department in life's university where they can learn to get to God. Any inmate that's managed to transform purgatory into a livable space can be an asset to our society. They know how to cut through bureaucratic spin and talk truth to kids on the streets; they know what it's like to step out of hell and be grateful for the air they breathe.

CHAPTER 21

Lines written in my late twenties:

It has never been easy for me to let go of egoistical images of myself that were buried beneath insecurity that encroached on every attempt I made to succeed. Perfection knotted my brain and kept me from ever taking chances. I lived on an economic and social precipice, poor, without many friends, introverted and angry at life, I hid from the world in a self-contained, false sense of security. I had revolutionary ideas about art and literature without strength to compete in the marketplace. There was so much mental and emotional baggage that weighed me down I couldn't tell the difference between depression and normalcy.

So much bullshit goes on in a world that not only caters to mediocrity, and places the trite on a throne for everyone to worship. Does it really matter? Why upset myself about things that can't be changed? I'm repulsed by a society that honors money and power above truth and beauty, a society that cheapens the most erudite of visions, that puts a dollar sign on everything. My only saving grace is a deep need to have a spiritual life.

Rudi recognized my struggle the moment we met. "I saw my son lost in the universe," he said to me a year later. "You were looking in the window of my shop, and I pulled you through the door. Human beings are spiritually starved creatures. They consume each other because they're not connected to God. You needed to let go, to make room inside yourself for higher energy to enter."

Stuart Perrin

*I've starved myself because I didn't know how to open. I've clung
to old habits that were killing me. What was I holding on to? What
was more important than being with God? Nothing comes to mind.
Then why was it so difficult to do? What purpose did these habits
serve? I can't breathe properly, I'm tense and unhappy, I'm disconnected from people and from spirit; I can't fully express myself,
and fear paralyzes creativity buried deep inside me. Do I want to
be happy? I don't even know if I can answer that question. I don't
know what happiness is. And on and on . . . a torrent of thought
forces me to re-examine myself and release a lifetime of crap buried
inside me. I'm afraid to open, to be hurt, and trust that life will
be kind to me. I replace kindness with anger, fear, arrogance, and
condescension, and hide behind masks without knowing what I am
doing. I pride myself on being artsy, bohemian, a non-conformist
who shuns society and its superficial ways. I'm a frightened little
boy who hides out on a glass island that will soon be shattered.
I've unearthed ancient tombs in which I've buried spirit and creativity—everything I need to live a happy life. When I break open
these mental and emotional tombs, I excavate joy, love, kindness
and gratitude. I've discovered that the world is no longer a place
that threatens me. I can deal with its multi-layered bullshit without
it turning me into a cave dweller. I am no longer judge and jury,
nor do I condescend because people see a different reality than I
do. My imperious, but fragile nature has disappeared. I am able
to embrace individual human beings and accept our differences.*

I asked Rudi if it's necessary to know what we surrender. He
smiled and said, "You don't have to pick through garbage to know
what you're about to throw out. If it sits any longer, rot and stink
will fill the house. Tension is human garbage. Either we learn to
convert it into compost [energy] that nurtures our inner life, or it
decomposes inside us and creates a killing field rife with mental
and emotional disease."

*I have to let go, but how does a pack rat free himself from a life-
time of bad habits? Do I analyze them, figure them out, and come
to terms with fear, guilt, anxiety, and unhappiness? Do I have to
know the underlying causes of my problems or do I just let go? I
have always looked for sensible answers when things went wrong.*

216

But when nothing changes, when I can't manage my tension, it's time to take a different approach. My inner life's a maze of mental and emotional problems that force me to live on the edge; and reason has done nothing but give me a headache. If a giant chasm separates my thoughts from my actions, if I can't build a bridge that connects my ideas to practical living, what good are answers to all my questions? They do nothing but frustrate me. They drive me deeper into a mental and emotional burrow—a shadow-like world where the mind divines solutions I can't use in day-to-day living.

"Don't create inner gridlock," Rudi said. "Just let go, trust that whatever you surrender will be replaced by higher energy."

I can only fit so much water into a glass. If I'm full of me there's no room for anything else. Does it matter if I know what is surrendered? Not if I feel a lightness of being; not if depression and anxiety disappear; not if I can fill my heart with joy and become a happier person, not if I'm no longer a nervous wreck, an anxiety-filled human being who can barely function. The pain in my chest has disappeared; my headaches are gone, and I haven't the foggiest notion what I surrendered. It's gone, that's all, and I can smile, and be happy, and enjoy my day. It's impossible for me to calculate the number of mistakes I've made in my lifetime, the people I've hurt, the time wasted, and the wrong choices that took me to dead ends. My internal filing cabinet is like some Kafkaesque office with thousands of cubicles filled with complaints. I'm on trial for assorted guilty acts no more important than a wrongful blink of an eye. The judge and jury, defense and prosecution don't give a damn if I'm innocent or guilty. They just need to prosecute somebody. Their minds aren't vast enough to wrap themselves around thousands of major and minor indiscretions. That thought alone could exhaust an army of therapists. Did I have to look through a mental haystack for needles buried beneath layers of tension? If I find one or two of those needles, what then? Do I have to get to the root of a problem? Does the why, when, and what happened in the past really matter? Will they rid me of depression, anxiety, headaches and chest pains? My inner life is so complicated it makes it impossible for me to take note of each thread of tension that's transformed into chi. I just have to reach a place in myself where

I can say, "Let go." I can't live with dysfunction any more. I don't want to be unhappy the rest of my life." The day that happens I will experience a lightness of being I've never known before. I'll have no idea what I surrendered, nor will I care, and it will be a joy to rid myself of a heavy burden.

Why I cling to old habits replete with tensions that have lingered inside me since childhood is difficult to understand. It's more of a mystery than the most arcane insights into metaphysics. Why I hold on to habits that are killing me; why I refuse to let go of inner blocks that keep my system from being in balance—these questions never seem to get answered. I've reached out to therapists, yoga instructors, sages, gurus, to anyone who could help free me from emotional and mental dysfunction. The question always arises: Is a spiritual life a lonely, monk-like existence that cuts a person off from the world? Can I have a social life, get married, have children, and attain material goals that are important to me?

I'd get so immersed in my own problems that I can't see two inches in front of my nose. I fabricate non-existent battlefields fraught with other people's tensions, not realizing that the only way to win the battle is to open inside myself. I can't support my own life much less the lives of others. "The only way to win the battle is to open," I laugh to myself. It's a different kind of recipe, one that I have never tried before because I hadn't learned how to do it. If I become big enough inside, I can support anything. Without that kind of bigness, every responsibility becomes a threat, every person a potential enemy. The best thing I can do for myself and everyone I know is to continue to evolve and grow closer to God. That will make room inside me to deal with any kind of problem that's presented without having to close up and feel threatened. People can live inside me. I can learn from them, grow because of what they bring to me, become more of a human being and work out my karma. It's an incredible way to use life, an incredible way to free myself from the one thing that has always crippled me: an inability to deal with my own and other people's tensions.

"Work brings more work," Rudi said after meditation class.

That's a misnomer because all my life I've tried to avoid work. I could never equate a lifetime spent in a corporate office with any kind of happiness. I'd rather wait tables, shovel shit, write poetry, tend bar, it didn't matter, as long as it wasn't a career. But that's not the kind of work he's talking about. What he's talking about is something much more difficult: inner work, change, and transformation of my tension into spirit. He's talking about a spiritual life, the single most difficult thing to do on earth. I'll have to overcome me. That's a real career, a lifetime of dredging up Stuart's crap, of taking some kind of cosmic pick and using it to break up my tension. It makes me laugh when I think that I stand in the way of my own enlightenment; that I am one of God's fools who'd give up everything to have a spiritual life.

"The best thing you can do for me is build your own connection with God," Rudi said. We had just left a movie and were taking a walk through Greenwich Village. "Learn what I have to teach and grow spiritually. That will free me. That's the best present a student can bring to a teacher." He looked at me and smiled, "A teacher's got to pass on his teachings or he's not a teacher. Take them and become a vehicle for higher energy."

The next day, in Rudi's store, a woman came in with a large bouquet of flowers. She gave them to him as a present. To my surprise, he returned them to her. She looked stunned. "You can't buy a spiritual life," Rudi said to her. "Those flowers don't come from your heart and I don't want them." He told me later that she had spent weeks trying to convince her boyfriend (a close student) to no longer study with Rudi. Her boyfriend had told her to stop or he'd get out of the relationship. "You've insulted my teacher. Make it up to him."

"There's poison in those flowers," Rudi said. "Just look in her eyes. She hates me. All she wants to do is keep her relationship."

The woman departed with her flowers. Ten minutes later a student of Rudi's came into the store. He was a young man who had recently started meditation classes. He gave Rudi a packet of M&M's. Rudi hugged him, thanked him and distributed candy to everyone in the store. It was as if Rudi had just received the crown jewels. "The M&M's came from his heart," Rudi said with a big smile. "A gift filled with love and gratitude." It wasn't the gift that mattered, it was unconditional gratitude and love, a lightness of being that came with spirit, recognition that we are all human and need to treat each other with kindness. When a cook puts love into his food, the guests can taste it. If a meal is cranked out without consciousness, without love and gratitude, with anger and resentment, even if the same recipe is used, the food won't be palatable.

I never visited Rudi without a gift of flowers, a plant, an ice cream cone, a bar of chocolate, something that said thank you. I didn't have money to buy expensive gifts, but a little token from the heart said a great deal to the person who saved my life. He devised the double-breathing meditation technique I practiced every day to tap vast resources of spiritual energy. He allowed me to spend a great deal of time around him though conversation with Rudi wasn't on my agenda. I just wanted to sit with him, draw his *shakti* into my chakra system, and strengthen my connection with God. If he needed a floor swept, a room cleaned, a statue delivered to a client, an errand here and there, whatever he needed never equaled what he had given me. Any resistance I felt had to be immediately surrendered. Though his meditation classes were free, early on I realized that if I wanted to have a spiritual life, it would cost me everything. I could never take any moment with him for granted.

Lip-service gratitude meant nothing to Rudi. No matter how many times I would say, "thank you," it never compared to meaningful acts of service that helped him get through his day. It never compared with a profound commitment to absorb his remarkable teachings. I'd ask myself, "What am I doing here? Is he a crutch, a railing for a crippled person to lean on, a voice inside myself that guides me on a spiritual path?" I didn't know the answer. I only knew that his presence forced me to work on myself. He had a commonsensical voice that defied all reason and hit me full-face with a simple reality: if I didn't work in depth on myself, my one chance at a spiritual life would pass me by. I had to take advantage of what God had given me. Then I'd ask myself, "Why me? There are millions of people in New York City." I'd often think, "What does it matter? How often does one get a chance to meet someone like Rudi? He's opened his door, welcomed me, and allows me to sit with him, meditate, and strengthen my inner life. His presence forces me to confront myself—the one person who keeps me from having a spiritual life."

"Who in their right mind," I thought with a smile on my face, "can confront their limitations day after day and not be perplexed by their own stupidity?" Who wants to look into a mirror and see what's really there, and not an overblown, distorted image of self that satisfies ego? Honesty is perhaps the most difficult of all things to accept. And Rudi . . . his very presence forced me to be honest with myself, a state of being too difficult to live with every day if I stopped my spiritual work. The reflection I saw in the mirror was living hell. It had to change if my life would amount to anything, and God had sent me Rudi. His divine presence stirred up in me a strange combination of inner turmoil and a masterful meditation technique I used to develop my chakra system and get closer to God. My subjective life became something more than a metaphysical chart that a scholar depicted in a book. Meditation practice with Rudi released a healing force that was hidden behind mental and emotional dysfunction, a force that transformed the reflection I saw of myself in life's mirror. "Every human being suffers," I thought. "I'm not the only one that's submerged in a whirlpool of tension." I had to look at people with a compassionate eye. Instead of judging them I had to find seeds of goodness buried beneath the surface. "If everyone has a chakra system, a mind, and breathes, why don't more people do something about themselves?" I asked Rudi. He replied, "They're not ready. Time has infinite patience with all of us. It provides thousands of lifetimes for people to get ready."

"Thousands of lifetimes," I said to myself, "of beating one's head against the wall, of chasing after illusion. It takes forever for people to wake up and do the obvious."

❖❖❖❖

Most people attend meditation classes to overcome serious mental and emotional problems. Rarely do they attend classes because they need to have a spiritual life. In time, problems dissolve, and they're confronted by a choice: do I want to continue and develop a spiritual life or have I had enough? A spiritual life can be seen as an airy-fairy goal that disconnects us from reality. It's intangible, out of reach, an ideal that transcends human understanding, that's difficult, almost impossible to recognize as something pragmatic. Many students have asked me if a spiritual life is even possible in our modern world. Concerned about immediate needs, spirit doesn't fit into their conceptualized box. People are so used to living in muck they can't see anything else. They're not cognizant that lotus flowers and lilies grow out of muddy water, that without darkness there is no light, and without light, no darkness. Both are essential to the wellbeing of the earth; both are essential to an evolution of human consciousness.

I had an ex-alcoholic girlfriend who claimed she had inherited the problem from her drunken mother. "It's genetic," my girlfriend said to me. It could be true, I thought. I didn't know. The unhappiness her mother caused, the anger and frustration, the lack of forgiveness, and the inability to truly open her heart, kept my girlfriend from moving on in life. Emotionally paralyzed and miserable, she often projected her resentment onto other people. When I gently suggested that she forgive her mother, she became so furious with me that it ended our relationship. I realized how difficult it is to surrender old habits. People would rather live in self-imposed hell than change. To say I am grateful is false if one's heart isn't open; to say I forgive you is nonsense if we still hold grudges; to say I love you has no value if a person doesn't mean it. Words without meaning cover up true feelings. For words to have meaning we must free ourselves from a past that's created deep-seated anger, resentment, and fear.

❖❖❖❖

Gifts are often used to sneak into another person's heart, a ploy that backfires if love diminishes and folks tire of each other. We can possess the body of another human being, but their soul is intangible, out of reach, a force that responds to unconditional love, to forgiveness, to a heart that is open. If we try to imprison it, the soul shrivels up and creates havoc with the body. What can be bought is a mind attracted to material things. When that body gets old and weatherworn, when the mind withers, when we're left with little or nothing for our money, the soul will pop its head out and say, "You traded me for material possessions and look what's happened. You've taken a walk to a grave where countless numbers of souls have gathered to tally their blessings."

My heart is a lonely place locked in remote and isolated chambers that are cut off from other people. Its anguish spreads bitterness in the world. My heart defers to the mind's logistical dictates that try to manipulate life and transform it into a dry, juiceless, hodgepodge of fleeting thoughts that imprison spirit in a conceptualized box. Love flounders, joy refuses to spread its wings, and the voice of reason burrows its way through my human interactions. I'm adrift in a striated fog that has no exit—an uncertain, hapless state of day-to-day ennui that creates a thick carapace of dead emotion around my heart. I listen to a silent, but deadly inner cry for help: a voice in the heart that languishes under the strict rule of a mind that extracts juice from life and transforms me into a flayed image of myself. There's no room for spirit in a closed heart; there's no room for me to live and breathe and to feel like my life has more to it than an automated puppet-like purpose. Gratitude diminishes to a non-factor and my heart has shriveled up and turns to ash. It must be resurrected, taught to love, to open, and to remove its death-like mask that keeps happiness at bay. Without love, without an open heart, I live in a mini theme park full of surreal, juiceless people that reflect sterile internal workings of a human mind. It's like trying to run an automobile without gas: no matter how many times I floor the pedal, it goes nowhere. If I don't refill its tank, the car will decompose in time and will be carted away to a junkyard. It's no different with me. If spirit doesn't nurture my heart, age and time will decimate my life force. My chakra system has to be retooled, my breath re-mastered, and my mind transformed into a surgical instrument that opens the core of my being. Dead parts of myself have to be resurrected. It's a big job. The alternative is scary: minds and hearts that fester, and bodies that limp to the grave.

Nothing is exactly what it appears to be. What I call reality is no more than a prismatic reflection of each person's thoughts. It has about as much substance as a shadow that follows me wherever I go. I've been lured into a web of illusion that dangles money, fame, sex, security, and a thousand other promises in front of my eyes. Once I attain them, I'm made to believe, they will provide some twisted form of self-importance. Of course they don't. What's missing is heart—its sublime and beautiful lens that takes the sterile out from life. It projects joy, love, and the highest levels of what it means to be human. Bleak landscapes return to life and people no *longer look like soulless creatures. I'm no longer an illusive person no one understands. I don't have to figure anything out. I must live it, that's all, and it turns a barren objective world into something lush and beautiful.*

❖❖❖❖

A serious falling-out had taken place between Rudi and one of his students. "His ego is the size of the cosmos," Rudi said to me about his ex-student. Years later that same student pronounced himself to be an avatar—a being so extraordinary that Christ and the Buddha were minor league players. I asked Rudi about this person. "He's crazy," Rudi replied, "and dangerous. He'll get his followers to worship him." After Rudi died I read articles about this so-called avatar, articles in which he used Rudi to promote himself. It was a sick portrait of spiritual ego at work, and it attracted many followers. I've learned that most people can't tell the difference between real spiritual teachings and cosmic neon glitz. They run anywhere crowds assemble; they're like moths attracted to the headlights of a car and they follow spiritual practices that often take them nowhere. Life has taught me that total surrender is essential if one is to become enlightened; a guru has to surrender his *guruness*, a saint his saintliness, a holy man his holiness, an avatar his birthright if they want to become one with God.

CHAPTER 22

After my first month of meditation practice with Rudi, I no longer took my health for granted, my diet, my living circumstances, my cleanliness, and a host of other things that I never paid much attention to before. Hallucinogenic drugs became a non-factor, both cigarettes and alcohol disappeared from my life. "My body's a temple and each chakra an altar," I thought. "I have to respect the sacred nature of the life I've been given." I didn't have to think about the changes that took place. They were organic life shifts that integrated themselves into my daily routine.

"If my body's a temple," I thought, "and if the seven basic chakras are altars in that temple, then it's my responsibility to treat body and mind with consciousness."

Besides the seven basic chakras, I discovered energy points in the palms of my hands and feet, in every joint in my body, in my fingertips; in fact, the human body was an intricate system of chakras that connected me to God. Rudi's *shakti* transmissions dissolved static pools of energy inside me and renewed vitality. "Anyone can sip brook water that flows down the side of a mountain," he said to me, "but once it becomes a lake, once it becomes stagnant, it attracts disease, insects, algae, and assorted other creatures that make the water impossible to drink."

Almost every ache, pain and illness is a product of stagnant energy—a weak immune system, heart conditions, dementia, cancer, and all prey upon the body because tension in people is so acute it creates immobile pools of energy that attract disease. We are victims of our own lack of consciousness. The body degenerates until nothing is left but a dysfunctional set of organs and bones. The food we eat, the water we drink, the thoughts that go through our heads, the people we associate with, and what we do with our time, are a by-product of inner development. We have a certain amount of time to spend on earth. If we grovel around in self-induced unhappiness and blame the world for everything wrong with us, tension will attract disease that plays havoc with body and mind.

In Denton I had a serious problem with calcium deposits in my knee. The pain was so unbearable I could barely stand up. Doctors wanted to operate but I said no. One day, in the apartment of a student, a copy of *Prevention* magazine lay on a table. I picked it up. I opened the magazine to an article about a man who had the exact problem that afflicted me. I read the article and now paraphrase: "Calcium deposits have nothing to do with excess calcium. In fact, it's exactly the opposite. If you are calcium deficient, the blood extracts calcium from your bones and deposits it in your joints. The calcium deposited in one's joints will cause excruciating pain." He prescribed a list of supplements he took to get rid of the problem. I went to the health food store and bought all the supplements. I took them according to the writer's prescription. In two to three days the pain went away. It never returned again. A week later, I began an exercise routine. Within a month, I was running at least two miles a day.

As we develop the chakra system, many mysterious forces are at work that change habits and teach us to trust ourselves and other people; forces that are so enigmatic no amount of study can ever explain how they work. Our faces and skin begin to glow, our activity level increases, our pain dissolves, we look younger and we no longer fear the unknown. That ragtag and lackluster sense of self vanishes and we feel at ease in our own bodies. Much of our tension assimilates into the flow of higher creative energy. We are reborn inside. The child of God has found a home inside us and that child radiates love and joy and raises the level of our humanity.

Enlightenment is a mysterious inner awakening and oneness with the universal soul that takes place when kundalini rises into the cosmos and embraces higher energy. It cannot take place if the heart is closed and we live without unconditional love. We must be responsible for our own wellbeing. The moment the chakra system opens and higher energy enters our system, the purification of body and mind becomes essential if we're to continue inner work. "That's all well and good, but Ramakrishna and Ramana Maharshi both died of cancer," a student of mine said. "We all die of something," I replied. "The difference between them and the rest of the world is that they told their disciples not to worry. 'This how God wants me to leave . . . why is everyone making such a fuss?'"

❖❖❖❖

Relationships teach us how to forgive and move on. They are always problematic but essential vehicles that provide love, companionship, and a mirror of our own inner lives and how evolved we are as human beings. They are a breeding ground for mistakes, for inappropriate communication, for fear, insecurity, love, and a host of other needs that put us on psychological and emotional treadmills. We run as fast as we can, but often wind up nowhere. If we don't acknowledge that the person we love has become our teacher; if we don't acknowledge that his or her presence requires us to listen without judgment, without opinion, and learn important lessons about ourselves; if we treat them cheaply and demand that they abide by life as we perceive it, the relationship is doomed to fail. The only real closure is forgiveness. It allows us to move on. "I would rather be wrong than right," Rudi said to me. "If I'm right, there's nowhere to go. If I'm wrong I can listen to and learn from another human being." There must be internal largess, bigness of soul and inner strength. A person with ego-based security won't give other people the freedom to be themselves. A strict set of rules will determine how "loved ones" should act. They're incapable of saying, "I'm wrong." It's the world according to "me" or no world at all. They create a tightly knit prison system and lock their "loved ones" in neon-tinted cells that keep them from ever exploring their own individuality—a pop-art version of hell that runs rampart through our world.

When I look back at the relationships I've had over the years, it could be easy to dwell on the negative. I have to remember that I shared a part of my life with another human being: I have to find the good in them, what I learned from them, and tap within myself a deep level of forgiveness and gratitude. Every relationship changed me. I wouldn't be who I am today without having had the experience. If bitterness is a dead end, if it does nothing to undo what happened in the past and disassembles one's life in the present, if I don't forgive and let go, a healthy, new relationship is almost impossible.

The past no longer exists. Why dwell on it, why be angry about it, why let it cripple me in the present? What happened ten minutes ago is already history. What happened ten years ago is ancient history. To dwell on shadowlike images from the past, to retain bitterness because someone once hurt me does nothing but damage my life today. If I cling to the past it depletes me of all creative energy.

The time I spent with another human being is valuable and shouldn't be disregarded. Why denigrate it, no matter how difficult the experience? It's impossible to relive the past, but it's possible to make use of its lessons for inner growth and development.

We've all blown it hundreds of times. So what? Who cares? Mistakes have their own graveyard. If they fester inside us, unhappiness and uncertainty are a given, the past dominates the present, and one continues to repeat those mistakes wherever one goes. Most people cripple themselves with guilt and remorse, and stand trial before a jury that exists in their own minds. Culpable and self-defeated, without enough inner strength to renew their lives, the past dictates to them every action in the present.

There are meditation students whom I've known for years. We've traveled bumpy roads together and have had some difficulties, but when I meet them today I don't dwell on any of it. I'm grateful to see how far they've come in their lives. The past has no relevance. Each meditation class is a new beginning, an opportunity to be reborn . . . and to grow. What happened ten or twenty years ago shouldn't affect the present. It's all dead and buried. The most important thing is to move on. It's the only way relationships can work. To hold a grudge is to destroy the bond we have with another person or group of people. It severs the connections. It's better to leave anger, resentment, and a lack of forgiveness behind.

❖❖❖❖

Rudi and I exited a movie theater. It was raining out. "Get that taxi," he said to me. I ran up the street, but the taxi was taken. He began to scream at me, "Where's the taxi?" Before I could answer he waved down another one and we got in. I had to listen to a thirty-second harangue about how dumb I was, how unconscious, how it's time to change . . . and whatever. I didn't respond because he wasn't talking to me. It was just excess tension that poured out of a person I loved more than anyone in the world. What did it matter? He burned up more of my bullshit than anyone I knew. The moment he finished the whole thing was forgotten. He spoke about next summer at Big Indian, about how grateful he was to Nityananda and the Shankaracharya of Puri. The entire energy changed. I smiled and hugged him. "He's my guru," I thought. "He gave me my life. What does it matter if he has to drop a little tension? Am I an over-sensitive little schmuck who can't forgive a person for being human?" In a matter of minutes we were laughing together about the movie, about something his mother said, about all kinds of stuff that related to the ashram. The drama of the moment passed. We moved on. The taxi pulled up in front of a restaurant in Chinatown. It was time for us to have dinner.

Forgiveness and gratitude make it possible for people to survive each other. God is perfect. The rest of us are a bunch of clowns in bumper cars at a carnival. Even gurus have problems or they wouldn't be alive on earth.

Rudi and I took a walk from his Seventh Avenue South Asian art gallery to the meditation hall on Tenth Street between Third and Fourth Avenues. He had had a difficult day: no-show clients, and his mother didn't feel well. From the moment we left his antique store he complained nonstop about everyone and everything on earth. As we walked east on Tenth Street, I discovered that there were more stupid people in the world than I could imagine . . . a lineup of incompetent human beings that knew little or nothing about life. I walked beside him and listened. I'd learned early on to refrain from judgment when I spent time with Rudi. It's just tension, I thought. The least I can do is help him get rid of it. If I keep my mouth shut and listen, I'd transform his tension into *shakti* and use it to strengthen my chakra system. Rudi had taught me this meditation technique, and I used it when interacting with most people. When we arrived at the meditation hall, he grew silent. "Let's get a couple of franks," he said. "Where?" I asked. "The Second Avenue Deli is just down the street." We ordered two franks with the works, one for each of us, ate them, and returned to the ashram.

Twenty students awaited Rudi in the meditation hall. He talked about the importance of unconditional love, spiritual malnourishment, the necessity of an open heart and quiet mind—words that were diametrically opposed to what I heard on the street . . . and required instant surrender on my part. Positive and negative are one and the same energy, I thought, and spiritual growth requires non-judgment. He had used me to drop his tension so the meditation class would be on a very high level. I didn't mind being used that way. It prepared me for difficulties I'd run into with other people. I wouldn't be intimidated by tension on the job, by my girlfriend's problems, by whomever I met in my daily life.

Rudi taught me to transform my tension into a strong chakra system. It was one of the most important lessons I'd ever learned from him. I discovered early on that he was an instrument of higher energy, a living example of spirit on earth. He not only saved my life, he opened a path for me that led to God. Nothing I knew of could compare with that kind of gift. Though he passed on over forty-three years ago, he still lives in my heart and teaches me every day.

❖❖❖

People slip into one persona after another. When they remove a mask, there's always another beneath it . . . and another . . . and another until the personality of a human being gets lost in a cluster of images that disappear into striated layers of self. The relationship children have with their parents creates doubt, insecurity, anger, and a host of other fragmented puzzle pieces that make up the sum total of a human being. It creates havoc of such a schismatic nature that forgiveness must show its head and demand that we listen. There isn't a child alive who, in one way or another, hasn't been damaged by their parents. What we do with that damage determines how we live the rest of our lives.

One can say, "They're my parents and I must love them. It doesn't matter what they did to me. Without them I'd never be

in the world." It's easy to say that forgi
ing on in life. Doing it is another stor
and the intentions are real, but we're
person whose hurt runs so deep they
graveyard. The work required to exc
human endurance. It's why there's
world. We mouth little niceties the
fester in unhappiness, so overwhelmed by hur
that forgiveness is the path to both happiness and enlighten
There will never be joy in a human being's heart until parents and
children make peace with each other.

"I chose you and mommy," my daughter said to me. She was
about six-years-old at the time. "I will always love you both
because you are the parents I chose before I was born." Wisdom
of children, I thought, with a smile on my face. I hope she doesn't
forget. "Do you remember choosing us?" I asked her. "Of course
I do, silly. How else would I know that?"

Life's well-traveled roads are strewn with forgetfulness. We
suffer profusely when there's a rift between parent and child. Does
it really matter what they did to us? Is it more important than our
own inner peace and wellbeing? Forgiveness requires a magnani-
mous soul—a generosity of character that transcends pain, insults,
difficulty, whatever reasons keep us from embracing our parents
or children. It doesn't come easy. It took me years to reconcile differences with my family, to overcome my petty prejudices, and to
recognize that they are human beings struggling with their own
lives. What they had done to me no longer mattered. They didn't
have to fit into my Hindu/Buddhist conceptualized box. It was my
responsibility to accept their way of life and not rebel against it.
The effort I made to change forced me to grow spiritually. I had to
open my heart and become nonjudgmental, accepting, and full of
love. I had to make room for my mother and father to live there. I
discovered they had already taken up residence there. They were
just waiting for me to come home.

In the mid 1980s, my mother told me that she had a tumor in
her breast. "Can you do healing meditation with me?" she asked.
"Yes," I replied. "We can start right away."

Twice a week for three months I went to her apartment in
Queens. She took to the meditation practice like a duck to water.

er went into remission and my mother insisted on
ng my Sunday morning meditation class in Manhattan.
udents treated her royally with big hugs and kisses. They
dn't do enough to make her comfortable. After class we'd go
ut for lunch, hang out, and then I'd put her in a taxi that took
her home. The dynamic in our relationship changed. I had been
the black sheep of my family, the crazy son who hitchhiked all
over Europe; a Hindu/Buddhist "nut" who practiced some strange
form of meditation in Greenwich Village. I knew that the beat
of my life would change as I changed. If I had patience, time
would heal my family relationships. All I had to do was work on
myself and let things evolve. The day before my mother passed,
I meditated in her bedroom. She was comatose and in bed. The
room was full of a celestial white light that shone on the body of
my mother. My father's soul hovered above the bed. "I've been
waiting," he said to her. "I can't move on without you." There were
tears in my eyes. We had all come home to a place in the heart.

I've heard countless stories of parental abuse: the horror of
being raped by one's father, a sadistic mother, parents that are
junkies or drunks or have been made dysfunctional by life, pre-
teen kids who were prostituted by parents to johns that got off
on ten-year-olds. How does one forgive such actions? It doesn't
seem possible. Yet we have to move on. Should we forgive abusive
people because we want to rebuild relationships with them? I
don't think so. We forgive them because it's the only way to get
past the nightmare. Happy people don't rape children, they don't
prostitute kids, turn them into slaves or beat them into submission. Everyone deserves a life; everyone deserves to be happy,
but happiness will elude us until we free ourselves from the past.
"Forgive them, they know not what they do," Christ said. He was
nailed to a cross, in terrible agony, yet asked God and people to
forgive the crucifiers.

It requires nobility of soul to forgive heinous crimes. It
requires growth like no other kind of growth to recognize that
our enemies are also people. They suffer, they are in pain, and
they, too, are adrift in an absurd world. We must forgive people
who "know not what they do." It's the first step in an attempt to
turn life's sideshow into a main stage filled with love. The person
we have to get free of in order to live happy lives is our self. It's

easy to blame other people; it's easy to listen to an inner voice that repeats, "I don't have to succeed in life because I was abused as a child. That's my excuse. I can hide out in some internal cave and never fulfill my karma . . . my destiny . . . what I was born on earth to do." No one escapes physical or mental abuse. It's worn like an honor badge stapled to the heart, a brand people display that personifies dysfunction, an excuse for humanity's inability to love and be loved. There's good in the world and life can be a friend, but it eludes us until we forgive abusive people and move on with our lives.

❖❖❖❖

The path to enlightenment is rife with obstacles impatience won't remove. There must be a need to grow that turns time into a friend when it's used consciously. Along the way we discover that time has a singular purpose: to get us to the top of the mountain. It doesn't matter how long it takes, it doesn't matter if we win or lose the race. What matters is that each step's a permanent one on the spiritual path. We discover that there's no competition on the mountaintop. We're free to breath a rarefied air and open to heightened consciousness. Anyone who makes it to the summit of that mountain understands how difficult it is to climb. It's clear to them that there will always be another mountain; it's clear to them that the struggle to the top is just as important as what we find when we get there. It's a treacherous climb, and every step must be taken with consciousness. The closer we get to the top the more everything we've learned must be used to assist us in the climb. We can't take the effort for granted, we can't forget fundamentals or ever assume that what we find on the mountaintop will be different than what's at its base. There will always be another mountain in front of us, and another, until we realize that the climb doesn't end and spiritual energy is without limitation. The moment we try to define it, we fall headfirst off a cliff.

❖❖❖❖

It's not easy to return to meditation class after a multi-year hiatus, and those that do return have trouble staying. The energy is much stronger than it was years ago, the level of teaching higher and the whole dynamic is different. When the meditation class ends, there's an inner quiet that affects everyone in the room. People hug me and thank me. New students tell me that they've never experienced anything like it before. Most of them disappear into the great maw of life. Without commitment, meditation doesn't work. If one hops from teacher to teacher, from event to event like a bumblebee seeking food in a flower garden, nothing inside them will take root and grow. It's a promiscuous use of other people's energy, a momentary high that doesn't last, and we become like bouncing balls in an animated movie. Forty-five minutes of deep meditation practice makes something major shift in me. I'm no longer the same person I was before the class started, and above everything else, I'm grateful to share my teachings with people who have made a commitment to build a strong inner life.

CHAPTER 23

Two Tunisian men picked up Marian and me on the outskirts of Tours and drove us all the way to Paris. It was late night when we arrived, and they took us to a hotel owned by a friend of theirs near Place Pigalle—a six-franc-a-night fleabag of an *auberge* that smelled from stale North African cooking and cigarette smoke. They invited us for a late night dinner. We declined. After two days and nights of hitchhiking, we wanted to sleep. "Hey! *Mon ami*, let's have an absinthe before you go to bed," they said to me in broken French. He stuffed a flaming hot pepper into his mouth and laughed. "No, thank you," I said. "I'm really freakin' tired. We'll see you in the morning." They had cockeyed schemes to make money when they got to Paris, and spoke about a harem of beautiful women millions of French francs would buy. "Paris! *Oui*. It's a place to get rich." Marian shook her beautiful Germanic head, laughed, and went upstairs to sleep. "*A demain*," I said. "Let's have breakfast in the morning." I joined Marian in our hotel room and fell asleep the moment I lay down on the bed.

I expected them to meet us the next morning for a farewell café crème and some croissants, but was honestly relieved when they didn't show up. We took the metro to the Left Bank, found a hotel on Rue Dauphine, and made plans for a trip to Sylt, Marian's island home off the coast of northwestern Germany.

I telephoned Charlie Berg, a good friend in Manhattan, and told him what happened in Spain. I asked him if he could send me a plane ticket from Paris to New York. "I've got fifty dollars to my name," I said. "I have to take Marian back to her home in northern Germany." "No problem," he said. "The ticket will be at the American Express office in a few days."

I hooked up with Raymond Ajavon, and he told me about art films he'd been making. He invited Marian and me to a screening. His idea of an art film was an eight-millimeter pornographic orgy shot in his apartment. "This shit sells, *mon ami*," he said. "I got twenty freaks lined up to buy every film I make. These Danish ladies love to be on camera." "Raymond," I said to him, "you're crazy. How could you film this crap?" "Don't you worry," he replied. "You and me we go to Dahomey. We be big shots. We ride into the village on elephants and use the money to build a hospital, to feed the poor, to fix the water, to do good things. When the money runs out, we come back to Paris and make some more art films." "Like sleazy Robin Hoods," I laughed. "Yeah! Yeah! Like Robin Hood," he said. "*Mon ami*," I said, "you're fuckin' nuts. I've got to take Marian to Sylt. Then I'm going back to the States." "I'm gonna miss you, *mon frère*," he said, "But I promise, someday we do somethin' big together."

Later that day in a café on Rue de Seine, I bumped into the producer and director who had auditioned me for their film. "I heard you replaced me with Pierre Clementi," I said to them. "Yeah. He had a few months off," the director said. "But we had to stop filming. We ran out of money." "Where the hell have you been?" the producer asked me. "Marrakech." "Oh, shit, that's cool. Did you bring back some hash?" "Yeah, but it's with the Spanish Government. I spent three weeks in an Alicante jail." They looked at me and shook their heads. "Well, welcome back to Paris," the director said.

I never saw them again. I don't know if they finished their film or any other film for that matter. It was a short-lived career for me as a movie star in Paris.

❖❖❖❖

Marian and I took a metro to the northern Parisian suburbs and hitchhiked to Sylt. It was a three-day trip through Strasbourg and north on German autobahns to Bremen and Hamburg. The last leg of our trip was a train ride from Hamburg to the North Sea island of Sylt. We were two lost children, dazed and unsure of ourselves, and beaten down by the short time we spent in prison.

We became distant from one another—a void suddenly opened up and kept us from real communication. There was silence, introspection, fear of the future, and not the faintest idea why life had brought us here. Intimacy vanished and we clung together more out of habit than as people who once loved and supported each other. We were both in a state of shock, and it would take time for the trauma to wear off. "I don't know anything," I said to her. "Where I'm going, what I want to do. I've been stripped to the bone. There has to be something more." She didn't say anything. She took my hand and we sat together for an hour and gazed at the North Sea. It was a cloudy day, misty and grey, and the waves of the sea pounded the shore.

Sylt was a Frisian island. Most of its thatched roof houses were built in a style that hadn't changed in a thousand years. "It's a famous nudist colony in the summer," Marian said to me. "A lot of celebrities come here." The place was beautiful in a dismal way, like something out of a Thomas Hardy novel, mysterious, aloof, quiet, and alluring. The sound of gulls pierced the air, and the sound of white-capped waves pounded the beach. There were dunes everywhere, some that rose twenty or thirty feet and were a city-block long—the perfect place for a drugged-out ex-inmate who had lost his way in life.

"I'm gonna return to New York in five days," I said to Marian. "I'll get an apartment for us and you can come later." I didn't know why I said that. It was more like, I performed my duty. Marian is home, safe, with a beloved aunt, and I can move on in life. New York will help me recuperate from nine months adrift in Europe. I had to make serious changes, but had no idea what they were, where I would go, or how I would live. The thought of a job in a restaurant didn't bode well with me, the thought of a position in corporate America was also horrendous. I equated it to a life without an exit. I wanted to write, but couldn't earn a living as a writer. I wanted a spiritual life, but my bohemian nature didn't quite fit into monastic settings, be they Buddhist, Hindu, Christian, or whatever. I had no allegiance to a country, but had faith that a divine entity watched over me. "It'll all work out," I said to Marian. "I don't know how, but it will. I'll find a way."

I took a train to Hamburg the next morning and hitchhiked to Bremen where an old friend of mine, Gerhardt A., lived. He invited me to spend the night at his apartment. I had known Gerhardt in New York City where he studied and worked and was fascinated by many ideas I had about art, literature and spirituality. He was mostly fascinated with me. Time and again he tried to get me to sleep with him. It never worked. We finally set the sexual part aside and became good friends. I had other friends in Bremen, but there wasn't time to pay social calls. I had to make a plane in four days. Paris was a long distance from Bremen for a hitchhiker.

Gerhardt had a managerial job at a famous nightclub in Bremen and returned home after work with his sixteen-year-old boy lover. I was half-asleep and out of it, but I could hear them snuggling in bed, kissing, farting, and screwing each other. It was like the Grand Ole Opry in German. It was one long sleepless night.

They were fast asleep when I got up the next morning. I wrote a note thanking him, got dressed, and left his apartment. I took a tram to the outskirts of Bremen and began to hitchhike. Three days later I arrived in Paris. The trip was kind of a blur: long winding blacktop roads through old towns and cities in France; a baguette and cheese was standard fare, something cheap and filling; occasionally a bottle of red wine and a ham sandwich; a cup of café crème and two croissants for breakfast. I slept in small, cheap *auberges* in towns long-forgotten on blacktops that seemed to go nowhere, a lot of grey skies, very little sun, and a deadline that I had to meet. If I missed the plane, I thought, I might have to throw away the ticket. Charlie warned me not to miss the flight. He couldn't buy another ticket.

I had a hitchhiker's faith in divine provenance. Two hundred cars would go by and one would stop. Why they stopped was often a mystery, but they did, and I'd be taken a hundred kilometers or three hundred kilometers, or whatever the distance was that got me closer to Paris. "I have a son who hitchhiked in England, and the Brits were kind to him," one driver said to me. "I once hitchhiked myself," another said. Another one had some perverted interest in getting laid. All kinds of reasons fit into a divine provenance that helped me make my plane.

It was early in the afternoon when I arrived in Paris. I went directly to the apartment of an old French girlfriend on Rue Guénégaud. "What happened to you?" she asked me at her apartment door. "Too much," I answered. "Are you hungry, tired, can I get you something?" "I'm starved," I said. "I could also use a good night's sleep. I'm flying to New York tomorrow afternoon." She put bread, pâté and some pasta and salad on a table and sat in rapt attention as I devoured the food and told her about my adventures. "A Spanish prison?" she said. "*Oui*," I answered. "One day was too long. Three weeks was an eternity."

Michele spoke perfect English and worked in a Parisian library. She was engaged to a man she didn't love, had promised to marry him, but had put it off at least ten times. "I told him that you and I lived together for a short while," she said to me, "and that we slept together for a longer time. He didn't care." He was so madly in love with her that nothing she said to him mattered. "Why don't you marry him?" I asked her. "He's kind to me, good to me, but I don't love him," she replied. "He's also old enough to be my father."

I hung out in Michele's apartment the rest of the day. We slept in the same bed that night. My horny ex-lover came on to me, but I couldn't make love with her. I was so beaten down by the events of the last month that sex for me was out of the question. There was also Marian. It had only been a few days since I left her in Sylt. Michele gave me a dirty look. "What's happened to you?" she asked. "Nothing. I'm just tired. I've been through too much. Maybe I'll feel better in the morning."

Morning came. She was up and gone, but left me a note: "I have to work. Have a great trip. Hope to see you the next time you're in Paris." It was the last time I saw Michele. I left her with memories of a half-dead American ex-lover, just out of prison, scrawny, tired, and listless, an American writer who couldn't satisfy her sexual needs. "Never knew him to be faithful to a girlfriend before," she probably told her friends. *Adieu*, Michele. Thanks for your help and some good memories.

The plane took off at two in the afternoon and landed at Kennedy airport about five p.m. I took a bus into Manhattan and a subway to Charlie's apartment on the third floor of a West Twenty-first Street tenement walk-up, a thirty-eight-dollar-a-month railroad flat, perfect for struggling writers too poor to live anywhere else. Charlie was at home when I got there. He took one look at me and sighed, "What the hell have you been through?"

"Just that," I said. "I've been to hell and I didn't like it there. Thanks for the ticket. I don't know how much longer I could have stayed in Europe." "Nothing serious, my friend. Welcome home."

We had long, riotous talks about drunken days and nights in Paris, about women, writers, and bohemian life on the Left Bank. It was good to see him. I was broke and without work and slept three weeks on the floor of his apartment. "Hey," he said to me late one afternoon, "let's go to that Middle Eastern restaurant in the Village. The food's great and cheap, and we both like it." "Sounds okay to me," I replied.

My strength had returned. With it came thoughts of the future. An artist friend, whom I had met on a trip to San Miguel de Allende, Mexico, insisted that I move to San Francisco. "It's your kind of city," he said in a letter. "They're gonna love your poetry here. The place is rocking with literary talent. I can introduce you to a lot of people." The idea was great. I wanted to write, but hadn't the chops to succeed in the New York literary world. San Francisco might be easier. The move was under serious consideration.

Charlie and I walked south on Eighth Avenue. It was a clear warm day, spring-like, and the streets were full of typical ragtag hippy types. We walked past luncheonettes and Chinese-Cuban restaurants, bodegas, head shops, and tired-looking pharmacies, flower stores, thrift shops, a host of run-down mom-and-pop stores that lined the avenue, and the Elgin movie theater where a nonstop slew of double-feature classical films was shown to the delight of film buffs. Before I left for Paris, I had been a steady customer. I'd go to Marx Brother Festivals, Janus Film Festivals, the movies of Truffaut, Orson Wells, John Ford, Ingmar Bergman, Fellini, Antonioni, Pasolini, and a host of others. I saw *Les Enfants du Paradis* at least five times at the Elgin and *The King of Hearts* more times than I can remember. It was a timeworn old theater that catered to the tastes of aficionados who loved good cinema. For a couple of bucks, you could spend three or four hours lost in the imaginary world of auteurs. The people that ran it had a curator's eye for top-notch flicks, and provided an entertainment forum for anyone with serious interest in the art of filmmaking. A sign on the marquee said, "Janus Film Festival—through the end of April."

"Let's take in a movie tomorrow," Charlie said to me. "It's okay with me," I replied, "but I've got to look for a job. The super told me the apartment down the hall from you is gonna be vacant in a few weeks. It's forty-five bucks a month. I told her I would take it." "What do you want to do?" "I can get a job as a waiter," I said.

❖❖❖❖

My thoughts returned to writing. I believed that the arts gave one entrée to a spiritual world. I believed that the goal of literature, art and music was to heighten one's perception and open a door to metaphysical experience. It was a naïve view, but one that catapulted me into visionary worlds created by Renaissance painters and composers like Bach and Handel. Truth in beauty couldn't be defined, but I wanted it to become part of my everyday life. Would writing ever take me there? Would the study of art and music? Would anything open that door? I truly didn't know the answer to those questions. I also didn't know if I was a good enough writer to get anyone's ear.

On Greenwich Street we turned left and walked east to Seventh Avenue South. There were a number of restaurants on this street, gift shops, frame shops, antique stores and boutiques that sold peasant dresses, sandals, tie-dyed clothes from India and paraphernalia that could be used to get stoned. "I'm starting to feel good," I said to Charlie. "It's like all that crap is far in the past. I really want to get on with things. An artist friend of mine asked me to move to San Francisco. He said the scene is amazing. My poetry would be a big hit." "Is it the apartment down the hall?" Charlie asked me, "Or San Francisco?" "I don't know, man. I just don't know." He shook his head and smiled. "You'd better find out," he said.

There was a no more confused person on the streets of New York City than I. I didn't want to just write, I thought. I wanted my writing to transform itself into living experience—a kind of utopian reality that gave me the strength to live in the light of God, a kind of inner work that could help me deal with my confusion.

I can see the finish line, I thought, but have no idea how to get there. It doesn't matter if I live in New York City, San Francisco or Paris or wherever, I still have to deal with me . . . a person who won't go away. I'd often wonder if Charlie had these types of feelings. He's secure in himself, I thought, capable of laughing at most things, unfazed by the nonsense in the world, a committed citizen of life, and never adrift on a raft that appears to be going nowhere. My mother would say: "He has his feet on the ground." I didn't even know if my shoes fit on my feet.

The sun's rays bounced off shop windows, blinding-type rays that made me wish I had a pair of sunglasses. We turned south on Seventh Avenue. "The restaurant's a few blocks from here," Charlie said. "Yeah, I remember the place. The food's very good." "Hey!" Charlie said. "Look at this shop." It was an oriental art gallery with an enormous bronze reclining Buddha in the window. There were also Tibetan paintings, cloisonné vases, Chinese porcelain dishes, and a host of other Asian objects displayed. "It's fantastic," I said. "Like a museum." "Why don't we go in?" Charlie asked me. "I'm broke, that's why, and this stuff must cost a fortune." "It doesn't cost to look," he replied. I smiled and said, "Okay."

Life-changing moments occur so unexpectedly that the shock of discovery takes years to wear off. A door opens into a magical kingdom that one reads about in books. It's beyond human comprehension, and there must be higher powers at work. When the door opened and I stepped into that oriental art shop I had the same feeling that Alice must have had when she entered Wonderland. It wasn't the abundance of art objects that filled the shop, it was the man who stood at the shop's center and welcomed me. He was about five foot eight, balding, quite heavy, but well built, and he resembled a Buddha in the shop's inventory. I was immediately drawn to him. He spoke in a jovial way, as if we were old acquaintances that met again by accident. "I just returned from India," he said. "I spent three weeks with my guru and got extraordinary teachings from him." He showed me a photo of himself lying on the floor at the feet of an Indian swami. Superimposed in his heart was a picture of another guru. He spoke about his own spiritual teachings in a way that made them so accessible I was immediately intrigued. I didn't say a word. As I listened to him, I could feel a powerful surge of energy enter my system. I saw light around him and his words uplifted me. I had never experienced anything like this before. "If you want to study with me," he said, "come here at five p.m. tomorrow evening. I'll show you the meditation exercise I teach, and we can go to class."

I heard myself say, "Okay. I'll be here."

As we left the shop, I turned and looked at the man again. A radiance of golden energy emanated from his heart, the same radiance I saw when I was sixteen-years-old in a hospital room just before my father died. "I don't know what happened in there," I said to Charlie, "but I feel like something's changed in me. I feel like I have to meet that man again." "Then go," Charlie said, "and find out who he is."

The walk to the restaurant, the dinner, and our entire conversation became a blur. I don't remember one particular thing that happened until we returned to Charlie's apartment building, climbed the stairwell, and were greeted by an elderly male neighbor who had an apartment on the same floor. I'd seen him before as he entered or left his apartment, on the stairwell, or in the building's entrance. I would nod pleasantly to him, but we never spoke. "How'd ya like to come in for some tea?" he asked us. "Sure," Charlie replied. He opened the door to his apartment. I stepped in and was shocked to see an extensive collection of oriental antiquities. It was like a small museum. I looked around. "Where'd you get all this stuff?" I asked him. "There's a dealer in Greenwich Village named Rudi," he replied. "I bought most of it from him." Rudi was the gentleman I had met in the Asian art gallery a few hours before. "You don't mean it?" I asked. "Yes," he replied. "About ninety percent of this art comes from his gallery." "I just met Rudi early this evening," I said to him, and turned to Charlie. "I have to go see that man again."

After tea and pleasant conversation, Charlie and I returned to his apartment. "The gods are talking to me," I said. He took two beers from his refrigerator and gave me one. "For once in my life, I have to listen. For once in my life I can't blow it." "Go see the guy," Charlie replied, "and find out what this is all about."

At five p.m. the next evening I went to Rudi's shop. He had assembled more antique Buddhas, Tibetan paintings, Indian stone carvings of gods and goddesses and decorative Oriental art than I'd ever seen in one place before. It was a treasure trove of Hindu and Buddhist antiquities. Seated in his chair next to a large Japanese bronze Buddha with a dark green patina, he smiled when he saw me and invited me to sit down. I had a million questions, but nothing came to mind. His energy was so strong it overwhelmed me. "I knew you'd come back," he said. "I knew it from the moment you entered my store." "I feel like I've known you all my life," I said to him. "This is no accident." "No," he replied. "Come, I'll show you the double-breathing meditation exercise." He went over the exercise twice, gave me a short class, and I experienced a flow of spiritual energy that transformed my tension into deep silence. It got me in touch with my breath and chakra system. "I'm gonna close the store," he said when we finished, "and we'll walk over to the meditation hall."

On our walk he talked about India, his guru there, and the incredible depth of inner work it took to open to God. He talked about how important it was for him to give away everything he'd learned in his lifetime, how a spiritual teacher dreams of great students; he also talked about how nothing works without surrender; he talked about how important it was to build the chakra system; he talked about stuff I'd read in books but never believed could be living reality. Before we got to the meditation hall he said to me, "No more drugs. It's the only thing I forbid in my practice." I was relieved to hear this restriction, and never touched pot or LSD or any other kind of hallucinogenic again.

"Am I walking on air or concrete?" I asked myself. "Will I ever come down from that class we had in his store? I've never felt this close to any human being before . . . and we've only known each other for about an hour. I've come home. It's taken nine years, but I've finally met the right teacher."

CHAPTER 24

I learned early on that meditation class isn't a spiritual life. It's like a gym where one goes to develop psychic muscles called chakras. If these muscles aren't developed in daily practice they atrophy, and whatever connection we have with spirit is reduced to a drip from a leaky faucet. A spiritual life is twenty-four hours a day, seven days a week, and meditation class is a place where we go to build a system that's strong enough to have a spiritual life. Consciousness isn't compartmentalized into activities we think are spiritual—be they vegetarianism, celibacy, fasting, attendance at churches or synagogues, religious persuasion, living in ashrams, monasteries or convents—consciousness doesn't wrap itself in feel-good environments that don't penetrate and heal dysfunction in people. The real test of an ashram and its meditation classes isn't the ashram. It's when we leave, when we enter a world that's foreign to our everyday experience and discover whether or not we find God there. To hide out in a reclusive space, to feel protected from life is the fastest way to guarantee oneself another incarnation. A great saint that lives in a cave must have been a profligate, a terrorist, a banker or lawyer, housewife or janitor in one or many of his or her former lifetimes. We carry inside us a smörgåsbord of experience. My teacher Rudi wanted "to eat from every dish on the table." There would be nothing to return for, nothing missing, not a morsel of life that he overlooked.

The very air we breathe is prayer—the *I AM* when we inhale becomes *THAT* when we exhale—a mandala or complete circle of energy that connects us to spirit. With every inhalation we ingest all of existence, and when we exhale we surrender to the

life, taken for granted by people that
st basic of all ingredients is breath: a
hens chakras and gives us the abil-
ll of humanity, be it religious people,
ain Joes that bumble through the day,
ival instinct tells us the alternative to
death. If we lose touch with the most
's no way we can move forward. God
mage of a kind or vengeful old man in
the sky. God is energy, all of existence, a life force that penetrates
everything on earth and in the universe, an unexplainable and
mysterious power that compels us to live more conscious lives.
It's both beauty and truth as well as all the horror and ugliness we
can conjure up; it's the movement of the universe, the pain and
joy we feel, the happiness and deep regret; it's birth and death
and everything in between—a life force no intellect can quite
understand, but every human being can experience if they learn
to breathe and use their minds properly. We are born with the
instruments we need to connect with spirit. We just have to learn
to use them.

Happy people don't terrorize other people. They look for the
good in humanity and accept differences of thought and opinion.
The moment we say, "My way is the only way," we become dangerous not only to ourselves but to the rest of the planet. We separate
people into well-defined boxes. They are black, white, brown or
yellow; they are Christian, Jew, Muslim, Buddhist, Hindu; they
are trapped within well-defined psychological and physical borders where signs are posted "No Trespassing, stay out, don't bring
your beliefs into this arena . . . or else." The question is, or else
what? A person could be shot, stabbed, strangled, crucified or
burnt at the stake because he sees God differently than someone
else, because his skin color isn't the same, because he doesn't
believe there's a kingly being who sits on a majestic throne in a
manufactured heaven that's like an animated movie produced
and directed by bigots and fools who have divorced themselves
from humanity.

In Marrakech, my policeman neighbor and I sat on the rooftop
of my house and smoked a *kief* pipe. The Atlas Mountains rose
high above us in the distance. "The great equalizer is death," he

said to me in French. "It shows no discrimination and welcomes everyone into its arms." From the mouth of a humble Moroccan policeman to the ears of the world, we all have to accept the meaning of equality. Death finally teaches us this lesson and destiny draws us onto a playing field that is truly democratic. It doesn't pick and choose. It reaches out to everyone and everything that lives on this planet.

❖❖❖❖

Self-involved spiritual teachers often compete with each other for positions of power, an ego-coated approach to life that radiates neon-coated auras that hypnotize naïve disciples. What they teach appears to be spiritual practice, but it has no depth. In February of 1973, the week after Rudi took his *samadhi*, communal closeness reigned in his Tenth Street ashram: hugs and tears and people that swore eternal allegiance to one another. The drama of the moment prevailed, the trauma of Rudi's death paralyzed his disciples and they supported one another. A few months passed. The communal spirit dissolved into a struggle for power. I never understood why Rudi had asked me to live in Denton. When power-hungry disciples struggled to take over the throne, it was the first time life in Texas made sense to me. I was far enough away from the battlefield to not be involved. The whole thing made me sick. There was a conscription phase: orange-tee-shirted mini-gurus did their best to convince Rudi's students to come live in their ashrams. I once heard Rudi say, "The best teachers have no students. They've built strong chakra systems in their disciples and given them their own connection to God."

God's children shouldn't be enslaved in the ashram of a spiritual tyrant who uses power to control his disciples. "You have to free the people you love," Rudi had told me, "Do not create more karma, more negative vibes than already exist in the world." Didn't these orange-clad predators learn anything? I thought with a smile. It really doesn't matter. My connection to God is more important than a coterie of disciples. This meditation practice isn't for the masses. It's for a chosen few that want their enlightenment. It's too difficult for large groups of people to do anyway. I have to respect the light that shines in every human being. I can't make use of charisma and personality to attract people to live in my demesne. Schisms will occur, people will rebel, there will be anger and revolt and students will break away and do their own thing. That has nothing to do with spirituality. It has nothing to do with divine light that nurtures people and helps them find their way. Rudi saved my life. He helped me to build an internal system that connected me to God. That's why I studied with him; that's what I must teach anyone who comes to study with me. The rest is nonsense that leads directly to the grave.

If a spiritual life is a twenty-four-hours-a-day, seven-days-a-week affair, there must be love, kindness, and compassion in our interactions with other people. And no one should be belittled because of their mistakes and limitations. Rudi helped to uplift his students, to give them the strength to overcome problems, to nurture them and teach them to transform their own tension into spiritual energy. He was a tough taskmaster, but kind and caring. His commitment was deep and real, and it nurtured those who opened to what he had to teach. The greatest treasure he bequeathed us was the double-breathing open-eyed meditation exercise. A conscious use of that exercise could help anyone attain spiritual enlightenment. He told me many times, "Don't love me... love God. One day I won't be here anymore. If you want to attach yourself to anything, let it be higher energy in the universe."

❖❖❖

Time and space are terms that are relative to each human being's level of understanding. Anyone can conjure up a personal definition. I once thought they were strictly scientific phenomenon, dealt with specifically by mathematicians and physicists. This idea stayed with me until the day I had my first experience of higher energy in the universe. The awakening of kundalini brought a renewed grasp of those abstract words.

After a few years of study with Rudi my crown chakra opened, and my soul moved through the cosmos to a place where my mind couldn't wrap itself around what I experienced. A sense of nothingness prevailed. Like the Mt. Meru vision in Tibetan Buddhism where a twenty-thousand-foot mountain is encircled by a chain of mountains half its height, and another circle of mountains half the mountain chain's height, and another and another until there was a mandala of thirteen mountain chains that made up the universe, I saw thousands of these mandalas move through time and space and into infinity. The macrocosmic transformed itself into a grain of sand on an endless beach.

Imagine yourself on a mountaintop. It's a dark clear night and there are millions of stars in the sky. Imagine the vastness of the universe reduced to a single strand of beads that connects all the stars; imagine galaxy after galaxy of stars and planets moving endlessly through the cosmos; imagine if that incredible vision is nothing more than a drop of water in an ocean. It's beyond human comprehension. It demands that we let go of preconceived notions about life and its meanings. We must go to the fountainhead of creation, a place that the human intellect cannot in any way grasp. Total surrender and oneness with higher energy guides the soul into the cosmos and outside the confines of time and space.

The question always is "How does one do this?" There's no immediate answer to that question. If one learns the craft of meditation and uses it under the guidance of a spiritual master for many years, if one develops a chakra system that's strong enough to support the energy of kundalini, the soul will rise up the spine and exit from the top of the head, move through time and space, and connect with the infinite. One has to experience a state of nothingness—a process that can take years to manifest. One has to prioritize a union with God, not as some abstract concept, but as a living reality that attunes us to higher energy in the universe.

If intellectual curiosity and humanity's adventurous spirit inspire us to explore the outer limits of time and space, if all manifestation exists within the realms of time and space, if what we comprehend fills nothing more than a metaphorical teacup, there's something wrong in this equation. The need to discover inspires us to explore unknown precincts, but logicians, scientists, and mathematicians often shrug their shoulders and say, "I don't understand. There must be something of a higher nature at work, something that transcends human logic and exists on a different plane." What that something is, we'll never know. It's elusive and out of reach, but it gives birth to all of creativity. Whether or not we accept the incomprehensible, it's always with us—a mysterious force that instills restless minds with an unquenchable thirst for knowledge, a need to explain the unexplainable and bring order to a disorderly world.

In my late teens and twenties I made every attempt to plumb the depths of the spiritual. Books I read ranged from the metaphysical to the psychological, from masters of literary fiction to philosophy and theology and the hagiographies of saints. I read and read until my head ached, and I still came up empty. I had no desire to understand spirit. I wanted it to become a living reality, but it always seemed to elude my grasp.

Under Rudi's tutelage the kundalini began to rise, and my soul force merged with higher energy. Death and rebirth became a reality, cycles made sense, and the transient nature of life was no longer a muddle in my brain. "I need to learn two things," I said to myself, "I need to work out my karma on earth and to connect with energy that transcends time and space." The marriage of the human soul with the universal soul created two rivers of energy, one that descended and entered my crown chakra and brought with it important elements of a spiritual life: wisdom, love, joy, foundation, the *Om* sound, a compassionate way of living, whatever was necessary to work out my karma. The second, an ascending river of energy transported my soul to precincts that rose outside the boundaries of time and space. My focus on the navel chakra during meditation enabled me to draw transcendental energy down and make conscious use of it in daily life. My mind, my emotions, my sense of attachment, all of it had to be surrendered. I experienced a state of nothingness that allowed higher energy to flow through my chakra system.

Rudi's meditation technique enabled me to build an internal life that was strong enough to live in the world and be free of the world at exactly same time. None of this can take place if one isn't grounded. None of this can take place if the heart is closed, and if sexual energy doesn't transform lower elements of life into a force that will activate kundalini. Rudi's meditation technique developed my chakra system and made it possible for me to work out karma and open to energy that's outside the realms of time and space. These are not separate activities. As I said earlier in this book, a human being is a vertex in an equilateral triangle that connects the inner and outer worlds with transcendental energy.

❖❖❖❖

Logic is a construct of the human mind. Once the chakra system opens and kundalini connects us to the soul of the universe, our consciousness will undergo a major shift. Infinite energy defies the mind's understanding and forces us to see the world differently. We can no longer rely on pat answer constructs to familiar situations in day-to-day life. A veil of illusion suddenly lifts, and reality no longer hides behind ignorance. We can "render unto Caesar what is Caesar's and render unto God what is God's," and we're no longer intimidated by pressure and don't judge foolishness in others.

Compassion is the main ingredient in one's newly discovered awareness, the ability to live in Caesar's world without being threatened by Caesar's requirements: deal with rent, work, relationships, laws and regulations, what we can and can't do. It doesn't mean that we let people take advantage of us. It just means that we've detached ourselves from Caesar's restrictions and no longer permit them to upset the balance of our inner life. Dramas that once drained us of our energy are reduced to soap operas that we can almost enjoy. We no longer have to consume people's energies in order to get through the day. The moment our consciousness detaches itself from the external world and connects with higher energy, that moment frees us from karmic bonds and allows us to become one with God. Whether we stay on earth or not depends on the work we have to do here. It has nothing to do with ego investment or greed. The life we live isn't our own; the time we spend here isn't our own; it's borrowed time given to us by the universe, time we must use to uplift our own life and the lives of others.

The chakra system is like a "tree of life," deeply rooted in the *hara*. Its branches extend infinitely into the cosmos. Just as a tree absorbs carbon dioxide from the atmosphere and transforms it into oxygen, the chakra system absorbs our tension and transforms it into *chi*.

If ambition becomes an end in itself, if greed and self-interest take over, we lose ourselves in the glitter of money and fame. If ambition helps us to recognize the transient nature of things, if we build an inner life that dwarfs the material plane, if we learn that the power of humility far surpasses the power of ego, ambition has served us in a profound way. It's easy to get swept away in ambition's river, it's easy to lose oneself in material success and inflated images of self, it's easy to get lost in poverty, failure and depression in whatever karma brings our way.

People are like predators in a jungle where one eats or gets eaten. They substitute ego for self-confidence, hack their way through life, and open paths to success by stepping over anyone in their way. Incapable of seeing beyond their own ambitions, they've lost all connection with spirit. The child in them has grown into a corrupt adult that feeds off other people's insecurity and tension. Internal growth has stopped. Their chakra systems atrophy, and what manifests is charisma and ego, masks that hide deep-rooted fears of old age and death's inevitability, stripping them of a lifetime's effort. They've substituted material gain for a spiritual life and have blinded themselves to the repercussions of ambition's shortsightedness. Life's most important treasures are overlooked: joy, love, and happiness get trampled in a quest for material gain.

❖❖❖❖

The thought of a trip to the crash site where Rudi passed on was anathema to me. "It will be a pilgrimage to a holy site," a student told me. "I've already been there," I answered. "It's not an easy place for me to return to. It's not easy to have survived a plane crash in which the person you loved more than anyone in the world died."

Most people need some kind of crutch to lean on, I thought, and forget that the real temple is a living force inside themselves. They need symbols of God to worship because they haven't developed their own inner life and connected to spirit. We substitute shrines, stupas, and temples for our own lack of inner development. It's easy to feel holy in a prescribed sacred place and difficult to feel holy at the grocery store, at work, in family disputes, when the minutiae of daily life become like chalk scratching a blackboard. We need megachurches and cathedrals, monuments, temples and shrines, to remind us of God. We forget that every breath is sacred, every experience takes place in a sacred temple called life. "It's the place where Rudi took his *samadhi*," the student replied. "I know," I said. "I was there. I tried to revive him. I tried to bring him back. I massaged his heart and breathed into his lungs, but nothing revived him. The plane was broken into pieces and scattered all over the place. The only way I survived was because he put his soul in me, and every time I look in the mirror I see a living miracle."

Early on I discovered that Rudi lives in my heart—a sacred place for loved ones, a temple created by God that's deep within me, a temple that opens its door when I feel gratitude and love, and elevates me to the highest levels of my own humanity. He is always with me, I thought. Why do I have to relive the experience of the crash? Why do I have to climb a mountain at Northlake to worship at a sacred shrine? Why do I have to relive that pain? There were no answers to those questions. I stopped asking them long ago and devoted my time and energy to the meditation practice I learned from him. Certain pains cut so deep the wound never heals.

At my Thirteenth Street gallery, clients and browsers would point at Rudi's photo and say, "I knew him. He died a tragic death, didn't he?" I heard stories about Rudi's death from people who had no idea what they were talking about. "He was a nice guy," I'd hear. "What a shame he died at such an early age." Others would say, "I bought great art from him. It was cheap. I don't think he knew what he had. His shop was like a supermarket full of Asian antiquities." On occasion, when the tales of his death became outrageous I'd simply say, "I was in the airplane with him when it hit the mountain." "You? Impossible. It's a miracle that you're alive!" "Yes," I said." "It's truly a miracle."

A group of my meditation students made plans to climb Northlake Mountain and visit the site of the plane crash. They wanted me to go with them. "Okay," I said after I thought for a moment. "I might as well get past my resistance. When?" "Next Saturday."

The moment of the plane crash was vivid in my mind as we drove from Manhattan to Northlake. Beau had cried out from the pilot's seat, "Oh my God," and everything went blank. When I awoke a few minutes later, my front teeth were missing. Blood poured from my mouth and soaked my jacket. "Rudi's dead," Beau whispered to me. "No," I said. "It can't be." I jumped out of the wrecked plane, kneeled over Rudi's body and tried to revive him. "You told me that you'd live to be eighty-four," I whispered to him. "We'd go to the Middle East and find the Aquarian Christ child together. You told me so much . . ." There were tears in my eyes and blood ran from my mouth like a waterfall. Dazed and in a state of shock I stood up, looked at him and thought, "Now I'll find out what the last six years were about. Now it's just me and God, and Rudi, dearest Rudi, you are alive and well in my heart. Thank you, for allowing me to be here the last moments of your life. I will do whatever I can to make sure you don't have to come back to earth again."

We arrived at Northlake and climbed a path that led up the mountain. There were blue markers every hundred feet or so and with each step I took, I experienced profound resistance in myself. There must be something important I have to do here, I thought. Why is there so much conflict in me?

We walked twenty minutes on a path that meandered up the mountain past a large boulder on a cliff that overlooked the Hudson Valley. "It's there," a student pointed. "How do you know?" I asked. "I came here a few weeks ago." We walked through fifty yards of brush and found plane wreckage—a wing here, another there, the body of the plane and every other part of the wreck covered with cryptic graffiti, names of people and dates.

Flashes of memory went through my head:

Beau, Mimi and I huddled around a fire. When dawn came, it took us five or six hours to walk down the mountain. We were dazed and in shock, and hobbled over paths that eventually led to people's houses. Without a clue to our whereabouts I moved forward step by agonizing step with one thought in my mind: Rudi's dead. We've left him behind. There wasn't much else we could do. Another day and night on that mountain and we most likely would have frozen to death. When I knocked at the front door of a house, a woman opened it and gasped, "My God. What happened to you?" "A plane crash," I replied. "Last night, we were in a plane crash in the mountains." "Come in, come in. I will call 911." "What time is it? I asked. "Eleven thirty," she answered.

It was unreal, dreamlike, a blur. Rudi was dead and no one in the city knew about it. We were certain they'd send someone to rescue us. "I have to call the city," I told Beau. "Go on," he said. This will be the most difficult phone call I've ever made, I thought. I couldn't pick up the receiver. "Go on," he said again, a little annoyed. "Call his mother." "No, I'm gonna call the antique store on Tenth Street." I dialed the number. "Hello, hello," someone said. "This is Stuart." "Stuart! Where are you? Is everything okay?" "I didn't want to call Rudi's mother direct." "What happened?" "Rudi's dead. He died in a plane crash last night." "Oh my God! This isn't a joke?" "No, it's not a joke. We're in the Catskill Mountains at someone's home. She's called 911. Here she is. She'll give you the address."

In a state of semi-shock, unable to move or think of what to do, I sat on a bench and waited in the woman's house. The tragedy had finally hit home. Rudi's death became a reality.

❖❖❖❖

Halfway through the meditation at the crash site, my thoughts stopped, and a wellspring of silence flooded my troubled heart with a sense of peace. My tension melted away. Rudi said to me, "It was my time to leave the world, my time to be with God. I had done whatever my karma required and could move on." He's home, I thought when I came out of the meditative state. He's finally gone home.

"Next summer," I said to a group of students, "I'm going to bring a busload of people here. We can meditate at the crash site, picnic and swim in the lake, and enjoy a day like Rudi would like us to enjoy it."

Each summer for the next five or six years, students from ashrams around the United States and I made a pilgrimage to Northlake. We paid homage to our teacher. We swam and picnicked, and, in a word, we had an incredible day at the *samadhi* site and the lake—a sacred place if there ever was one.

❖❖❖❖

The six years I spent with Rudi transformed a neurotic and insecure young man into a person who had developed a spiritual life. It was impossible for me to take him for granted. His energy was too strong. I rebelled a bit because of demands he made on me to change. But I never treated his meditation techniques cheaply. "This opportunity could easily disappear," I said to myself. "I would be left with the old Stuart, a person I don't want to return to." Each meditation class was an opportunity for me to move forward. It never occurred to me to put off until tomorrow what God had provided for me in the present. To take this gift for granted would have been a foolish attempt to destroy myself. I needed what Rudi had to teach. I had to have patience, I had to hang on.

Necessity demanded that I go to meditation class. Necessity demanded that I listen to Rudi, learn from him, grow inside myself until neurotic me disappeared; necessity also demanded that I never take his meditation practice for granted. I didn't want to become overly familiar with the most important gift that I had ever received. "It's not going to work if you procrastinate," I said to myself. "It's not going to work if you disappear for months at a time." As much as I couldn't stand to dredge up nightmarish me, I knew that if I ran away it would be the end of my life. I didn't want to waste my time and Rudi's time. I couldn't do that to either of us.

There are always blue markers on the spiritual path. We just have to recognize them. Simple signs of growth: a word here, a person there, a kindness offered, a sense of balance, memories of what life was like pre-Rudi, a change of job, more responsibility, signs that inspired me to work in greater depth on myself. A deep sense of gratitude never permitted me to treat life cheaply. Signs of growth came early in my spiritual development: the rekindled love for my mother, the respect I gained for people that lived in Rudi's house, the ability to surround myself with Asian art, the discovery that my father, on his dying bed, became my first teacher, and so much more. They were all steps on a ladder that enabled me to climb out of the basement and find the light of day.

Most of his disciples assumed Rudi would live another forty years. His premature death upset many of them who believed that there was a great deal of time left to master what Rudi had to teach. He told me a hundred times: "Don't take one day for granted. Learn what I have to teach. It's the most important gift that I can give to you. Do the work while I'm here and get your connection with God. When I leave you might have to wait ten thousand lifetimes for energy like this to come again."

"I will be in a plane crash in the Middle East, disappear for ten years, and re-emerge as the teacher of an Aquarian Christ child," he told me one day in his gallery. It never occurred to me that the plane crash would take place in the Catskill Mountains . . . that it would end Rudi's life. There would be no more meditation classes with him on East Tenth Street. A plane crash in the Catskill Mountains had turned one second into an eternity. No one lives forever, not even Rudi, whose life touched so many people.

A fellow student of Rudi's asked me if I had ever thought about a career. "No," I answered and shrugged my shoulders. "My career is getting to God. That's it, the only profession I want." "Can you earn a living doing that?" "I don't know, but I will certainly find out." That was my commitment. My bags were packed and I was ready to move to the Middle East, China, Tibet, Burma, anywhere Rudi wanted to go, anywhere I could receive his teachings. The alternative was to sit wide-eyed on a riverbank and watch enlightenment float downstream. Money will come when necessity makes its demands, I thought, but spiritual opportunity can slip through karmic cracks before anyone takes notice.

❖❖❖❖

I'd work when I needed money as a young man, but rarely stayed with a job for more than three months. My ambitions weren't economically motivated. I believed that fine art and literature would open doors to spiritual realms. When I studied acting in New York City, insight into human nature by playwrights, directors and actors was more important to me than pecuniary recompense. Money never entered my life's equation until I reached my early thirties. I had literary goals, artistic goals, poetical goals, but never gave thought to financial success.

The profound truth and beauty I found in sculpture and on canvases inspired me to write. I was shown what was possible but not how to get there. If I had been born with painterly gifts they would have determined the course of my life. But something was missing in the lives of artists. Van Gogh painted masterpieces of a spiritual nature but lived the life of a mad man; Caravaggio was no different, nor was Michelangelo or Gauguin. When I left a museum full of artistic insights I wanted to put on paper, my thoughts were elevated, but the rest of me was in the lower depths. Momentary happiness flitted through me and vanished. I assumed that suffering was all that there was. Without it, creativity was impossible; without it musicians couldn't compose and artists couldn't paint. Suffering was responsible for masterpieces that come down to us through the ages. There has to be more, I thought, but in my early twenties I didn't know where to look. It upset me no end when I read in Plato that art and music were secondary to the ideal. They rendered truth and beauty but weren't its source. What eluded me was the source of creativity, the wellspring, the inception and birthplace that would connect my consciousness to higher energy. Manifestation, no matter how profound, no matter how closely it touched on truth and beauty, was not the source itself. It did nothing to transform my inner life and develop a connection to God, and finally, it brought me no peace of mind.

❖❖❖❖

Later on in my life I discovered that ambition and goals were important. They attracted karmic situations I had to work through. If goals become ends in themselves, if money, success, and power were godlike entities, if nothing existed beyond them, these illusive endgames would poison my vitals. They would placate my ego and create a false image of self, one that dissipates in time.

"What is their purpose, if any?" I asked Rudi.

"We can't free ourselves from what we haven't experienced," he replied. "It's easy to reject money and success, but rejection doesn't build internal strength. There's always something missing. Money is just a form of energy. It gives life if we use it properly. A monk who lives in a cave and meditates all day must have been very rich in a past lifetime."

How much money does it take to get through the day? I asked myself. At what point do money and success become nothing more than greed and gluttony? There are only so many houses we can buy, boats, cars, art and antiques before we can't inventory what we have. At what point does money do nothing else but make more money? It's always the next deal and the next, a nonstop, out-of-control diesel-like ambition that will eventually derail itself and cause a great deal of pain. Twenty-five years of art and antique dealing enabled me to make a great deal of money. It also revealed to me the transient nature of things. I'd buy and sell statues from the fifteenth century, paintings and porcelain that were hundreds of years old, objects that could tell great stories if given the opportunity. "Nothing is an end in itself," I thought, when I handled these works of art. "It's all so transient." I was grateful to have the money, but I never let the money have me.

The art world was full of Jekyll-and-Hyde-type characters that would shift and change in front of me. The light in people's eyes went out the moment money was involved, and one could easily be stabbed in the back by a best friend. The friendly dinners, the social gatherings, the smiles and hugs vanished when the conversation turned to money. There were many sophisticated people in the room, but few human beings. Beneath the glitz and glitter was a shark's tank of voracious predators who thought about only one thing: the next sale. Great art became a commodity and, like any other commodity—pork loins, soybeans, corn, lentils, or whatever—it had only one value, what price could it bring in the marketplace? I not only learned about art, I was given an education in human nature and the force of greed.

❖❖❖❖

The moment we shed ambition and step off the karmic merry-go-round, spiritual enlightenment ceases to be a goal. It becomes a state of being that weaves the past and the future into the present, and time and space become drops of water in a vast ocean. There are markers on the path to nirvana: happiness, detachment from material possessions, freedom from anxiety, fear, guilt, and a compassionate life. These markers raise our humanity and open doors to enlightenment.

CHAPTER 25

Rudi taught us a street-smart, survival-type yoga that was a tight fit for a place like New York City where goody two-shoes, holier-than-thou approaches to meditation and spiritual practice didn't quite come up to snuff. He was a Jewish guy from East New York, born into a slum, and raised by a mother who was a chorus girl and close friend of members of the Mafia. Not quite a Buddhist beginning, but a significant one, because he was able to fight his way out of the slums of Brooklyn to become one of the most important spiritual teachers of the twentieth century. With his no-nonsense, no bullshit approach to life and God, his charismatic nature attracted many people. His incredible sense of humor could alleviate any tense situation, and his wisdom far surpassed anything I'd ever heard before. He was the most sacrilegious person I knew, but had such a deep and pure spirituality it cut through the tightness of organized religion. "I'd be the first one to leave," he once told me, "if my meditation center became institutionalized." He was Rudra incarnate, the earliest form of Siva, a gifted yogi who was strong enough to transform the chaos of New York City into a temple. He had only one rule in his meditation practice: no hallucinogenic drugs, a rule that eliminated problematic students who wanted to get stoned and not have a spiritual life. "Drugs work in the same area as kundalini yoga," he once told me, "but they drain your energy and destroy the chakra system. They're also illegal, and who needs all the problems attached to them?"

The first six months of classes were a revelation. I saw light and color around Rudi, and the souls of ancient gurus streamed through him and into me. Tears flowed from my eyes. After every class my shirt or t-shirt was soaking wet. They were tears of joy, of surrender, of letting go of a lifetime of pain. I can be with God, I thought. I can attain everything I've wanted since I was a teenager. It was an extended honeymoon of the first order, a marriage of student and teacher that was arranged by higher energies. I would visit his store three or four times a week, sit with him, and absorb his teachings, sometimes in the form of words, but mostly from meditation classes we had together.

My ordinary life was no different than pre-Rudi. I worked as a waiter to pay rent and eat, a job I hated but suffered through because it put money in my pocket from day one. I'd often work until three o'clock in the morning. Tired and without enough sleep I'd get up at seven a.m. on a cold Saturday morning and walk to Rudi's meditation center to attend class. I'll sleep later, I thought. The class was more important. I had never worked for more than three months at any restaurant job. I'd either quit or get fired, but in either case, the time would come for me to leave.

Rudi had many rich, celebrity-type clients and friends, but his commitment to his meditation students, no matter what their background, superseded friendships. The downtime in his gallery enabled me to visit him quite often. I didn't understand why he let me get close to him, but I never questioned the blessing. I went to his gallery whenever opportunity made it possible. The one-on-one meditations were a privilege. They helped me develop a profound connection with Rudi, a connection that serves me to this day. I had never had a relationship with anyone like him before—a spiritual master who ate in Chinese restaurants, the Second Avenue Deli, pizza joints, and loved pecan pie and sloppy Joe sandwiches. It was a refreshing change from lineages that preached vegetarianism, celibacy, and hundreds of rules and regulations that kept me from participating in life. There's nothing wrong with vegetarianism and celibacy and religious dogma, I thought, if righteous people didn't insist the rest of the world follow suit.

Obsessed with the written word, I spent every spare moment immersed in novels by masters like Tolstoy, Flaubert, Dostoyevsky, George Eliot, Dickens, Kafka, and Turgenev. I wanted to extract technical aspects of prose from their books and become a writer.

In awe of their masterful accomplishments I still couldn't put five words together to make a sentence. I was a writer who couldn't write, an insecure person who didn't trust himself to put original ideas and thoughts on paper and create a novel or short story. I wasn't able to overcome confusion in my own head.

Joyce's *A Portrait of the Artist as a Young Man* and Hemingway's *A Farewell to Arms* struck a literary chord in me and loosened my writing chops. I liked the freedom in their prose, understandable stream-of-consciousness-type writing that made it possible for me to transmute thought into words on paper. I was taken with playwrights of the 1960s that transformed stodgy and structured theater into absurdist plays that no longer relied on set dramatic themes, and storylines developed into tragic or comic circumstances—playwrights like Beckett and Ionesco, who, for a brief period of time, changed the shape of theater.

There was no shortage in me of what to say, but I hadn't as yet found my own voice. It will come, I thought, but when? How long will I have to wait? Could I ever make a literary career for myself? There was another problem: literature had deep spiritual implications for me. I didn't want to just write another novel. My words and insights had to explore esoteric realms. They had to open inside me a path to enlightenment, an approach to art and writing that I didn't find in stylistic geniuses like Hemingway, Turgenev, Dickens, and other writers, masters of craft who had great insight into the psychological makeup of people but rarely stepped through a door to transcendental experience. The poetry, paintings, drawings and prints of William Blake took that step. The poetry of Rimbaud and Rilke, the novels of Herman Hesse and Dostoyevsky explored human suffering and spiritual elevation. The poems of Rumi and Japanese haiku touched a deep chord in me.

I found myself adrift in a literary ocean without the foggiest idea how I would get to shore. I'd tread water in shadows cast by Kafka and Tolstoy. I didn't want to compete with them. I wanted to learn from them, find my own voice, and publish my writing in the future. Why should these great masters intimidate me and shake the mind and heart of a seeker after truth? I thought. They had something to teach, and I would learn. That's all it amounted to. If I invested time and energy and believed in myself, someday

I would write a decent book.

Literature was my magical garden, a place I retreated to when I wanted to escape life's frenzy. I never spoke about it to anyone, not Rudi, Charlie, not even Marian when she came to live with me in New York. I believed that the study of art, music and literature would deepen my spiritual life. When I discovered the shitty lives most artists and writers lived, how self-centered they were, how critical, how they were obsessed with their own position in the literary or artistic world, I surrendered my fanatical need to be a writer. I wrote because words flowed through me and had to manifest on paper. Whether my books were successful or not didn't matter. What mattered was whether or not the people that read them would derive benefit and explore their inner lives a little differently.

When Marian and I lived together in New York, I had to split my time between her, Rudi, a job, and my writing. I wasn't strong enough to do it all. She never interfered with my meditation classes, but was shocked to discover how serious I was about spiritual practice with Rudi. She had no interest in meditation. In her mind, Rudi was more important to me than her. At first, it wasn't true. I just didn't know how to balance both. "It'll take time," I told her. "I can't give this up. I've been looking for it all my life." "How long do I have to wait?" She asked me. "I don't know." "Do you expect me to become a Hindu/Buddhist?" she said. "I don't understand any of this crap." "I don't understand it either," I said, "but it works for me and that's all I have to know." "Great," she responded. "I've come here from Germany to find out you're married to a cult."

Sunday morning pre-class breakfasts were a weekly tradition at Rudi's house. I invited Marian to attend. My hope was that she'd meet Rudi and the people who studied with him; my hope was that she'd realize I wasn't involved with a cult. My hope was that she'd make friends with some of the people that attended meditation class. She'd see that Rudi was a person that could be trusted. He would never try to get between her and me. The exact opposite happened. Intimidated by the openness of people there, resentful that she didn't feel part of the group, Marian hid out in a corner and spoke to no one. We left early. The walk home was a nightmare. Neither of us spoke.

The relationship fell apart. We didn't argue about anything. There was just distance, that's all, time spent apart, her with friends at the bar where she worked, and me at meditation class, writing, and working in a restaurant. We didn't speak much to one another. "I'm going to move," she said to me one morning." I had expected it. She had gotten close to a bartender. They had gone out a few times after work. "Are you sleeping with him?" I asked her. "Not yet," she replied, "but once I leave here, I'm gonna move into his apartment. I've got to get out of this place," she said. "Whatever," I replied. "I'm going for a walk."

I couldn't blame her for being upset with me if she believed I'd attached myself to a cult-like spiritual practice she couldn't relate to. Some guy named Rudi who was all-powerful and controlled her boyfriend. Her thoughts were simple: Stuart's adrift in a spiritual fog and there's no room for me on his raft. I'd rather be involved with a bartender, a waiter, with anyone who has practical interests, anyone who would make me the center of his life. How can I compete with spiritual fanaticism?

I went into the Eighth Avenue flower shop and bought a very large bouquet for Marian. "What's the point?" I asked myself. "She's gone. There's no more relationship and you want to return to something that doesn't exist." I went directly to Rudi's gallery and gave him the flowers. "They're for you," I said, "with gratitude for what you've done for my life. I can never repay it, but I hope these flowers say something."

❖❖❖❖

Rudi's meditation practice was anything but fanatical. He asked me to sit for half an hour a day at home and attend four hour-long classes a week at his center. What Marian had trouble with were profound changes that had taken place in me. I wasn't the person she fell in love with. She was living with a stranger. I couldn't return to the pot-smoking mystic who chanted *Hare Krishna* and immersed himself in arcane and esoteric books, ate macrobiotics, and pretended he was having a spiritual life. My past was dead. To exhume it would have been suicide.

I missed her warm body next to mine, the lovemaking, a beautiful Valkyrie-like lady who wanted to share my life, the good and bad experiences we lived through in Paris, on the road, in Morocco, and in Spain. But that was all in the past. I now had to focus on something I'd wanted since I was sixteen-years-old—a spiritual life, a conscious connection with God. I stepped through the front door of my life like a man who had nothing to lose. The daily drudge had to stop; the unhappiness, the existential two-step that took me nowhere. The answers were directly in front of me. For the first time in my life I focused on inner growth and refused to be distracted. I had stepped through a magical door and there was no turning back.

CHAPTER 26

Spiritual talk often manifests as words that drip with false wisdom when spoken by people that have read books but never listen to their gut. Two pundits can say the exact same sentence—from one it might sound like empty words in a dark tunnel, from the other, deeply rooted wisdom that comes directly from their soul. I knew it was impossible for me to mimic Rudi. If I tried, my words would sound so false that no one would even pretend to listen. I didn't want to be a second-rate Rudi. I realized that it was going to take a great deal of time to become a first-rate Stuart. It wouldn't happen in a day or two, or a year or two, but it would happen if I kept my focus and sustained inner work.

The ashram on East Tenth Street was more than just another loft building. It was my spiritual home, the place where I got training, where Rudi's presence demanded that I connect with God. It not only contained a wealth of museum-quality Asian paintings and statues, it also housed a ragtag group of assorted hippie-types that had come to New York City from all over the United States to study with Rudi. It became so crowded that on any given night I had no idea where I would sleep.

The solitude I once enjoyed vanished when I went to live on the second floor of Rudi's house. I said farewell to any thought of privacy. When I discovered that real solitude is an inner state, when I learned that every person who lived in the ashram was there to teach me detachment, my heart opened, and I made room for people to live around me. "You can relax, Stuart," Rudi said to me. "I'm gonna send them all home." "You can invite twenty more people," I replied. "They've all taught me so much about myself."

"That's why I invited them here in the first place," he smiled. "You had to learn this or you'd never be any good to yourself or anyone else."

❖❖❖❖

Life never works the way we expect it to. It's like a comedic improvisation with strong touches of tragedy—a play in three acts without denouement, without plot, with absurd characters that grow more absurd the moment they try to manipulate the world—a foolish quest for money, power, and self-aggrandizement that hasn't changed in thousands of years.

We still haven't learned that revenge doesn't work, that anger creates more anger, that there's never a real winner in war, that the solution to most problems is kindness and love. Instead of carpet-bombing other countries, political leaders should divest themselves of righteousness, hatred, self-importance, and bring sensible tactics to the table: compassion for human suffering, the realization that every action has a reaction, and no matter how powerful the forces of revenge, they will always kick mud in one's face.

The heart has been taken out of being human. We're left with bodies that are like empty shells and minds that tick like time bombs. We try to fix the unfixable and use the wrong tools to repair a world that's out of joint. It's like a plumber that uses a hammer to fix a water pipe. Every time he strikes the iron or plastic fitting, the problem gets worse. Every bomb we drop creates more hatred, more angry, disheartened and homeless people that want to take revenge. It creates hordes of migrants that look for safety in countries not torn apart by war. It creates erudite diplomats that meet in secure countries to discuss the fate of innocent people being slaughtered in their war-torn homelands, diplomats that dine in five-star restaurants and stay in palatial hotels while their constituents are being blown to pieces by carpet bombs and religious fanatics. This senseless waste of human life creates well-paid jobs for political hacks that have wormed their way into power. Deals are made, pacts are signed, and armies exhaust themselves, withdraw, build up their resources again and prepare for the next confrontation. To the satisfaction of industrial, technical and defense industry greed, forces of evil always manifest somewhere on earth, and kill countless numbers of people.

❖❖❖❖

Anyone who runs for President of the United States should be required to ride New York City subways north of Ninety-sixth Street at least four times a week and connect with the people they want to govern—members of the ninety-nine-and-nine-tenths percentile of American citizens that have no voice in the halls of power, the beaten-down and overworked populace that barely make ends meet. Politicians that promise to fix health care and poverty at election time would keep those promises if they interacted with constituents. It's probably been thirty years or more since any U.S. president has visited the Southeast Bronx. Travel to Asia, Europe and Africa is easier than to the poverty-stricken enclaves that house the lower depths of our society. The real blights aren't in slums and indigence. They're in the slipshod consciousness of egotistical fools that govern us, in the black holes that are embedded in politically ambitious minds that keep elected officials from compassionate interaction with humanity. No wonder it's difficult to believe anything politicians say. Their lies usher them into the halls of power, a place where fabrication and self-aggrandizement are the accepted norms.

If one looks into the glazed-over eyes of political power brokers, it's easy to see why so little truth comes out of their mouths. If politicians listened to humanity's heartbeat and responded with compassion and not false promises, every act would be one of kindness, every act would help to uplift people. Remarkable men like Mahatma Gandhi and Martin Luther King devoted their lives to serving humanity. In every generation there are many great souls who perform unconditional service and refuse to accept praise for their actions. They rarely, if ever, step into the limelight. A love of life has taught them to give and to receive unconditionally.

❖❖❖❖

"I've never met an easy person," Rudi said to me. "There are no angels on earth, just human beings that struggle with tension."

❖❖❖❖

On a hot summer's morning in Big Indian, we dragged dead trees and branches down a slope and burned them. The idea was to clear the hillside and make room for an apple orchard. It was exhausting work and the heat weighed on me, but Rudi had an apple orchard vision that couldn't be stopped. The dead trees had to be removed. Periodically we'd rest and drink some water.

People at the Big Indian ashram fought with each other, complained all the time, and refused to take care of their responsibilities. Some of them threatened to leave. Angelic and soft-spoken on the outside, they sported auras of superficial sweetness; vegetarians and celibates that practiced hatha yoga and the martial arts, but beneath their spiritual veneer was a hotbed of tension, insecurity and anger…and even worse, a righteous approach to life. "What's going on with these people?" I asked Rudi. "I always thought that Big Indian was a place where one came to develop an inner life." "Don't worry about it," he replied. "In twenty years, none of them will be here. None of them will continue to study with me. You will be here. I know your commitment and I'll give you all my teachings." He smiled and gave me a hug. "You will never need another teacher," he said. We walked to the dining hall for lunch.

❖❖❖❖

Ten p.m. Sunday night, Rudi and I had just returned from a movie. We stood on the second-floor landing of his house on Tenth Street, a house sacred to me where I had received profound spiritual teachings. "Good night, Stuart," he said. Before he went upstairs to his apartment, he looked at the stairwell, shrugged his shoulders, and said to me, "Five years after I leave this place, they will pee in the hallways."

It didn't take five years. Six months after he took his *samadhi*, Tibetan and Indian antique statuary were stolen by one of his students. His disciples vied for power, and a sacred spiritual center turned into a mini-sanitarium. It was a different kind of piss that was dumped in the hallways. His mother called me at my home in Denton. "Stay away from those people," she said. "They are dangerous." "Yes, I know, Rae." "Rudi loved you," she said to me. "He always believed that you would carry on his work." Her phone call brought tears to my eyes. My commitment to his spiritual practice deepened. It saved my life, I thought. It gave me a connection with God. There is no way I could ever turn my back on him; there is no way I could discontinue his meditation classes. Nothing had to be changed. Why tamper with what works? Why add on rituals he thought were nonsense? There's no need to add on superficial spiritual window dressings if an honest practice of his meditation opens doorways to enlightenment.

❖❖❖❖

"There's a young boy in the Middle East," Rudi said to me, "who was born in an Egyptian brothel and might still be living there, a young boy who's destined to be a Christ-like avatar for the Aquarian Age. Are your bags packed? I want you to go with me to the Middle East. That child needs to be trained in the meditation we practice."

The idea captured my quixotic fancy, but, more importantly, it represented an opportunity to develop my spiritual life. It didn't matter to me where Rudi taught. If the Aquarian Christ child lived in an Egyptian brothel, if he was supposed to be a disciple of Rudi's, if Rudi's spiritual teachings would help thousands if not millions of people, that suited me fine. It didn't matter to me whether I was in New York City or Cairo or on the moon. My main purpose was to get to God. Each day, my inner life strengthened. I could feel that I was getting closer to my objective.

I've always had a bit of wanderlust in me. A journey with Rudi to the Middle East sounded like a scenario that would fit perfectly into my life, something biblical and so outrageous it could be a script for a movie: two New-York-City-born yogis on a quest to find a spiritual teacher so powerful he could change the world. "It's better to train Christ than be Christ," Rudi said to me with a smile on his face. "Who needs all the drama?"

His plans changed, but I wasn't at all upset. One never knew when a great spiritual student would come along. The important thing was to continue to work inside myself and trust that God would take care of the rest.

❖❖❖❖

Is the Aquarian Age teacher alive and well today? Is he still in an Egyptian brothel? I have no idea. My door is always open. I never know who's going to show up next, the kind of potential they will bring, and where it will lead. New students force me to change patterns in myself and adjust my chemistry to their uniqueness. They help me to explore inner territory I've never been to before. The rough-and-tumble of "begetting" spiritually awakened students is an adventure that touches the core of my being. The mantle must be passed on to a new generation, and my job is to train people in Rudi's meditation. The rest will take care of itself. Over the years thousands of people have come to study with me, and a handful got the teachings. As they say in the Bible, "Many are called, but few are chosen." I can't remember one student I've ever had who hasn't taught me something important about myself, essential things like: I have to move on and not hold on to bygones; I have to let both positive and negative situations find their watermark; I have to learn and to grow from them, surrender whatever happened in the past, and continue to develop my inner life.

Some people teach a watered-down version of Rudi's meditation technique. They sit on an altar with a photo of Rudi above their head and never tell their students to focus on the *hara*. They chant and sing and swathe themselves in orange robes and substitute form without content for a raw gutsy meditation practice that transmutes life's roughage into spiritual enlightenment. Most students can't tell the difference. Rudi has become a folkloric-type figure that died two generations ago, and they have no idea what he taught. Whatever people are told they believe, and the orange-robed "swamis" dilute his practices into a thinly veiled version of Rudi's remarkable meditation technique.

We all have chakras, mind, breath, need and will. Whether or not it's one's destiny to pursue a spiritual life depends on the evolution of their soul. The tools are all available. People have to learn how to use them. Easy, feel-good routes to a spiritual life are almost always a waste of time. Read the hagiographies of Christian, Hindu and Buddhist saints and see what they endured to elevate their consciousness. There is no easy way for a human being to get enlightened. We don't have to manufacture problems for ourselves. Every human being has enough internal blockage to damn up the Hudson River. We can't escape who we are. We can change our inner makeup by committing time and energy to deep meditation practice.

In the Old Testament there are many pages written in which people "begat" others. It's like an interminable stream-of-consciousness writing that takes one from generation to generation without a clue as to what happened to the different characters mentioned. I'm not sure if I've ever focused on the names of the people. I certainly don't remember them. It was always a mystery to me why those pages were included in such a masterful work until I realized that mystical Jewish lore needed to be passed down from generation to generation. Knowledge of the interlinear had to be taught, knowledge of a sacred Hebraic language, of a Sephirotic Tree and its system of energy centers that connects the human to the Divine and reveals a pathway into those "caverns measureless to man" that Samuel Taylor Coleridge wrote about in his poem *Kubla Khan*.

My family spoke of the Jewish people as a "chosen" race. It never made sense to me; I never felt chosen or special or that Judaism made me more important than any other person on earth. My circle of friends included Jews, Italians, African Americans, Puerto Ricans, and a host of other young people from assorted races and religions, and it never occurred to me that there was anything chosen about being Jewish. The very thought left a bad taste in my mouth.

In my early twenties I rejected the Jewish religion for a more humanist approach to life. I didn't reject the art and architecture of medieval and Renaissance Europe, masterful works that touched on deep levels of spirituality and inspired my own search for enlightenment. I didn't reject Hindu and Buddhist sublime depictions of gods and demi-gods in a cosmic world replete with beauty and spiritual energy. I'd often wonder why twentieth-century Western artists, musicians, dramatists, and writers had transmuted spirituality into a vacuous, almost substance-less vision of the modern world. If form follows function, then the human mind dictates all activity. We live in conceptual little boxes that are more like prisons than organic expressions of creativity. Illusion becomes tantamount to anything spiritual as humanity indulges (almost tongue-in-cheek) in futile efforts to make sense of a senseless world. In my early twenties, though young and quite innocent, it was clear to me that I needed something more. I didn't know exactly what I was looking for, but recognized it the moment I met Rudi.

He used every method at his disposal to break me down and transform my ego into nothingness. He used everything from heartfelt love to "calling a schmuck a schmuck" when the situation warranted it. In fact, "Schmuck-dom" often became a rite of passage. It reminded me that I had a great deal of work to do on myself. He told me that he would never take another student like me again. "Thank God I made the cut," I said to him and laughed. His no-holds-barred approach to a spiritual life was raw, and demanded work of such depth on myself that I couldn't take a moment with him for granted. It also reassured me that I could tough it out, get strong in myself, and master his teachings. I'd often ask myself: do I have the stomach to take it? Could I transform my naïveté, my insecurity, and my lack of consciousness into a spiritual life? Both Rudi and I understood that I wasn't going to run away. If my ego was bruised, so what? Let it be bruised. The idea was to eliminate ego, to free Stuart of encumbrances that blocked the pathway to God. I had no need for an "I'm alright, you're alright" approach to spiritual practice. In my short twenty-five-years of life, I'd been through enough to know that nothing real came easy. As a kid I thought if I survive the Bronx I can survive anything. I later learned that the Bronx was no match for Rudi's version of kundalini yoga. It required me to slay my internal dragons, to take any punch thrown my way and transform it into chi.

Rudi's idea of the rough-and-tumble was a quick jab to the ego followed by a delicious hug. Nothing was ever done maliciously. It was done with such fine-tuned precision that he'd poke at a person's ego when the person was ready to take an important step in his or her spiritual life. It always made me work harder on myself. I would get livid for a moment, but the anger dissipated when I realized that Rudi's meditation technique helped me to overcome the problem. His pokes and prods were essential because I was a complete mystery to myself.

The mind's devious and complex nature makes it easy for us to get lost in a febrile collection of thoughts and impulses that dominate our actions. It creeps up on us when we least expect it and derails every effort we make to grow spiritually. It took four years for me to learn how to use it properly, four interminable years in which I had to listen to nonstop chatter in my brain. The chitchat in my head was so severe I had no choice but to master its endless cacophony. "Bring it into the chakra below the navel," I heard him say a thousand times. I'd focus there, I'd bring my anger and unhappiness there, my anxiety and neurosis, but moments after the meditation class I'd return to a montage sequence of thoughts and images that bedeviled my brain. One day the noise stopped. I don't remember exactly when, but the anger dissipated, the anxiety fell away, and I could keep the focus of my attention in the *hara*. I was able to transform what was killing me into life-giving energy.

The door to enlightenment must never be shut. One never knows who will step through it. I was once a lost soul who stepped through that door. It was like Alice tumbling down the rabbit hole, like the armoire in *The Chronicles of Narnia*—a mystical, magical world that opened and freed my soul from its prison. The next person who walks through that door could be responsible for the enlightenment of thousands of people—like Rudi's Aquarian Christ child, like a re-incarnated *rinpoche*, or like a kid from the South Bronx or Brooklyn who had to walk through that door or perish. There's a whole new generation of young people who have come to earth to learn important lessons that will help them get to God. Most of them get lost in an underworld of suffering and unhappiness.

The chosen few don't have to be born Jewish. They just have to be born, and they'll find their way to an open door. There's no throne to inherit, no rightful heir, and no religious caste system that keeps hordes of people in chains. What determines spiritual progress has nothing to do with birth, ego, or charismatic image of self. There are no winners or losers in the struggle to get to God. Every soul has its chance; some do it in this lifetime, but most do it in lifetimes down the road. It depends on whether or not it's walked into enough dead ends to realize "that the best way out of town is up." Then the real work begins: an internal battle waged by the soul to transmute lifetimes of tension and bad habits into a state of nothingness. There's no feudal system that determines enlightenment, no lineage or birthright. Democratic principles are at work here, and the door is open to anyone who is ready to build an inner life that will connect them to God.

Rudi refused to run a private kundalini sanctuary for privileged western or eastern *sadhus*. The guru has only one purpose: to give away the teachings. And only God—the universe, higher creative energy, whatever one wants to call it—determines the next generation of real disciples. The door has to be kept open for people to find their way in. If the real *guru* is life, a kundalini master's responsibility is to train his students to learn from life. The belief that life begins and ends with mind and matter and doesn't extend into the unknown is a misconception. There's enough mystery about spiritual practice without gurus and practitioners of meditation that clothe it in more mystery. God didn't create a special club for an elite few that are "bound for glory." The difficulty of inner work sifts through long lines of people. It determines who becomes enlightened and who will use whatever they've learned in a future lifetime. It's an open-door policy. Anyone can enter and receive teachings. The guru's role is like Johnny Appleseed. He plows inner turf and plants seeds that germinate and sprout in either this or future lifetimes. Not everyone is ready for spiritual enlightenment, but no person should be denied the next step on his or her journey.

In the Jewish religion they say, "If you save one life in your lifetime, the gate to heaven will open and welcome you." That life was my life: an innocent schmuck on a leisurely walk down Seventh Avenue South with his friend Charlie. As a drugged-out ex-inmate from a Spanish prison, I entered a door and found something I'd been looking for since I was sixteen-years old. There are no accidents, just chance karmic occurrences that transform the lives of people that are ready to change. It's why the door has to always remain open. One never knows who will walk in.

❖❖❖❖

"There are no bad students, only bad teachers," Rudi said in one of his talks. It's a difficult piece of wisdom to digest but readily understandable. If a teacher works on himself in enough depth, he will find God's seed in anyone who studies with him. He will nurture that seed until it germinates and the student begins to have a spiritual life. Failure to do this isn't necessarily a negative thing; it's nothing more than a learning process, a step on a teacher's inner growth ladder, the recognition that perfection is in the realm of the gods and we all fail at something. If we learn from that failure the next go-around will have better results. It's another way the universe teaches us to develop an inner life, another way we learn to serve higher energy.

For many years I lived with the thought that Rudi's meditation practice was a be-all and save-all for anyone who practiced it. It was basic common sense to me. Develop the chakra system, build inner strength, and connect to God. At the same time karma will work itself out. I never took into account the individuality of students, the size of egos, and the need in people for self-importance. It never occurred to me that a person would use their spiritual practice to gain power over others.

When I first noticed the sizable egos in people and how important they felt when they sat in front of a group of innocent spiritual seekers, it not only shocked me, it forced me to re-evaluate teacher-making. Many of these mini-gurus turned on me. I even heard them say that Rudi had made them teachers. Years ago, there was a student that I not only made a meditation teacher, I convinced Rudi to consign to him an enormous inventory of Asian art. He wanted to open a gallery that would support an ashram. "What should I do?" Rudi asked me. "It'll help him grow and build his ashram," I answered. A few months subsequent to Rudi's death, in a dubious Tibetan painting deal, this student's greed caught up to him. He made a promise to me and then reneged. "Stuart isn't my teacher. He's my friend," he told someone who relayed that message to me. "God sends me my students," I replied. "I pick my friends very carefully."

Minutes after I taught my first class in Big Indian, Rudi, in a succinct but whimsical voice said, "Next summer at Big Indian, first I'll teach, then you'll teach, then we'll show cartoons." When I think back about that moment with Rudi, it makes me laugh. Over the years I've had to deal with many oversized spiritual egos. It dawned on me that we had entered an animated era of kundalini yoga. Let God take care of it, I thought. My work is to continue to build my inner life.

People's egos are no longer offensive to me. I've learned that priorities differ for almost every human being. My expectations have diminished and I react to what people bring me, not to a delusional image created in my brain. It's become clear to me what I should support. Many students have dropped out of my life. It no longer bothers me that people sit beneath pictures of Rudi and teach some twisted version of his meditation practice. "Everyone chooses where they want to be," I remember Rudi saying. "Don't feel pity for people because they're attracted to fools and quacks. Just do your inner work and get closer to God."

His words provided a profound insight into what it means to teach. They helped me to realize that a lack of consciousness in this world is God's problem, not mine; and He's created a solution—time, reincarnation, a continuum of events that barrage people with their own foolishness until they finally see what's real. I was up against my own foolishness for a long time. It turned around when my heart opened and I felt gratitude for every person and situation that's ever been in my life. There's so much negativity on this planet, I thought, but I'm not going to allow other people to interfere with my spiritual process. Rudi's meditation practice is a treasure. It's not for everybody, but it is for me, and I have to remain as truthful to it as possible. It saved my life and I've seen it save the lives of many other people—an antidote to my youthful impetuosity, to my drug-filled days when I wandered with aimless abandon around the world.

❖❖❖

In Charlie Chaplin's movie *Modern Times*, there's a character trapped on a conveyor belt, packaged, and made ready to be shipped off to a department store and sold to a friendly consumer. We've become so much a product of a mechanized society that our inner lives salivate like Pavlovian dogs. We're hypnotized by video games, hooked on movies, TVs and cell phones. We're creatures of such habit we can't function without some kind of an external stimulus. We have to fill every moment with something to do. The alternative is to be alone with one's self—a scary

proposition when solitude reveals a person we've been hid
from most of our lives. Each moment must be filled with the
clamor of video-game death and destruction; no wonder there's
so much violence in the world. It reflects dark forces at play in
every human being.

Beneath a crusty layer of unhappiness there lurks a febrile need
to love and be loved, a need so prominent in our society that it's
the main theme of popular songs, novels, and romantic movies.
We wander blindly through a wasteland of dried-up tears and
parched terrain and try to restore it with anything that will make
our spiritual hunger go away. Although nothing of an external
nature works, people continue to stuff themselves with illusion.
Their hunger is never satiated because they feed themselves the
wrong food.

Pop culture tells us to find somebody to love. One's internal
discomfort will be eased when a mysterious stranger appears
who's the right fit. This is often a lifelong quest. We bounce from
the arms of one mysterious stranger to another, and never fill a
void in our own heart. The person we embrace can easily become
a person we learn to hate. It's too great a burden to dump one's
need for happiness on another person's shoulders. It weighs them
down with an impossible task: to make another human being
joyful all the time. Years ago I discovered that I'm the only person
who can make me happy; I also discovered that if I don't do that
for myself, no relationship will work. I no longer needed outside
stimulus to make my life wonderful: my heart was open and full
of love, and every breath I took was wonderful.

Weighed down by excessive baggage we bring to relationships,
it's naïve to think we can leave it all behind. When the baggage is
unpacked people are shocked to discover that the person they're
married to is different than the one they initially fell in love with.
They've embedded themselves with a stranger. There are kids,
financial entanglements, social and family commitments, and a
host of other pieces to a puzzle it took years to assemble. They're
forced to live with a mysterious stranger. They're forced to rekin-
dle magical love that has morphed into something else. They're
forced to accept that people change and that no relationship is
going to work if we cling to the past.

It's unfair to dump my need for happiness on another person.

own unresolved problems; they can't light up at the drop of a hat. If I don't build an inner life ugh to sustain an open heart, if I don't take full r the ups and downs of my daily life, if I don't gratitude is the quickest way to open my heart, then I have no one to blame for my unhappiness but me.

The self is a cryptic entity enshrouded in mysterious mental, emotional, and spiritual integuments. No matter how much time we take to understand this illusive creature, we always come up empty. It's easier to see other people's faults than our own. "First you have to know yourself," is proclaimed by educators and religious figures throughout the world. It's a daunting proposition that sends people on a wild goose chase in terrain so foreign to them it's easy to get lost. The human mind can't wrap itself around the sheer magnitude of "self." There are too many nuances at play: thoughts and memories, emotions and instincts, a landscape so vast it's impossible to grasp the full depth of "self" in one lifetime. No one has time anyway. They're too busy chasing success and money, they're too busy raising families, they're too busy being busy. They're also too busy running from "self" to ever stop for a moment and look at its magical kingdom. If they took time to peruse this mysterious place, they'd discover behind all the chaos and confusion, there's a door that opens and reveals a pathway to enlightenment.

CHAPTER 27

I lived in a railroad flat on West Twenty-first Street between Eighth and Ninth Avenues. It had a bathtub in the kitchen and a toilet in the apartment building hallway. Twenty-five-years-old and broke, I worked three or four nights a week as a waiter in a restaurant. What little money I made was spent on utilities, rent, food, and other basics. I invested the few dollars left over every month in Asian art that I found in Rudi's store: Tibetan *thangkas*, a Japanese screen, a large Siamese Buddha, Chinese scrolls, Indian miniature paintings, pieces that were very inexpensive by today's standards. I paid a hundred dollars for a nineteenth-century *thangka*, three hundred dollars for a seventeenth-century Kano School screen, and five hundred dollars for a large Siamese bronze Buddha. They transformed my dingy apartment into an exotic living space. I slept on a futon that was surrounded by the Japanese screen I had nailed to the wall. When I woke up in the morning, Zen monks greeted me. They lived and meditated on craggy mountainous cliffs and in caves. The only pieces of furniture I had were a large writing table that came with a chair and a low table surrounded by pillows on which I'd eat my meals. I purchased them from a Salvation Army thrift shop. There was no television set or radio, but I did buy a stereo system and a sizable collection of Western and East Indian classical music as well as jazz. It was a small apartment, uncluttered, and suited to my taste. I didn't mind going to bed at night and waking up there in the morning.

After Marian and I broke up I remained celibate for a long time and focused my attention on Rudi's meditation practice. My chaotic mind's rambunctious prattle yakked nonstop from morning to night, and my overactive brain focused on every woman who walked past me on the street. One thing was certain: I had to master my inner life. The first time I tried Rudi's meditation technique at home I came up empty and couldn't sit still for five minutes. My head was like a birdcage full of a thousand chirping canaries. My heart was a closed vault, the navel chakra nonexistent, and a drip-drip of energy flowed through me that felt more like a leaky faucet than a strong current of *shakti*. I needed Rudi's presence to help me focus. Though my thoughts prattled on in his classes, I never listened to them, and I tried to direct my attention to the navel chakra. After many weeks of internal struggle, success finally came. An ocean of quiet flooded my system, along with renewed vigor and a sense of balance I'd never known before. It wasn't just Rudi who sat in front of me, but Swami Nityananda, the Buddha, and a host of other spiritual teachers bathed in white and golden auras. I witnessed a psychedelic light show without having to take drugs, the likes of which I'd seen only in mystical paintings of great Western and Asian masters. At the end of the class I lay down for about fifteen minutes in order to absorb the experience. "What happened?" I asked Rudi just before I left the ashram. He smiled and gave me a hug. "You have a gift," he replied. "It will take time to develop it, but you definitely have a special gift."

A month of meditation sessions at home brought results. My mind became less chaotic, and I could focus on the navel chakra. A flow of energy moved from the *hara* through my sex to the base of the spine and awakened kundalini. I sat for twenty minutes to half an hour without a problem. My classes with Rudi went much deeper, but I accepted the importance of both. It was essential for me to attend his classes. I couldn't master this by myself. It was also important for me to sit at home and learn to meditate by myself.

❖❖❖❖

I found a job in a honky-tonk New Orleans-type banjo-thumpin' beer hall in Greenwich Village that catered to tourists. The music was so loud and raucous and the guests so drunk and rambunctious that by the end of the evening my brain was fried. The band played a two-hour set of Dixieland music that consisted of up-tempo versions of "When Johnny Comes Marching Home Again" and "God Bless America." A hundred and fifty drunken tourists stood up and cheered. The tips I made just about paid my rent, put food on the table, and helped me give Rudi small sums of money every month for art I purchased from his gallery.

Dressed in black trousers, a white shirt, a red-and-white-striped vest and a panama hat, I not only had to wait tables, but I had to sing and shout and get the crowd in a frenzy. It wasn't difficult to do. Most of the people were drunk and ready to party. "Hey, Perrin," the manager said to me one evening. "Want to earn some extra money?" "Yeah," I replied. "What do I have to do?" "Warm up the audience at the Johnny Carson show," he said. "You kidding me?" I asked. "No. The whole thing takes fifteen minutes and you'll make forty bucks." "Count me in." "Good," he said. "Come tomorrow at four thirty. Bring your waiter's outfit." He gave me the address.

The NBC Theater was full to capacity with tourists from all over the United States. They waited patiently for Ed McMahon to cry out, "Here's Johnny!" Before McMahon made his appearance, the Dixieland warmer-uppers, eight high-energy young men in striped vests and panama hats came on stage. We sang stuff like, "When the Saints Come Marching In," and "Over There" to the sound of two banjos, a bass guitar, and a trumpet. The entire performance lasted ten minutes. By the time we finished, the audience was ready to tear the theater to pieces. They screamed like hyenas when we left the stage. I repeated this ten-minute comedy romp a dozen times on a dozen different days before I told the saloon manager that I quit. The music began to wear me down. The four a.m. beer hall closing time was hard on my body and mind. By the time I got the Dixieland cacophony out of my head and fell asleep, the sun had already made its way into the eastern sky. I'd wake up at one in the afternoon with a chorus of "Over There" ringing loudly in my ears.

❖❖❖❖

I'd visit Rudi at least three or four times a week. We'd meditate together and I'd listen to him talk. His Asian art emporium was another world to me. Nothing in New York City compared to the exotic inventory that filled the gallery. Large bronze antique Buddha statues from Burma, Thailand, Japan, and China; medieval stone carvings of gods and goddesses from India; antique Tibetan paintings and statuary, Chinese and Japanese cloisonné, jade, and porcelain—a four-hundred-square-foot space filled to the brim with Asian artifacts. There was barely room to walk. My eyes roamed from statue to painting. They were covetous eyes that wanted to collect Asian art. Before this, it had never occurred to me that I could decorate my apartment with exotica from the east.

"It wasn't always like this," Rudi said to me.

When he first opened his store on Seventh Avenue South, Rudi had to wash dishes at the Village Vanguard to make ends meet. He rented a U-Haul truck every Wednesday and scoured Manhattan for old furniture people left on the streets, often two buildings ahead of a city garbage truck. "I had to work like an animal to build this business," he said, "but you know something . . . I'd give it up in a moment if it ever interfered with my spiritual life."

He'd confide in me about his trips to India, about visits to Ganeshpuri, and the struggles he had with Swami Muktananda. "Baba took me apart piece by piece," Rudi said on more than one occasion. "It was painful and difficult, and I wanted to run for my life." "Why'd you stay?" I asked him. "He was the only person I'd ever met who was strong enough to break me down," he replied. "The pain was worth it, the mental anguish, the magic games, the wrestling match in the astral, it was all worth it. I came away with a stronger connection to God. Big chunks of me were left on his ashram grounds. I could barely recognize myself after a week with Baba."

In Rudi's world there were no negatives. Reality was a hodge-podge of divergent experience one used for their spiritual growth. The lessons of life ran the gamut from sugarcoated pleasantries to difficulties that tested one's resolve. Roughage was essential. "We need it to digest our food," he said many times. "We also need it to build an inner life that's strong enough to transform tension into spiritual energy." Positive and negative were like conjoined twins that couldn't be separated. Both were products of the human mind, both walked a fine line that separated illusion from reality, both had a singular purpose: to remind us that polar opposites needed to be transformed into spiritual energy.

"I'd love to go to India," I said to him. "To do what?" "Find a guru. Do spiritual practice." He smiled and said. "The only thing that would grow in India is your ass." "What do you mean?" I asked him. "You'd chant for days and months and years. You'd get up at four in the morning, go to the temple, meditate and do prostrations, but when the time came for the teachings to be passed on, a Westerner wouldn't qualify." "You got them." "Yes," he said. "I survived Muktananda's torture rack. I became a swami in order to qualify. Do you think I wanted to be a swami? The whole thing is dumb in the West. It's embarrassing, but here I am, Swami Rudrananda. It was the only way I could get spiritual teachings in India."

He was the most sacrilegious spiritual master who ever wore an orange robe. He had no patience with ritual or dogma . . . anything that denied him freedom to explore his life. "Work brings more work," he said one day in a meditation class. "That's the best return you can get for your effort. There's no easy means to attain enlightenment."

Until I met Rudi, work was anathema: the drudgery I had to endure to pay for basics like rent, food, utilities; the hours spent at jobs I hated; the unhappiness I saw in people's eyes; the toll money took on their lives. At first I shied away from Rudi's work ethic. In time Rudi's classes transformed me to such a degree that a poem written every now and then did nothing to satiate my creative needs. I quit my restaurant job and started a house-painting and carpentry business. I returned to college, taught Hatha Yoga, and went to Rudi's classes at the ashram. When he'd go out of town I'd teach the kundalini yoga classes. There wasn't a spare moment in any given day. I focused my energy and worked five projects at the same time. Indolence and lethargy vanished. I sought out creative projects to make me work harder on myself. "A diamond is a product of fifty-thousand years of the earth's pressure," Rudi repeated again and again. I needed that kind of pressure. I needed something to make demands on me that I couldn't make on myself. Rudi sensed my need. He asked me to go to Denton, Texas, to run an ashram. "Go for three weeks," he told me. Three weeks turned into nine years of the most pressure-filled lifestyle imaginable. A neophyte meditation teacher became a well-balanced human being who could deal with whatever the universe sent his way.

❖❖❖❖

Five years of Rudi's meditation practice prepared me to run the Denton ashram. It was an arduous five years. Not only did it test Rudi's patience, it tried my own. I was sexually inactive for long stretches of time. Horny, and on edge, I'd relieve my tension with occasional one-night stands. Women were attracted to me, but nothing clicked but platonic friendships. Though relationships complicated my life, I still craved a partner: someone to sleep next to, someone to make love to, someone I could trust and who would participate in my life. Rudi's meditation practice forced me to confront inner dragons that raged day and night. "I'm messed up," I said to myself when I first recognized the problem, "and there's nowhere to hide. But so what! There's a metaphorical pot of gold on the other side of my dragons. If I don't slay them no one else will. If I don't manage my inner chaos this is what I'm up against for the rest of my life."

"This is almost impossible work," I replied, "the most difficult I've ever had to do." He smiled and shook his head. He never turned his back on me. He got pissed off and would relegate me to the kingdom of "Schmuck-dom," but his teachings were profound, his *shakti* healed me, and wisdom inspired me to work harder on myself. "The only person you have to overcome," he told me in his store, "is yourself. Once you do that, the rest is easy." "Is there anything harder?" I laughed. "No," he replied, "but the answer to your problem isn't so complicated."

The answer to my problem, I thought. I don't know if there is an answer. I don't even know where to go in myself to find the source of the problem.

Day after day I excavated buried parts of me but never came up with an answer. In one meditation class with Rudi I discovered that there are no answers, that I would never know myself, that my inner life would always remain a mystery. "Let it all be and grow a step at a time," I said to myself. "You can make mistakes.

You can bumble about in the realms of Schmuck-dom without guilt, without fear, without any encumbrance. There's no rush to become enlightened, no goal to reach, no external force of evil that will keep you from God. You can finally grow at your own pace."

When Rudi was out of town and I taught a sparsely attended meditation class, there were five or six wide-eyed students present. I realized for the first time that I wasn't supposed to teach them. I was there to learn from every person in the room, I was there to channel spiritual energy. My job was to get out of the way, to be nothing, to keep an image of myself from interfering with the process. It lifted an enormous weight from my shoulders. My mind and emotions were quiet. An internal balance sustained itself throughout the class, and I couldn't recognize myself when the session was over. A new person lived in an old body, and I was surprised that everyone still called me Stuart.

❖❖❖❖

Rudi spoke about an undercurrent of tension on the ashram second floor. It needed to be dealt with. "If it persists," he told me, "I'll send everyone home." Much of that tension was directed at me. Petty jealousies formed in people who thought I was high up on Rudi's totem pole. I would teach classes when Rudi left the ashram, I would cook breakfast almost every morning, and there was a special bond between Rudi and myself. He had even asked me to sleep in his apartment when he was out of town. I avoided the jealousy like a plague. I buried my own insecurity beneath false bravado and an insular personality. I was an intense young man, shy and aloof, and I had trouble making friends with people. It was difficult for me to interact with Rudi's students, and most likely that's what turned them off.

"I live in this ashram for only one reason," I said to myself, "and that is to get Rudi's teachings."

After the meditation class he held special hands-on healing sessions for those of us who lived in his house. My spiritual life was more important to me than people's petty opinions and I paid little or no mind to them. They're just people, I thought, and that's what people do. They compete with one another, they find fault in others to justify their own lives.

"Have a talk with them," Rudi said to me. "They're a good group and I want them to grow, but the tension has to stop."

The next day I met with a group of meditation students who lived at the ashram. "I'm here to learn from you all," I said to them. "Problems can be solved if we listen to each other." I apologized for inappropriate and aloof behavior on my part, and told them I would do my best to never let it happen again. "Each of you has something important to teach me and I thank you for that. We're here for one reason, to study with Rudi, to master his inner work, and get to God. It doesn't matter what we think of each other. What matters is that we grow every day and live with open hearts."

There was a deep silence in the room, uninterrupted and profound. When I rose, one of Rudi's students came to me and said, "Thanks for your words. I needed to be reminded of why I was here." He gave me a big hug. "Thank you," I replied. "We need to remind each other."

The tension on the second floor dissipated, and Rudi's students made a deeper commitment to the meditation practice. A few of them left the ashram for one reason or another. Some went to live at the Big Indian ashram. Other students came. There were never less than six people (plus guests) who lived on the second floor. I learned to thrive in a communal environment without letting people's tension bring me down. My likes and dislikes were of no importance. I internalized my anger and no longer judged other people. I used everything that happened to me as an excuse to deepen my inner work. Life on the second floor had its highs and lows, but one thing was certain, everyone there had come for the same reason: to study with Rudi, absorb his wisdom, and use his meditation technique to develop a spiritual life.

❖❖❖❖

"I want you to get a college degree," Rudi told me one afternoon in his store. "You'll probably teach one day at Big Indian, and you'll need a means of supporting yourself."

It had always been impossible for me to sit in a college classroom and listen to the drone of tenured professors reiterate the same stale lessons they'd taught for twenty years, lethal voices of tired, bored and erudite teachers that lacked improvisatory skills. They took the juice out of poetry, fiction, and philosophy. The thought of returning to educational purgatory made me shrivel up inside and want to run away. "Are you sure?" I asked Rudi. "Yes, I'm sure. You've got to learn to finish cycles. You've run away from most everything you've ever started in your life." "Except your meditation," I said. "Yes," he responded, "but now you've got to apply what you've learned from me in a practical way. Get a degree. Finish up with college, and great things will happen for you." "A degree in what?" I asked him. "Education . . . whatever. . . something practical that will enable you to get a job."

I had re-registered at Hunter College three years before I met Rudi and planned to get a degree in English literature. I was in my junior year. By the second week of the semester I was so bored with the environment I began to poke holes in everything that was being taught. In a psychology class the professor showed a short film that explored the work of highbrowed behavioral psychotherapists experimenting with children. I raised my hand and asked who experimented with the brains of these so-called erudite doctors. "Why don't they let kids just be kids? Why do they have to twist their heads around in the name of advanced psychological research? It's all nonsense to me." My question so upset the teacher she almost threw me out of the room. "Is everything nonsense to you, Mr. Perrin?" she asked me. "Not everything. But to experiment like this with the minds of children is concentration-camp-type stuff. What right do they have to do it? What makes these doctors so imperious?"

Whether the class was literature, French, philosophy, or whatever, it was all the same to me. The college had placed me on a gurney and rolled me into an operating room where an expert anesthesiologist put me into an hour-long coma two or three times a day. Desensitized and oblivious to what was being taught, I'd daydream about trips to France, Italy, India, anywhere but the stifling environment of a classroom. I'd write haiku in my notebook and other poems about mystical and far-off places. The badly written textbooks were not only expensive they were tedious and paralyzed my mind. After five weeks of this torture, I left Hunter College and never returned.

Did Rudi want me to re-register at Hunter College? Did he

want me to return to purgatorial irrelevance?

A friend of mine suggested that I check out the New School for Social Research. They had an avant-garde educational program in its second year. "You can even design your own courses and study at home," he said. "You'll never take a test. You just have to write papers and prepare a thesis in your senior year that will determine whether or not you graduate."

I made an appointment with an administrator at the New School. "Have you finished your sophomore year with at least a C average?" "Yeah," I replied. "I've finished my sophomore year, but I don't know my exact grade point." I did know. It was below C. She gave me a brochure that explained everything. "The cut-off date for applications is a month from now. The interview is very important and you must write two essays on books of your own choosing."

I read through the brochure and wrote two essays, one on Albert Camus' novel *The Stranger,* and the other on Franz Kafka's short story, *The Metamorphosis.* I filled out an application form and submitted everything to the New School's admission office. Two weeks later I went for an interview. At best it was a hope and a prayer. My grade point average at Hunter College was well below C. The interview and the essays had to be stellar. To my surprise and great pleasure a month after the interview, I received a letter of acceptance from the New School.

"This must be an avant-garde college," I said to a friend. "I wrote two essays on existential writers that were more like prose poems than intellectual studies. I start in January. Let's see what happens."

❖❖❖

My first six weeks at the New School made me feel like an avant-garde college was as much hype as institutional learning. The teachers were less than stellar. They were self-centered, erudite, and a bit insecure in their approach to the humanities. My old persona emerged—a know-it-all little bastard who would bug his teachers to no end, who had to juice up the classroom or he would have fallen asleep. "I will never survive two years of this shit," I said to a friend. The first six weeks were torturous. I enjoyed the essay assignments, but two or three lecture classes a day almost drove me to distraction. I was ready to develop a home-study program that would get me a degree.

Late one afternoon in Rudi's store he spoke to me about cycles and how important it is to know when they begin and end. He spoke to me about finishing cycles. "It's the only way to work out karma," he said. "There has to be completion. If not, we're suspended in space.'"

"Am I suspended in space?" I asked myself. "Have I ever finished a cycle? Have I ever finished anything?" His words struck a deep chord in me. "Is it a karmic necessity for me to finish school?" I thought for a moment. "Yes, it certainly is. I'm in school for only one reason, to complete a cycle and transfer that know-how to whatever else I do in my life."

I didn't attend the New School to study philosophy, literature, and history. Those subjects I could learn on my own. I was there to change my work ethic and to make an impossible situation possible. "Teachers shouldn't be targets for my verbal abuse," I reasoned. "If I listen to them perhaps I will learn something. It's time to finish up with my all-knowing and arrogant persona." I was an egotistical jerk who covered up deep insecurity with a veneer of false knowledge and would fight to my last breath to prove a point. "And where will I wind up?" I asked myself with a smile. "On a road that goes nowhere. Maybe it's better to be wrong. This righteous crap always leads me to dead ends." What I liked or disliked about the curriculum and how they taught it was less important to me than a newfound sense of humility. "If I shut my mouth and listen," I said to a friend, "I'll finally get a degree and be finished with college."

The next year and a half of college was a breeze. Many of the teachers became friends, and those that I pissed off in the first semester recognized that something had changed in me. I wrote prose-poem literary essays that explored the inner lives of fictional characters. The response varied from teacher to teacher. One even asked me if I'd ever published anything. Others demanded that I comply with strict essay-writing rules and made me re-do papers, but no one blocked my path to a degree.

The New School College required a final thesis to graduate. I would be grilled for three hours by a panel of teachers. No thesis, no degree, and my advisor asked me to submit an outline of my intended project. "How about an analysis of Coleridge's poem, *Xanadu*," I asked her. "Fine," she replied. "Just bring me the outline."

When I first read the poem by Coleridge, it struck me that his opium reveries tapped into the mystery of Kabbalah.

Where Alph, the sacred river, ran
through caverns measureless to man
down to a sunless sea.

Alph was synonymous with Aleph the first letter of the sacred Hebrew language. Other elements of the poem were of such a mystical nature that I could easily make the analogy. I wrote a two-page outline and submitted it to my advisor. At our next meeting she threw the two-page outline in my face. "This is not only nonsense," she said to me, "its madness. Bring me something else." "But . . ." She didn't let me finish. "Bring me something else." She pointed at the door. "Now get out of here." I shrugged my shoulders and left.

What the hell am I going to bring her, I thought. If I fail to do this thesis, there's no degree. The cycle starts over again. I thought seriously about the paper for half a day. "Okay," I said to myself. "I know what to do." I'll write an essay on the *Om* sound. I'll break it up into four component parts: A, U, & M, and the entire sound of *AUM*, and show how each component is relevant to spiritual enlightenment. This idea is more outrageous than my analyses of the Coleridge poem, I thought, but so what? I need something interesting to work on. I submitted an outline to my advisor. The next time I met with her, she green-lighted the project. "I can't wait to see the actual essay," she said to me. "Be sure you have footnotes." "Don't worry," I replied. "There are plenty."

It took a week to write the essay. After I submitted it, my advisor called me to tribunal. If I fail this freakin' interview, I thought, two years of work go down the drain. I had no idea what was going to happen.

Three staid and solemn teachers sat behind a table. I parked my butt on an empty chair and faced them from the other side of the table. The three of them studied me in a strange way. "Shit," I said to myself. "They probably thought my essay was written by a mad man." "Mr. Perrin," one of them said. "I'm Doris M . . .

And my colleagues are Melissa R . . . And Joan W . . . " I nodded hello. "This interview will determine whether or not you graduate from the New School," Doris said. "Yes," I replied with some trepidation. "Okay, let's proceed," she said. Doris asked the first question. It was about Buddhism. I answered it as best I could. What followed was a deep silence. There were no more questions. "I loved your paper," Melissa finally said. "It was original, insightful, and like nothing else submitted." The other two agreed. The next two hours and fifty minutes were spent in a friendly discussion about my life. All three teachers were intrigued. They assured me that each of them would write the highest letter of recommendation to any graduate school I wanted to attend. "Have you thought about that?" one of them asked me. "Not yet," I answered. "But if I decide to go to graduate school, I will definitely get in touch with you." We shook hands and I was on my way. "I've graduated," I said to myself. "I've finished a cycle. Something I've never done before in my life."

I told Rudi that I had graduated from college. "Good," he said. "We'll go to Chinatown tonight and celebrate." I was a little sullen. "Is there something wrong?" he asked me. "No, it's just that you told me when I graduate, extraordinary things were going to happen." He looked at me for a minute. "I want you to get a master's degree," he said. "A bachelor's degree is worthless." "Are you kidding me?" I asked. "No, Stuart. I also want you to stop teaching meditation. You need a break." In one fell swoop, he undercut my entire life. The thought of getting a master's degree was repulsive to me. I had done my time in educational purgatory. "A master's degree in what?" I asked him. "You figure it out," he said. I was at a crossroads. I could have easily said, "Fuck this," packed my bags and left. But Rudi's teachings were essential to my life. I was well aware that I couldn't just skip out. "A master's degree," I thought as I left his store and walked around the corner to the ashram. "What the hell am I going to study? Maybe theology or kundalini yoga or Asian art history or anything to finish another cycle and move on with my life."

I went into the ashram meditation room and sat in front of a photo of Swami Nityananda. "Baba," I said to him. "Tell me, my grandfather, how do I go on?" I had a special connection with the Indian saint. He always came to me in my meditations. "You remind me of a young Nityananda," Rudi had told me many times. I was upset with Rudi, with life, with the idea of a master's degree. I entered a deep meditative state and began to smile. "I'm pissed at Rudi," I said to myself, "but here I am using his meditation technique to resolve my problem. The whole freakin' thing is crazy." As I continued to go deeper into myself, Nityananda manifested and sat cross-legged in front of me. "What has Rudi done to you?" he said. "It takes two years to get a master's degree. If you do what he asks, he will pass on his teachings to you. You will become a master of kundalini yoga, of tantra, of the highest spiritual practices." "But he took away my teaching!" "So what," Nityananda replied. "He's pruned the tree. He's taken away another obsession. For the first time in your life you will be able to grow like a healthy plant."

I meditated for about half an hour, rose, and left the ashram building. A weight had been lifted from my heart and I understood that one has to pay a price if they want to receive great teachings. "No matter what the cost," I said to myself, "it's cheap when I compare it to what Rudi has given me. I will get a master's degree and my enlightenment." I returned to Rudi's store and hugged him. "Thanks," I said to him. He smiled and returned the hug. "I didn't think you'd get it this quickly," he said. "We'll go to Chinatown tonight and celebrate your degree and your spiritual awakening."

After an intense summer of spiritual and physical work at Big Indian, I had changed so much that Rudi told me to forget about a master's degree. "I want you to go to Denton, Texas, for three weeks," he said. "What am I supposed to do?" I asked. "What do you mean?" he replied, a little upset. "You told me I'm no longer a teacher," I said. He smiled and said, "You're learning, aren't you? I want you to go there and teach my meditation practice."

Before I left for the airport, he took me aside, "If anyone ever asks you who the guru is, just say the guru is life." It took me twenty years to absorb that simple teaching, to become detached enough in myself to sit before life and let it be my guru.

CHAPTER 28

Gratitude unlocked my closed heart and transformed ego-based self-interest into humility. It enabled me to communicate with other people in a profound and compassionate way. I've never forgotten my mental and emotional state the day before I met Rudi. Strung out and unhappy, self-involved and incapacitated, it was difficult for me to make it through a day. The post-Rudi life I lived over the past decades fills my heart with undying gratitude for his patience, care, love, and spiritual teachings. He bequeathed a meditation practice that needs to be shared: the double-breathing technique he developed from years of Hindu-Buddhist studies that strengthens the chakra system and connects the practitioner with higher creative energy in the universe. He would often speak about his own gratitude. "If it wasn't for the love and blessings of Swami Nityananda and the Shankaracharya of Puri," he'd say, "I wouldn't be alive today. That's why I teach. Out of gratitude to them for the life they gave me." Though his relationship with Muktananda was rough-and-tumble, he expressed profound thanks to Baba for *shaktipat* transmitted that broke him down and guided him on a path to enlightenment. He never forgot where he came from, what he had to overcome, and the effort it took for him to build his inner life.

I've said it before and it bears to be repeated: "The only successful people on earth are happy people." I wasn't born here to waste time and energy on petty and useless activity, to satisfy self-aggrandizement until it becomes an overblown, caricature-like float in my own personal parade. What I hungered for was unconditional love that could be shared, a heart that was replete with trust and compassion. I discovered that no matter how difficult one's journey is through life, the seeds of happiness germinate when the heart is full of gratitude.

Without enough inner strength to sustain an open heart, I couldn't tell the difference between what turned me on and real happiness . . . and substituted one for the other. Lost in a tenuous world of high pressure, family, and money, and a belief that objective cures would solve deep inner problems, I discovered that objective cures didn't solve anything. They'd patch up my problems but never got to their source. Caught up in life's game, I could think of nothing but victory, but whether I won or lost did little to change my inner condition. It gave me momentary highs and lows that floated away in turbulent rivers. I was on to the next game, and the next, until I'd thoroughly exhausted myself and my inner life. I walked into hundreds of dead ends and finally said to myself, "there has to be another route."

Shakespeare's *"whips and scorns..."* reminded me that the world was a dream-filled caravan of events that slipped away into nothingness—a show staged by buffoons and clowns, fools and heroes, that repeated itself over again without anyone ever learning real lessons. Would I ever learn to uproot problems at their source, or would I continue to apply bandages to symptoms and postpone deeper answers for another day? I once believed that money, success, and literary prowess could replace unconditional love. I didn't know the difference. Could material things make that much of a difference? Sex? Power? Success? I certainly thought so. But none of them were a permanent solution. They got me through the day, they reassured my ego, but never reached deep enough inside me to tackle the root of the problem.

I'm often reminded of a Bill Gates interview I saw on television. "I have difficulty sleeping at night," he said. "I'm afraid my empire will be gone in the morning." Someday, his empire will be gone. So will he and I and the entire cast of characters that makes up the twenty-first century. Impermanence stares us all in the face. Human greed and its penchant for money and power won't vanish; what also won't vanish is a hunger for love and a need to transform suffering into enlightenment.

Karmic coordinates come together at a particular point in time and space and make it possible for gurus and disciples to meet.

It has nothing to do with human will. A higher power makes sure that spiritual teachings are passed down from generation to generation. As the aphorism says, "When the disciple is ready the guru will appear." It all seems predetermined, almost destined, but coordinates can diverge and move in other directions if either the guru or his disciple has ceased to focus on inner work. The moment the disciple's heart closes and gratitude diminishes, material and mental obsessions intercede. The wiring in the house short-circuits.

The goal of kundalini yoga is to open the heart chakra and transmute angst and suffering into joy and love. The goal is to help the soul fulfill its destiny on earth, to build inner strength that allows one to step off the karmic merry-go-round and merge with higher energy, to free body, mind and spirit from a lifetime of pain and dysfunction. When my heart first opened in meditation class I discovered that my inner child could laugh and dance on God's playground. If there's anything like utopia on earth it exists in the human heart, a place where love is unconditional, where happiness welcomes one to a sanctuary that houses the highest level of human attainment.

Other Books by Stuart Perrin

A Lotus Flower In Muddy Waters

Little Sisters

Rudi: The Final Moments

Moving On: Finding Happiness in a Changed World

A Deeper Surrender: Notes on a Spiritual Life

Leah: A Story of Meditation and Healing

The Mystical Ferryboat

Author's Biography

Stuart Perrin, an American spiritual master of Kundalini Yoga who has been quietly teaching small groups of students around the world for over 40 years, and is a direct disciple of Swami Rudrananda, more commonly known as Rudi. Stuart studied six years with Rudi. In 1973, Rudi died in an airplane crash and Stuart was one of three survivors.

Stuart Perrin was born in the Bronx, New York. The first child and only son of Sylvia and Michael Perrin, he began his spiritual quest at the age of sixteen. Sitting at his father's deathbed, he was shocked and awakened to a simple reality. "Why," he asked himself, "is it the first time I've seen my father in such a profound state of inner peace? Why did he have to wait until the last moments of his life to be filled with so much love and serenity?"

In his early twenties he studied acting in New York and wrote visionary poetry. In search of a spiritual teacher he spent a good deal of time in Europe, and North Africa. When he met Rudi in 1967 the entire trajectory of his life changed. He had finally found someone who showed him a meditation technique that developed the chakra system and made the esoteric into something practical. He now teaches Kundalini meditation in New York City and holds monthly intensives in centers around the United States. He has written and published many books on the subject of meditation and spiritual practice as well as novels and short stories.